WALLACE STEVENS

Literary Lives
General Editor: Richard Dutton, Professor of English
Lancaster University

This series offers stimulating accounts of the literary careers of the
most admired and influential English-language authors. Volumes
follow the outline of the writers' working lives, not
in the spirit of traditional biography, but aiming to trace
the professional, publishing and social contexts which
shaped their writing.

Published titles

Cedric C. Brown
JOHN MILTON

Peter Davison
GEORGE ORWELL

Richard Dutton
WILLIAM SHAKESPEARE

Jan Fergus
JANE AUSTEN

James Gibson
THOMAS HARDY

Kenneth Graham
HENRY JAMES

Paul Hammond
JOHN DRYDEN

W. David Kay
BEN JONSON

Mary Lago
E. M. FORSTER

Clinton Machann
MATTHEW ARNOLD

Alasdair D. F. Macrae
W. B. YEATS

Joseph McMinn
JONATHAN SWIFT

Kerry McSweeney
GEORGE ELIOT

John Mepham
VIRGINIA WOOLF

Michael O'Neill
PERCY BYSSHE SHELLEY

Leonée Ormond
ALFRED TENNYSON

Harold Pagliaro
HENRY FIELDING

George Parfitt
JOHN DONNE

Wallace Stevens

A Literary Life

Tony Sharpe
Senior Lecturer and
Head of Department of English
Lancaster University

St. Martin's Press
New York

WALLACE STEVENS

Copyright © 2000 by Tony Sharpe

St. Martin's Press, Scholarly and Reference Division, 175 Fifth Avenue, New York, N.Y. 10010

First published in the United States of America in 2000

This book is printed on paper suitable for recycling and made from fully managed and sustained forest sources.

Printed in Great Britain

ISBN 0–312–22069–3

Library of Congress Cataloging-in-Publication Data
Sharpe, Tony, 1952–
Wallace Stevens : a literary life / Tony Sharpe.
p.   cm. — (Literary lives)
Includes bibliographical references and index.
ISBN 0–312–22069–3 (cloth)
1. Stevens, Wallace, 1879–1955.   2. Poets, American—20th century–
–Biography.   I. Title.   II. Series: Literary lives (New York, N.Y.)
PS3537.T4753Z7658   1999
811'.52—dc21
[B]   99–13314
                                                  CIP

For Eva and Ned
Two sure answerers

Here lurks an immense homage to the general privilege of the artist, to that constructive, that creative passion, . . . the exercise of which finds so many an occasion for appearing to him the highest of human fortunes, the rarest boon of the gods. He values it, all sublimely and perhaps a little fatuously, for itself – as the extension, great beyond all others, of experience and of consciousness.

(Henry James, from his preface to *The American*)

' "Oh-ho" dit-il en Portuguais, une langue qu'il parlait très bien.' (Marcel Duchamp's remark, as reported by Walter Arensberg to Wallace Stevens)

There are things in a man besides his reason.
Come home, wind, he kept crying and crying.

(from the poem 'Pieces')

Contents

Preface

On holiday in Connecticut last summer, one hot afternoon I paid a visit to Wallace Stevens's former house on Westerly Terrace, Hartford, and to Elizabeth Park nearby. The imposing residence (now owned by a local church and not open to the public) is situated on a quiet street of similarly stockbrokerish dwellings that must, when Stevens moved there in 1932, have identified their occupants as Americans who had 'made it'. There is nothing to declare the house's link with the poet, and as I stood in the (possibly uncharacteristic) sunshine, with my ever-so-slightly-bemused family and our escorting American friends, the place's anonymity struck me as both poignant and appropriate. So it was, again, on my discovering how relatively unremarkable Elizabeth Park is: smaller and less distinctive than I had supposed. The plaqueless house and the modest park in which he had so regularly walked were eloquent, in their omission of precisely that factor of the extraordinary his poetry can evoke, even by denoting its absence. And indeed, I reflected as I sat in the rustic arbour amid the park's rose-beds, Stevens had already imagined his own absence from these places (see 'Vacancy in the Park', for example), and had foreseen how little of what mattered to him in them might be recoverable by others (see 'A Postcard from the Volcano'): in his writing, the necessary angel is the one that has just vanished, and his poems indicate the oscillating threshold between plenitude and vacancy.

In his essay on Marvell, T.S. Eliot asserts that the great and perennial task of criticism is to bring the poet back to life; yet imagining Stevens, that exponent of American loneliness, can seem like conducting a continual conversation with a silent man. It was the spirit that I sought, on my naively archaic pilgrimage to Hartford, but what perhaps I sensed was what he called the 'literate despair' of a spirit storming in blank walls, whose poems were rooted in a life unlived: which nevertheless became an exaltation of that life, both jocular and uncompromising. The jubilant weather and the prosperous neighbourhood, together with my awareness of Stevens's not-being-there, were a minor enactment of the connection, in his poetry, of opulence with absence: a plain sense of things he expressed in a contestingly extravagant language. In *Notes toward a Supreme Fiction*, he coined the phrase 'sensible ecstasy', which is an oxymoron that brings to birth a combinatory third thing: in microcosm of the way he felt poems served to mediate between the worlds of common sense and imaginative transfiguration.

I have wanted to write about Stevens, because his poetry has been a significant influence on the way I think about literature, for over twenty years; I found his presence asserting itself when I was addressing the work of other writers. To some extent, then, this is a (not uncritical) personal statement, deriving from my particular view of the man and his work, that is itself a consequence of what he would have called my own peculiar plot. Implicit in my approach is that I am a British critic beholding an American poet, and my reading both of the life and writing is on occasions adversarial: for what writer of importance does not at times infuriate the reader? The kind of book this is has been further shaped by the requirements of the series and this subject. The exploration of a writer's 'literary life' need not in principle involve a large amount of literary criticism as such, since the emphasis falls more on biography and the shaping of a career in letters; but it is obvious that our interest in the life originates in a prior engagement with the art. Stevens's development as a writer is in itself interesting; but I have supposed that, in addition to learning what happened, any reader will also wish to see how this affects our reading of the poetry: the more so, as the poetry in question is generally considered to be difficult. Throughout this study, therefore, I try to suggest ways in which certain poems can be read in the context of my general exposition – without in any way pretending that such a reading exhausts their interpretative possibilities.

For a long time, Stevens remained an invisible poet, high and aloof; now we hear more about the man than the mandarin, and are encouraged to attend to the contexts in which his poetry came into being. His can appear to have been an eminently sensible ecstasy, with the insurance man safely bankrolling the poet; yet for all the reassuringness of his bourgeois exterior, I think much of Stevens's continuing significance lies in the inherent extremism of his belief in the 'precious scope' of poetry; a belief whose stature derives from the depth and extent of his commitment to it: as he declared to Henry Church in 1943, 'The belief in poetry is a magnificent fury, or it is nothing' (*L* 446). In part, I read his life as a dialogue between the requirements of sense and those of ecstasy, with his successive books as stages in the debate. I read it, also, as a continued awareness of fathers and fatherhood, with the particular complications wrought by his Americanness; and as a simultaneous compliance with and revolt against convention, in both life and writing.

When I completed my doctorate on Stevens in 1978, Holly Stevens's editions of her father's letters and journal, together with fragmentary reminiscences by her and some others, represented the sum of what was biographically available, not greatly augmented by S.F. Morse's 1970 study. Since then the situation has been transformed, chiefly by the labours of Peter Brazeau, Milton Bates, Joan Richardson and Alan Filreis, who in their various ways have brought into the open a considerable body of unknown or previously unpublished material relating to Stevens's life. My debt to their researches is explicit in what follows; but the exhaustiveness of detail available in those studies enables me to proceed more selectively, in offering an interpretative narrative of Stevens's literary life, which I hope will enable a reader to assess the significance of his contribution to twentieth-century poetry, as well as to engage with individual poems more knowledgeably and enjoyably.

I pay attention to the formative years before he published much, and to the domestic circumstances in which his poems were produced, as well as to the cultural and historical background of his publishing career. Although the sequence of chapters is largely chronological, on occasions I refer forward to poems written outside the period under discussion, where this might be helpful; certain poems, such as 'Earthy Anecdote', 'Anecdote of the Jar', or 'The Snow Man', I allude to quite frequently, since they seem to me to offer useful triangulation points from which to map Stevens's poetic terrain. On occasions I allude to a phrase from a poem not directly under discussion; and when I think it would vex a reader not to be able to locate this, I give a page reference; but sometimes these echoes are part of the ordinary fun of writing and reading. Similarly, I hope in my endnotes and bibliography to provide the reader with everything necessary to establish my sources and extend the contexts of my argument; but I have not given exact references for quotations from canonical nineteenth-century writers such as Emerson or Hawthorne, which I assume to be easily traceable in a variety of sources. My bibliography is also intended realistically to indicate useful further reading, and by no means exhausts what I have myself read or what is of value in the field.

Although this book has been new-written, my manifold debts go back a long way: to my research supervisors at Cambridge, to undergraduates and research students at Lancaster I have myself supervised, and doctoral candidates at other universities whose dissertations I have examined; in their various ways all have stimulated me in my own conceptions. My chief debt is to Lancaster University, which granted me study leave to write the book as well as helping with the unexpectedly high US permissions fees, and to those American scholars who have done so much to raise the level of writing about Stevens in recent years. The General Editor, Richard Dutton, offered helpful comments, as did my wife Jane; who saw that I was moved by seeing Stevens's house, and may, now, see more clearly why.

Note

Those unable to visit Hartford in person can pay a virtual visit to Stevens's haunts in the city on the website run by the Hartford Friends of Wallace Stevens (http://www.wesleyan.edu/ wstevens/stevens.html). Here there is an illustrated 'walk' from his office to his house (pictured in snow, and described as comfortable but modest for a senior executive), as well as photographs of his grave, and links to other sites. The city of his prolonged residence does not wholly neglect his memory, therefore. The recent appearance of a Stevens volume (edited by Frank Kermode and Joan Richardson) in the 'Library of America' series seems to indicate the permanence of his literary standing.

List of Abbreviations

I have used the following system of abbreviation to give references for Stevens's writing in the running text. Fuller details may be found in the Bibliography.

CP: *Collected Poems*
L: *Letters of Wallace Stevens*
NA: *The Necessary Angel*
OP1:   *Opus Posthumous* (first edition)
OP2:   *Opus Posthumous* (second edition)
Palm: *The Palm at the End of the Mind*
SP: *Souvenirs and Prophecies*

WSJ: *Wallace Stevens Journal*

Acknowledgements

Material has been quoted from the following copyright sources:

From *Letters of Wallace Stevens* by Wallace Stevens, ed. Holly Stevens Copyright © 1966 by Holly Stevens. Reprinted by permission of Alfred A. Knopf Inc. and Faber and Faber Ltd.

From *Opus Posthumous* by Wallace Stevens, ed. Samuel French Morse Copyright © 1957 by Elsie Stevens and Holly Stevens. Reprinted by permission of Alfred A. Knopf Inc. and Faber and Faber Ltd.

From *Souvenirs and Prophecies: the Young Wallace Stevens* by Holly Stevens Copyright © 1966, 1976 by Holly Stevens. Reprinted by permission of Alfred A. Knopf Inc.

From *Collected Poems* by Wallace Stevens Copyright © 1954 by Wallace Stevens. Reprinted by permission of Alfred A. Knopf Inc. and Faber and Faber Ltd.

1

The Métier of Nothingness[1]

'I have no life except in poetry', wrote Stevens in one of the aphoristic memoranda to himself that he composed during the latter part of the 1930s and entered into private notebooks as his 'Adagia' ('adages'). This declaration emphasises how important to his sense of self the poetic occasion was, constituting what he defined, at the beginning of *Notes toward a Supreme Fiction* (1942), as the 'central' of his being. Here, in his most ambitious poem, we are again made aware of the exclusive nature of Stevens's fictive music: for its first line – implicitly addressed to a personification of the 'Supreme Fiction' – asks, 'And for what, except for you, do I feel love?' (*CP* 380). Not fully living 'except in' and not fully loving 'except for' experience as poetry: this all seems rather shockingly dismissive of the world beyond the poem or outside the book, offering in Wallace Stevens a literary life that looks like the accomplishment of an extremist in the exercise. Of all the major figures of Modernism in English, it may be that only James Joyce led a life in writing as intense, as quintessentially constitutive of the man, as Stevens did.

Important as books and writing were to Stevens, however, there was always a world elsewhere: in full, what he wrote was 'I have no life except in poetry. No doubt that would be true if my whole life was free for poetry' (*OP2* 200). Clearly, he accepted that the whole of his life was *not* free for poetry; and however challengingly exclusive the opening question of *Notes toward a Supreme Fiction* seems to be, this self-consciously major poem starts with the self-consciously minor word 'And', as if to emphasise its connection to a precedent less exalted state – much as the grandiose resonance of the title's 'supreme fiction' has already been modified by the provisionality of 'notes toward'. Indeed, the question of what else he felt love for may not have been entirely rhetorical; Stevens asserted in a letter to Henry Church, the poem's dedicatee, that he liked wine, grapes, cheese and books as much as he liked supreme fiction (*L* 431): and if we were to speculate on other possible answers, we might come up with items such as 'money', 'power', 'prestige', 'security', or 'comfort' – all of which derived from his life beyond the existence as man of letters, but each of which related to it as well.

1

If Stevens is known (an 'if' more substantive in Britain than America), he is known for the apparent oddity of his having combined a full-time career as an insurance executive with his life as a poet. More specifically, at his death in August 1955, aged 75, he was still employed as Vice-President of the Hartford Accident and Indemnity Company (one of the largest in the USA), and had earlier that year received the National Book Award for his *Collected Poems* (1954), a volume of 534 pages. Having started in an era before the writer-in-residence became an institution of the American campus, it is not odd that Stevens, with no independent income, was obliged to earn his living in an occupation unrelated to literature. What is notable, however, is the apparent dissociation between the sensibilities directed to each sphere of his activities: for whereas one might deduce from reading William Carlos Williams's poems that he knew something about medical practice, or from reading Robert Frost's that he was 'versed in country things', it is not easy to locate the world Stevens knew as a businessman in the poetry he wrote.

The myth of a bifurcated life came into being, not wholly discouraged by Stevens himself; as when he told a correspondent that he tried to maintain a definite line between poetry and business (*L* 615), or when he cautioned a young scholar of his acquaintance, on the threshold of the supposedly prestigious Canoe Club in Hartford, that 'we do not talk poetry here'.[2] As early as 1922, when asked for a biographical note to accompany a group of poems to be published in the *Dial*, he begged to be excused: 'I am a lawyer and live in Hartford,' he tersely confessed, 'but such facts are neither gay nor instructive' (*L* 227). It was not true, however, as some believed after his death, that colleagues at the Hartford were astonished to discover his poetic side: for years he had been in the habit of getting his secretary to type up drafts of poems, as well as using her for his literary correspondence. He would send office juniors to the reference library in Hartford to look up obscure words in the *OED* (sometimes, one of them recalled, trawling as far as the twelfth meaning), for filing with the notes for poems which he kept in the bottom right-hand drawer of his desk. He had also grown adept at parrying – 'squashing' might be exacter – any attempts made by his colleagues to draw him out on the subject of his own verse. Nor was his situation quite as anomalous as might appear: both Benjamin Lee Whorf, the linguistician, and the composer Charles Ives worked in insurance at Hartford at the same time as Stevens, and in Whorf's case, for the same firm.

As a very senior executive of what became a very large company, another myth was engendered, of his prodigious wealth. In his Dream Song 219 about Stevens, John Berryman called him a 'funny money-man'; and much earlier, in a letter of 1944, he had reported to his mother that Stevens 'makes $85 000 a year'.[3] From about 1917 onwards, Stevens was never less than financially comfortable, although he sometimes affected not to be; but although early (in the case of Walter Arensberg) and later (Henry Church) he associated with millionaires, he was far from being one himself: according to Brazeau, at his death his estate was assessed at under $100 000; in 1944 Stevens earned $20 000 from the Hartford, and although his salary was raised the next year, according to company records it never reached $25 000. Whilst this is substantially less than Berryman believed was the case, it still represented good money for the times. Although, for example, his salary was reduced from $15 000 in 1929 to $13 500 in 1932, Stevens was virtually untouched by the Depression, and as that receded his earnings recovered to $17 500 in 1934: 'a heck of a salary ... in those days', recalled someone whose own father, during the period, was 'probably earning two thousand dollars' as a doctor (Brazeau, p. 237). It may seem irrelevant or even slightly vulgar to dwell so much on money (as if none of us needs it!), but Stevens himself would not have thought so. 'Everything was in terms of dollar bills to Stevens', remembered Samuel French Morse, an early critic-biographer (Brazeau, p. 152); and although later in life Stevens was remembered for advising younger writers, such as Richard Wilbur, to pursue a monkish devotion to their art, for his own part he did not seriously regret the path he had chosen, and uttered a profound and slightly shocking truth, for himself, when in another of his 'Adagia' he recorded that 'Money is a kind of poetry' (*OP*2 191).

W.H. Auden, in his elegy for Yeats, asserted that 'executives' would never bother themselves about poetry and its remote sources; the case of Wallace Stevens the executive disproves this. He was not, however, a businessman in any simple sense of being involved in the manufacture or sale of anything; rather, his was the highly specialised area of surety bonds, where his legal training came into play (a recent critic of Stevens has noted that those hostile to his writing tend to define him as a businessman; those sympathetic, as a lawyer).[4] The work entailed was not entirely legalistic; a surety bond was a form of insurance whereby a party contracting to have work undertaken (for example, a public authority) would be protected and compensated should the work fail to be completed or to be satisfactory. This could involve substantial projects and large sums of money; as the agent of the company issuing the bond, Stevens's job – in which he achieved national eminence in the field – was to assess the grounds for and extent of any liability arising, to consider the most effective ways of meeting any obligations, and to authorise the release of funds as appropriate. This area of the insurance market was a considerable source of revenue for the Hartford, especially in the post-Depression years of the New Deal, and then of the war economy; and it was Stevens's particular fiefdom within the company.

The importance of his job to Stevens is attested by the simple fact that he never retired from it: the Hartford's regulation that its officers leave at 70 was relaxed in his case (as apparently in some others). In November 1954 he wrote declining the offer of the Charles Eliot Norton professorship at Harvard for 1955–6, for fear that this would make inevitable the retirement he so wished to postpone; and, even though his health would in fact have prevented him from taking up the position, this refusal is the more significant in that, in making it, he denied himself the opportunity to attempt his project of formulating a theory of poetry as 'a normal, vital field of study for all comers' (*L* 853), which had been dear to his heart for more than a decade. There may have been domestic reasons underlying Stevens's desire to keep up his office routine for as long as possible; but this episode underlines the significance, for him, of the life that he led outside of poetry – which has been increasingly the focus of researchers in the field. As the poet John Malcolm Brinnin puts it, 'I used to see Stevens as a delightful exotic. Now I see him with oats in his teeth' (Brazeau, p. 194).

'Every great and original writer', declared Wordsworth in a letter, 'in proportion as he is great and original, must himself create the taste by which he is to be relished'. Wallace Stevens's poetry did not inaugurate a revolution of taste comparable with that wrought by the *Lyrical Ballads*; nor did he manage during his lifetime to define and influence his own readership to the degree that his contemporary, T.S. Eliot, did. But the comments Stevens contributed to the 1938 issue of the *Harvard Advocate* in honour of Eliot's 50th birthday show him to be aware of the drawbacks of such success. He started his brief 'tribute' by declaring that Eliot's 'prodigious reputation' itself constituted an obstructive element for the reader; and for the writer, whilst 'more or less complete acceptance' such as Eliot had achieved could help create his poetry, 'it also helps to destroy it' (*OP2* 240). Stevens went on to say that he could only enjoy Eliot's poems when able to forget their eminence – 'reading Eliot out of the pew' was his slightly mischievous phrase for this procedure, which was necessary to counteract the less desirable consequences of the process outlined by Wordsworth in his letter. For however much issues of 'greatness' and 'originality' figured in Stevens's conception of what a poet should be, he was also consistently clear about the need not to become so accepted as to achieve an institutionalised immobility: as he explained in 1954 to Robert Pack (who would write the second book-length study of the poet), 'that a man's work should remain indefinite is often intentional' (*L* 863). It was this quality of unfixedness that has enabled Stevens's poetry – as Brinnin's comment above suggests – to reveal its different aspects, or to reflect different preoccupations of the reader, at different times. This has been a significant factor in the development and establishment of Stevens's reputation since his death.

Also implicit in Brinnin's contrasting views of Stevens as 'exotic' and 'with oats in his teeth' is the change, from seeing the poet as somehow at odds with American writing to seeing him as the home-grown product. This to some degree reflects the alteration in the dominant critical perceptions of his work: one of the earliest books in which Stevens's poetry was discussed, René Taupin's *L'influence du Symbolisme français sur la poésie américaine* (1929), tried to annex him to a French tradition, whereas a half-century later Harold Bloom's massive *Wallace Stevens: the Poems of Our Climate* (1977), as its title makes equally clear, is concerned to argue Stevens's centrality to an American tradition. The need to find a French antecedence for a Modern poet was partly in order to conform to the template offered by Eliot, who (even by 1929) was well known for having been crucially influenced in his development by Laforgue and Baudelaire; and I suspect that the example of Eliot conditioned critical perceptions of Stevens in various ways. When critics praised Stevens for his abstruseness and difficulty, or for the philosophical/theoretical content of his poetry, it may have been in part to show how he fulfilled Eliot's criterion that modern poetry should be 'difficult'; at the same time, however, their praise implicitly celebrated an American exponent of intellectually ambitious writing who, unlike Eliot or Henry James before him, had not found it necessary to leave America. If the first step was to see Stevens as somehow mentally rather than physically expatriate – which felt much less like rejection than did Eliot's desertion of his native land – the second was to see that Stevens not only stayed at home but was at home, all along; and there is some truth in each of these positions. It also seems to be common for a critic to be unable to appreciate the poetry of both Stevens and Eliot: the cases of Harold Bloom (who admires Stevens and deplores Eliot) and Hugh Kenner (who admires Eliot and deplores Stevens) are notable instances of this condition.

As his 1938 remarks showed, Stevens kept any admiration for Eliot well within bounds; and (having declined to contribute to a *Harvard Advocate* issue on Stevens in 1940) Eliot returned the compliment in spades, in his statement to the *Trinity Review* (Hartford) in 1954, which struck a tone of rather emphatic blandness: Eliot defined himself as 'admirer' of Stevens and as director of Faber & Faber, his London publishers – also letting slip that it hadn't been his own idea to publish Stevens; he had imagined some other British firm to be responsible, but now that Faber's was doing the job, albeit belatedly, he supposed that the more people who read Stevens's poetry, the greater would be the opportunity for some to like it. Eliot's ability to have overlooked Stevens reflects the poet's marginalisation by the Anglo-American Modernists; in Ezra Pound, for example, he provoked aggressive perplexity: 'Stevens?????? the amateur approach, the gentle decline to take responsibility of being a writer???' – where the tally of question marks seems rather to indicate certainty than interrogation.[5] Across the Atlantic, however, doubts about Stevens's stature and achievement have been progressively dwindling, to the point where a recent study of his canonical incorporation can adjudge his status to be 'perhaps more secure than that of any American poet of this century'.[6] Such 'complete acceptance' of Stevens brings destructive dangers with it, as he would himself have acknowledged, and there is a value in retaining some, at least, of Pound's question marks in respect of Stevens's career. A British critic may therefore be better placed than an American to read Stevens 'out of the pew'; and this is what I wish to undertake in this book.

It was not only in 1938 that Stevens was alert to the dangers of solidification: throughout his poetry, statues and states of immobility are regarded with amusement or distrust. In a letter of 1954, having mentioned his decision not to attend a celebration of Robert Frost's 80th birthday at Amherst, he went on to acknowledge that Frost was greatly admired by a wide readership; Stevens himself held off from such admiration (through insufficient familiarity with Frost's work, he claimed), but recalled for his correspondent having some years previously seen a bust of Frost in Harvard's rare books library, commenting that he supposed he himself would 'never be eighty', no matter how old he became (*L* 825). The publicly acclaimed Frost, in other words, as virtual poet laureate had achieved a highly undesirable embeddedness in the official scheme of things, which in Stevens's eyes marked an inevitable petrifaction. He felt no confederacy with Eliot or Pound; but neither did he embark on a campaign, as Frost did, to entice the 'general reader who buys books in their thousands'. In his 1954 letter, Stevens noted that Frost's work was 'full (or said to be full) of humanity' – his disdainful parenthesis signifying a refusal to confer belief in, or value on, such an achievement. During his lifetime, commentators had remarked on the absence of such a note in his own work, and he never completed an envisaged section of *Notes* entitled 'It Must Be Human'; yet, as his already cited view of poetry as a 'normal, vital field of study for all comers' shows, this was not because he affirmed a marginalised elitist role for the poet. To return to the declaration with which this chapter opened, it is because according to his own account of the matter Stevens's was in its most significant dimension an intensely literary life, that he is so appropriate a subject for the present study.

Given the intensity of his commitment, evidenced by the fact that Stevens carried on writing good poetry virtually to the end of his life, it is interesting to remember Pound's thinking he exemplified the 'amateur approach'. Presumably what Pound had in mind – suggested by his amplification that Stevens avoided taking the full responsibility of being a writer – was that because he did not rely on his pen for his living, Stevens took no risks in the service of his art (as Pound himself undoubtedly did), and by implication relegated it to the status of part-time pursuit. Since Pound had been unable to appreciate the contribution made to Eliot's peace of mind and therefore creativity, by his years of employment by Lloyds Bank (1917–25), he was not well qualified to make a just assessment in Stevens's case. The connections and disconnections between 'work', 'money', and 'poetry' were highly significant for Stevens; but we get nowhere if we force the first and third of these terms into a non-negotiable opposition. It would be truer to say that 'work' permitted and necessitated 'poetry': for if Stevens went on writing to the end of his life, it has already been observed that he went on working, as well. Another possible construction of Pound's remark might be that, for him, Stevens's irresponsible amateurism was to be seen in the failure of his writing to address social or political issues; for while Pound was devoted to the cause of good art, this was because he saw good art as both sign and prerequisite of the good society.

Since Stevens's death, what had once seemed the self-contained isolation of his *oeuvre* has been modified, by a twofold development of the recent criticism: in the 1980s, building on his daughter's edition of Stevens's letters (1966) and journals (1977) – as well as on her brief essays of reminiscence – and on research into unpublished materials principally held at the Huntington Library and oral memoirs of those acquainted with the poet, a considerable amount of biographical detail became available; and in the 1990s, building on all this, a good deal of work has been undertaken to demonstrate Stevens's connectedness with the times in which he lived. The notion that he was thoroughgoingly a mandarin in an ivory tower is now obsolete, and is being replaced by a perception of the ways in which his writing interacted with the political climates of America in the century's middle decades. Stevens's kind of engagement was much less direct and interventionist than Pound's, in part because he lacked the latter's belief that ultimately the poet should be an acknowledged legislator rather than an unacknowledged one; but Pound's career hardly offers an irrefutable argument for his own position on the matter.

With Stevens, the kinds of knowledge now available can be problematical; the life he led is not immune to ridicule, as even admirers acknowledge. In the mid-1960s Frank Kermode suggested that the poet could seem to be a sort of Hartford des Esseintes, pestering acquaintances to send him exotic items from China and ordering paintings from France as substitutes for the Peking and Paris he denied himself the pleasures of ever visiting – even though he could have afforded to. This was a (particularly American?) form of consumerised imperialism, yet at the same time it was also of real personal value to Stevens, an affair of the spirit rather than the wallet that finally seems, more truly and more strange, a mark of his resourceful destitution rather than of a pseudo-touristic acquisitiveness. We can now see how quickly Stevens's marriage became an unloving emptiness that not even the eventual birth of a child could revive; we learn of cases of wine smuggled into the basement after dark, of bottles hidden in the former maid's room upstairs, of cigars smoked furtively at the end of the garden. This behaviour of a man in fear of his wife is sad to know about, as also is the absence of hospitality in their desirable residence: for wine, cigars, and a comfortable house are pleasures greatly diminished when enjoyed in solitude. We can infer, too, the degree to which Stevens himself contributed to an atmosphere in the household that reduced their home help to a state of nervous prostration, and led to his daughter's reminiscence that her earliest memory was of planning to run away from home. Yet this unwelcome knowledge of a life lived in constraint is the context for a juster appreciation of why what mattered to Stevens, such as poetry, mattered so much: a plain sense of things that helps to render insignificant the distraction of his having had a lot of money, comparatively speaking, and that helps us better understand what he meant by 'poverty' – an important term in his writing. 'World without Peculiarity' (1948) suggests some of the elements Stevens wove into the song of himself:

> He, too, is human and difference disappears
>
> And the poverty of dirt, the thing upon his breast,
> The hating woman, the meaningless place,
> Become a single being, sure and true.

> (*CP* 454)

One of the more influential of Stevens's recent critics, Helen Vendler, has insisted on a note of austerity as the defining tone of his poetry – notwithstanding the gaudiness and verbal exuberance which have preoccupied some other commentators. Vendler's emphasis risks undervaluing the element of playful excess in the poems, but it helps to define an aspect in which Stevens can be seen to be characteristically American, or to confront a phase of experience almost self-consciously so: described in his poem 'The American Sublime' (1935) as consisting of the 'empty spirit' situated in 'vacant space' (*CP* 131). This radically reductive state, in which the self confronts a 'new' world cleansed of precursive intentionality (and therefore perceived as a 'sensible emptiness', to borrow Thomas Traherne's sombre seventeenth-century phraseology), is potentially both daunting challenge and exhilarating opportunity. It is the site of possible despair and defeat, or victorious self-affirmation, or – as Stevens's enigmatic 'Anecdote of the Jar' (1919) may have it – the site, simultaneously, of both. The relevance of the radically reductive state to the reductive radicalism which gave birth to the United States should not need underlining; 'reductive' is not used pejoratively in either formulation, but denotes a fundamentalism which requires confrontation of a minimal existence as the basis for any reconstruction – required, Stevens would put it in 'The Plain Sense of Things' (1952), as a necessity requires.

The process involves a rebuttal of precedent and an implicit affirmation of American uniqueness. The unprecedentedness of the experience is frequently imagined in terms of the European coloniser's first sighting of some aspect of the new continent – such a moment as compels the silence on the peak in Darien, with which 'stout Cortez' (in an appropriate Keatsian disregard of history) first saw the Pacific Ocean. More relevant to the generation of American national mythology than Keats's sonnet (which uses this American uniqueness as a simile for the poet's discovery, not of a new-found-land, but of his originary forefather Homer), such an initiatory experience is commemorated in William Bradford's history *Of Plymouth Plantation* (1630–50), describing the landfall of the Pilgrim Fathers and their company in November 1620:

> Being thus passed the vast ocean, ... they had now no friends to welcome them nor inns to entertain or refresh their weatherbeaten bodies; no houses or much less towns to repair to, to seek for succor. ... Besides, what could they see but a hideous and desolate wilderness, full of wild beasts and wild men – and what multitudes there might be of them they knew not. ... Which way soever they turned their eyes (save upward to the heavens) they could have little solace or content in respect of any out-ward objects. For summer being done, all things stand upon them with a weatherbeaten face, and the whole country, full of woods and thickets, represented a wild and savage hue. If they looked behind them, there was the mighty ocean which they had passed and was now as a main bar and gulf to separate them from all civil parts of the world.

Although the biblical allusiveness of Bradford's account implies how confrontation of the 'wilderness' denotes a time of trial taking place within an ultimately providential divine scheme, his early representation of 'America' as a literal and metaphorical rite of passage, requiring separation from old ways of being and the apprehension of an unconstructed landscape, is a notable example of the inflections given by a mythology to its region.

This depiction of America as a land of lack may surprise, in the context of contemporary and subsequent European portrayals of America as a land of plenty (e.g. Captain John Smith's or Crèvecoeur's), but the notion of America at its truest consisting in an absence of the known is encountered elsewhere: in Thoreau's removal to his lakeside cabin in *Walden*, for example; and in Henry James's notorious itemisation, in his study of Nathaniel Hawthorne (1878), of all the social and civil amenities of which Hawthorne was deprived by his choosing – unlike James – to stay for the most part in America. There were no palaces, ivied ruins, cathedrals, great universities or public schools in the USA ... James's list is longer, and well known enough not to require quotation; but what is less often dwelt upon is the conclusion to his confessedly 'ludicrous' enumeration of 'the absent things in American life', in which he asserts, 'the American knows that a good deal remains; what it is that remains – that is his secret, his joke, as one may say'.[7] By stripping away all the elements that make the Old World what it has been, you come to the 'secret' core of America, the world whose difference lies in its declared quality of being 'new': the absent things define the present essence.

All this has bearing on the attempt to see what makes Stevens an 'American' poet, with a sensibility distinct from that of a British writer; and for Stevens, as for some others, part of the effort to be American involved repudiation of any British lineage, a process which, metonymically, was akin to looking at a landscape uninhabited by his forefathers. It is, admittedly, old-fashioned and slightly politically incorrect to talk as if an essentialist version of 'Americanness' could have any objective reality, independent of its use as an ideological construct; but, as Sacvan Bercovitch has argued, such ideas *have* had political, social, and historical consequences, as well as a mythological continuity. D.H. Lawrence, in his idiosyncratically seminal (in all senses) *Studies in*

Classic American Literature (1923), defined what he described as the dual rhythm of 'American art-activity' as '(1) A disintegrating and sloughing of the old consciousness. (2) The forming of a new consciousness underneath';[8] therefore, at the end of Stevens's 'The Snow Man' (1921), when the listener in the snow, 'nothing himself, beholds / Nothing that is not there and the nothing that is' (*CP* 10), he may be thought to engage in a definingly American procedure.

These repeated nothings have been compared to those in *King Lear*, but it seems to me that the more useful contrast within English literature is to be drawn with Jane Austen's *Emma* (I do not claim a direct connection, although we know that Stevens possessed a copy).[9] In Chapter 27 of what may be as English a novel as *The Adventures of Huckleberry Finn* is American, Emma has gone to the village shops with her protegée Harriet and, while that slightly empty-headed young lady takes large time over small purchases, Emma goes to the shop-door to survey the scene:

> Much could not be hoped from the traffic of even the busiest part of Highbury; ... and when her eyes fell only on the butcher with his tray, a tidy old woman travelling homewards from shop with her full basket, two curs quarrelling over a dirty bone, and a string of dawdling children round the baker's little bow-window eyeing the gingerbread, she knew she had no reason to complain, and was amused enough; quite enough to stand still at the door. A mind lively and at ease, can do with seeing nothing, and can see nothing that does not answer.

The sense of inertia at the end of 'The Snow Man' – of a perceiving mind that is so far from being 'lively' as to be almost not alive at all ('nothing himself'), and of a grammar that has exhausted its own logic (the poem is a continuous sentence) – is banished by the participial forms which predominate in the excerpt from *Emma*, and convey the ongoingness of life. Both pieces are to do with necessarily reduced expectations, but Austen's is a celebration of the responsive mind in a social context, a mental adequacy that makes nothingness impossible; whereas Stevens's unpeopled scene, its only occupant a man of snow, expounds mere being. A sense of community would impair the snow man's arctic integrity because of what it implies, not only about contingent lives in place, but about the continuity of lives in time: a snow man is created, not begotten, existing without ancestry as if – to use Stevens's words from the end of 'Sunday Morning' (1915) – he could truly be 'unsponsored, free' (*CP* 70). Jane Austen's Highbury, with its old woman and its dawdling children, bespeaks the succession of generations, implies the actuality of history in the present moment; but Bradford's 1620 America, with 'no houses or much less towns', is an ahistorical wilderness permitting (and necessitating) self-authorship: 'the moment's being, without history' (*CP* 427).

This last phrase comes from Stevens's poem 'The Beginning' (1947), and the issues here have very much to do with beginnings and originations. In his short book *Nature* (1836), Ralph Waldo Emerson made what have subsequently become influential opening remarks:

> Our age is retrospective. It builds the sepulchres of the fathers. It writes biographies, histories, and criticism. The foregoing generations beheld God and nature face to face; we, through their eyes. Why should not we also enjoy an original relation to the universe?

As Emerson's writings made clear, the young American was best placed to break such craven habits of retrospection; and in the American context 'fathers', defunct authority figures burdening the present with authorised versions of all their yesterdays, have to be understood as European – specifically British – ways of seeing, being, and thinking. Although it is also dear to the Romantic tradition in Europe, which historically coincided with America's achievement of self-determination, the quest for an original relation to the universe has been a particularly American project. It implies a belief in beginnings that explains the availability, in American history, of a wide range of dates and occasions from which to count the commencement of the new and the abandonment of the old: 1620, 1776, 1865, the New Deal, the New Frontier – these are the more obvious choices. American writing has many *loci classici*, depicting the point from which Americanness begins, in addition to Bradford's: young Ben Franklin getting off the boat in Philadelphia in 1723, buying his 'three great puffy rolls' from the baker and, starting from scratch, embarking on a life's journey which would see him instrumental in ejecting the British; Hawthorne's Robin, in 'My Kinsman, Major Molineux' (1832), disembarking from the ferry on his quest for the powerful relative in the colonial administration whose patronage he hopes for – only to find that worthy being expelled from the town in tar-and-feathers. The tale ends with one of the republicans telling Robin, 'If you prefer to remain with us, perhaps, as you are a shrewd youth, you may rise in the world, without the help of your kinsman, Major Molineux'. Thus are the Emersonian 'fathers' to be dealt with, by the free, unsponsored sons who make their way without any illusory benefits of patrimony: types of 'ephebe' (the arcane term Stevens used, denoting a 'young citizen'), obeying the instruction to 'begin'.

Emerson almost implies that it is unnecessary even to inter these dead fathers; but Hawthorne is alert to the problems inherent in declarations of independence (his tale 'Roger Malvin's Burial' deals with the consequences of an unburied parent): for in the story's title and its closing words, Major Molineux remains Robin's 'kinsman'. For Hawthorne there is something painful or dishonest in dissociating from the past, producing in him a distrust of those dramas of rebirth or disconnected inception, which abound in America's stories of itself and of its origins. As Eliot notes in *Little Gidding*, 'What we call the beginning is often the end', and Stevens's poem 'The Beginning' turns out to be, in part, about the end (of summer); his writing, too, shows sharp awareness of the downside of a gospel which cannot progress beyond the phrase, 'in the beginning...'. His poetry acutely renders the suppressions required when establishing 'an original relation to the universe'; for there has to be not only 'nothing' outside his snow man, but virtually 'nothing' inside him either: a state of amnesiac unhopefulness.[10] For Emerson, this sacrifice of self accompanied an influx of power, as seen in the famous visionary passage, taking place 'in the woods', in the first chapter of *Nature*:

> Standing on the bare ground, – my head bathed by the blithe air, and uplifted into infinite space, – all mean egotism vanishes. I become a transparent eye-ball. I am nothing. I see all. The currents of the Universal Being circulate through me; I am part or particle of God.

Here, being nothing means seeing all, whereas in 'The Snow Man' being nothing means beholding nothingness; and I think Stevens's poem 'A Rabbit as King of the Ghosts' (1937) offers a satirical commentary on this passage in Emerson.

Although forgetting or disowning one's ancestry (and all that entails) may have been one prerequisite for the American attainment of an original relation to the universe, another was that one suppress any sense of there having ever been a precedent aboriginal relation. The 'wild men' and 'savages' of Bradford's account could be of little consequence to his narrative, except as inhabitants of what Cotton Mather later described (in his *Wonders of the Invisible World*, 1692) as 'the devil's territories', their significance confined to acting as Satan's agents or, like the land itself, manifesting usefulness through conversion. They could hardly be accorded the status of being viewed as the rightful occupants of the land they happened to be living in: and the happy accident of Columbus's misappellation 'Indians' (supposing he had 'discovered' the Indies in 1492) precluded until recently the awkwardness of having to consider these to be the true 'Americans', in defiance of a huge accumulation of myth – which sees, in a blatant example, how the West was 'won', rather than that it was lost.

The point and force of seeing America 'for the first time' is seriously diminished if the Eurocentric gazer has to yield precedence to the countless eyes of 'Indians': and so their claims were sidelined by an imported rhetoric establishing that incomers from another land had magically acquired prior rights to their territories. It was important that those rights were 'prior': 'The land was ours before we were the land's' runs the first line of Robert Frost's 'The Gift Outright' (1942), recited at the Kennedy inauguration in January 1961; and this shows how a state of mind (Americanness) was seen as having greater validity than a state of affairs (primarily British colonial rule, but equally applicable to the existence of resident natives unseen in the poem, albeit faintly heard in the name 'Massachusetts'). Such a belief legitimised the ensuing expropriations which chiefly characterised white America's behaviour toward the tribes, whilst at the same time enabling it all to be seen as the fulfilment of national destiny rather than as a process of neocolonialist expansion or imperialist aggression. Displaced from their tribal lands, many gravitated to Oklahoma (set aside as Indian territories in 1836); and despite Stevens's assertion that he had actual animals in mind (*L* 209), the 'bucks' clattering over Oklahoma in his poem 'Earthy Anecdote' (1918), in fruitless evasion of the persistent 'firecat', may – albeit at the twelfth level of meaning – also evoke the Indian braves saddled up for yet another act of removal in response to the authorised 'land-runs' of homesteaders (in 1889, 1891, 1892, and 1893); a progressive settlement whose culmination was the incorporation of Oklahoma into the Union in 1907, when Stevens was 28. 'To us, of course', an American historian drily declared near the time of Stevens's birth, 'the American Indian is no longer a mysterious or even an interesting personage – he is simply a fierce dull biped standing in our way'.[11]

It would be no more than appropriate if, thereby, 'Earthy Anecdote', chosen to begin his first published volume in 1923 and retained as the opening poem of his *Collected Poems* (1954), were to manifest some sense of the compromised nature of even the freshest-seeming beginnings – such as Oklahoma's, or America's. Stevens's own beginnings as poet, husband, and father may reasonably be described as delayed; and a sense of deferred inception is to be observed in *Notes toward a Supreme Fiction*. For although its first section starts with the imperiously unambiguous 'Begin, ephebe, ...', this has been preceded by eight prefatory lines starting with 'And for what...?', printed underneath the title and dedication, and inevitably read first by all who encounter *Notes*: the poem is one in which it seems formally impossible to begin at the beginning. Other American writers have in various ways interrogated the myth of their nation's 'immaculate beginning' (*CP* 382): Hawthorne, in *The Scarlet Letter* (1850), found that from the outset the New World had required Old World appurtenances such as gaol and cemetery; and at the end of *The Great Gatsby* (1925) Fitzgerald has Nick Carraway imagine the Dutch sailors' first sighting of the 'fresh, green breast of the new world': an irretrievable beginning that is also an ending, as man comes 'face to face for the last time in history with something commensurate to his capacity for wonder'. Their 'aesthetic contemplation' is in essence outside history, a 'transitory enchanted moment', immediately supplanted by the historical processes whose agents they are, as they move in upon the virgin land.

The relation of the 'aesthetic' to the historical was a major concern of Wallace Stevens, who also saw its connection, in the American context, with origins – and therefore, with originality. It is also a major concern of recent literary criticism of his writing, in its attempt to diminish the sense of the poetry's existing in an aesthetic vacuum. 'Originality', the decisive difference from precursive models – for Wordsworth, as we have seen, the function of a writer's greatness – was of considerable importance and a source of some anxiety to Stevens, who (like Eliot) desired to be original at the same time as he recognised that desire to originate in defensiveness. In 'The Comedian as the Letter C' (1922), his long, extravagant poem of occluded autobiography in which he gave one version of the growth of a poet's mind, the 'poetic hero', Crispin, having discovered his 'still new continent' of America, conceives his project there to be to 'drive away/ The shadow of his fellows' and 'from their stale intelligence released,/ To make a new intelligence prevail' (*CP* 37). These 'fellows' are the Emersonian 'fathers', his literary precursors; and Stevens's formulation is an almost perfect illustration of the 'dual rhythm' of American art-activity, expounded almost simultaneously by Lawrence.

The poem 'Celle Qui Fût Héaulmiette' (*CP* 438), with its Villonesque title, seems to address many of the issues so far touched on, and can be read as a poem about the stage immediately following that radical reductiveness which was – considerably earlier in Stevens's career – the closing note of 'The Snow Man'. Set, like some others of his poems, at the moment when winter gives way to spring so narrowly as almost to be undiscernible, signs of seasonal change nonetheless operate as if they constituted 'a meaning in nothingness': for if the first step for the American artist is to confront nothingess, the next is to locate meaning. The poem's girl (a tentative creature who personifies the uncertain inception of this process) seeking and finding shelter and form may, it is acknowledged, simply have happened upon mere 'American vulgarity'; but all the same this functions as her 'native shield', and establishes her, not in the chilly ancestorlessness of the snow man, but as the daughter of 'a mother with vague severed arms' (which I take to denote the Venus de Milo, functioning as metonym for European artistic inheritance) and a father 'bearded in his fire' (primordial America figured as the sun).[12]

Written in the late 1940s, this poem of apparent accommodation between America and Europe, between the self without history and the self as an historical consequence, is an appropriate point at which to conclude. This chapter has tended to perceive Stevens's *oeuvre* as a set of poems in dialogue with each other, existing in the simultaneity of his 'collected works'. I believe this not to be an invalid or misleading way of approaching the material, as it reflects the experience of any reader sufficiently immersed in Stevens's writing, as well as corresponding to the way in which he himself felt his poetry to constitute a whole. It has also enabled me to present certain general and particular issues which I think are helpful to an overall view. Nevertheless, it is with the literary life that this book is concerned, which develops in time and is marked by the successive publication of the material on which his reputation rests. Subsequent chapters, therefore, will be more chronological in their approach, and more attentive to the kinds of decision involved for Stevens in the publication and organisation of his poetry. The increased availability of the facts of Stevens's life cannot be overlooked in a study such as this, but I hope to remain alert to the dangers of reducing poems to incidents of autobiography. In common with others of his generation, Stevens lived in a period during which America transformed itself more rapidly and more radically than ever before, and quite possibly more than it could ever do again. He was born in 1879, 14 years after the end of the Civil War, ten years after the opening of the first transcontinental railroad, three years after the Second Sioux War; the gunfight at the OK Corral had not yet happened, the frontier was still open (it was declared closed in the 1890 census), the Klondike Gold Rush had not taken place. The great nineteenth-century poets, Walt Whitman and Emily Dickinson, were still alive (the latter, of course, hardly known); *The Adventures of Huckleberry Finn* had not yet been published, and (later) Stevens would read Henry James as a contemporary author. In the year of his birth, the electric light bulb was simultaneously invented on each side of the Atlantic (the older Stevens would save used bulbs and return them to the power company so as to achieve a small reduction on his electricity bill). By the time he died, Stevens had lived through the two world wars, into the atomic age; he had seen the development of the car (he never owned one) and of the aeroplane; during his lifetime, techniques of mass production and mass communication (and mass destruction) transformed the nature of the market-place and the relations between people. All of this had consequences for the possible meanings of art – as commodity or enchanted moment – that are particularly relevant to Stevens's development into what he became: a major poet of the twentieth century.

2
Starting with Nothing

Keats's assertion that a poet 'is the most unpoetical of any thing in existence' seems to be borne out by Wallace Stevens, whose own existence apparently enshrined a kind of ordinariness embodied as high principle. Not for him the mannerisms of dress and bearing by which a Yeats or a Pound declared that they were poets; not for him, even, the more restrained dandyishness glimpsed in T.S. Eliot; not for him, certainly, the projected wiseacreishness of Robert Frost. He is remembered as having gone so far as to wear pastel-shaded shirts with his customary suits of solemn grey, at a time when white shirts were overwhelmingly the norm in the business community; but that was his only gesture toward the kind of sartorial extravagance yearned for in his poem 'Disillusionment of Ten O'Clock' (1915), or toward the ceremonial purple robing his speaker in 'Tea at the Palaz of Hoon' (1921). Whatever the verbal excesses of his poetry (and these were great), Stevens himself for the most part preserved an impeccable formality of bearing behind which – trespassers could find – lay a glacial aggression; the snow man was not there to be played with, and even his high spirits could take a violent turn: punching Ernest Hemingway on the jaw, for example, or kicking a tray of drinks out of a waitress's hands. By some accounts he could be stunningly rude: late in his life, at a reception held in the house of a trustee of the college awarding him an honorary degree, on being invited by the owner to admire its interior decor Stevens is reported to have replied that he and his wife had taken great care in their own home to avoid creating just such an effect! When a British philosopher, to whom Stevens had been introduced, asked if he might call on the poet at home, the answer was brief and absolute: 'No'.[1]

Indeed, few trespassers ventured to 118 Westerly Terrace, the sizeable house in Hartford where Stevens spent the greater part of his writing life (1932–55); fewer still penetrated its interior, where they would have seen an immaculate white rug on the living-room floor – and might have been forbidden to walk on it. The British philosopher was probably lucky, in having been prevented by Stevens's discourtesy from proceeding further with his scheme of sociability; for had he managed to avoid being insulted by Stevens, it seems quite likely that the poet's wife would have done the job herself: whatever effects of interior decor Wallace and Elsie had taken trouble to create, they had been wholly successful in achieving a reputation of legendary inhospitableness amongst his business colleagues – 'I never did get in that house', recalled one.[2] Stevens's occasional rudeness may have been, in part, the behaviour of a man of power who had no need of anybody's good opinion but did need to demonstrate the fact (which suggests a certain insecurity, despite appearances to the contrary). It is true to say that throughout his life Stevens seems to have sought for and been most at ease in relationships with those who could be considered his inferiors, whether through age, talent, social class, or by virtue of their position in the company hierarchy; and this has a potential relevance to his poetry. Is the reader's role that of a subordinate, who can be flattered by the appearance of confidence but who can always, within the implicit power structure, have it made quite clear just where the limits of intimacy lie? 'Begin, ephebe...': these are the words, maybe, of an uncle who observes one through the frostiest of monocles. Underlying much of Stevens's behaviour was the issue of privacy; poetry was something which, for him, fell into the area of 'private', and the maintenance of this attitude – in spite of the apparent paradox of publication – seems to have been important. Whatever public function he envisaged for 'the poet' as generic type, it was of clear psychological significance for him personally to regard poetry as a form of retreat (*L* 230), a making interior of the exterior, an act of disengagement rather than the reverse (although he was not absolutely consistent in this attitude). In a poem celebrating Stevens, Theodore Roethke wrote that he 'never met him'; and not meeting Stevens, in one way or another, seems justly symptomatic of his reclusive predilections.[3]

To echo James on Hawthorne, enumeration of the 'absent things' in Stevens's life could run to quite a list, although its effect might rather be poignant than 'ludicrous'. Apart from a visit to Cuba he didn't travel abroad, he didn't have any really close friends, he didn't have a happy marriage nor happy family relationships with his own parents and siblings, nor, subsequently, with his daughter (except latterly); despite his final eminence in poetry and business, his funeral was sparsely attended. To be sure, his poems, the 'present things', are a substantial mitigation of all this; but even so the life in which they originated was, in its external forms, such as to justify his label 'neither gay nor instructive'. It seems less eventful and stimulating in its contexts than the lives of Yeats, Frost, Pound, Eliot, or Williams: for unlike all these others, Stevens kept his distance from literary associates and associations (with the half-exception of his early years in New York). Always he seemed to prefer people on paper to the real unpredictable thing; he could, for example, adopt a tone of unbuttoned friendliness in his letters to Williams, but when the latter came to visit Stevens put him up in a hotel. Yet, to revert to the terminology of 'The Snow Man', he was an accurate observer of the nothing that *did* happen; and if Thoreau was right to assert that the mass of men lead lives of quiet desperation, there are aspects of Stevens's life which make him a more truly representative man than any of these others.

Home is where one starts from. In Stevens's case, this was a large terraced (or 'row') house in Reading, Pennsylvania, where on 2 October 1879 he was born the second son of Garrett Barcalow Stevens and his wife Margaretha Catherine Zeller; his brother, Garrett Jr, was 18 months older, and their parents – both in their early thirties – had been married just under three years. The family subsequently enlarged with the births of John (1880), Elizabeth (1885), and Mary Katharine (1889); the other children were given family names, but Wallace owed his to a politician prominent at the time. He was exceptional, also, in being the only one of the entire family to reach and exceed the biblical threescore-years-and-ten: both his parents died in their early sixties, and by the spring of 1943 all his brothers and sisters had predeceased him. The youngest, Mary Katharine ('Catharine' to Stevens), was the first to die, of an illness contracted as a Red Cross nurse in France in May 1919; and that same month Stevens wrote about it to his wife, imagining how Catharine must have been looking forward to returning home even though, as he immediately added, in fact she had no home to return to (*L* 213).

The desire to recover a state of being no longer accessible is a classic theme, on which Stevens's writing wrought particular variations; six years earlier he had revisited Reading (after the deaths of his parents), and reported the experience to his wife, herself a native of the place: 'Reading was very – unsympathetic, I thought. The trouble is that I keep looking at it as I used to know it. I do not see it as it is. I must adjust myself; because I do not intend to shut myself off from the heaven of an old home' (*L* 181). Repeating that last phrase, he modulated into a reminiscence of du Bellay's famous sonnet of homesickness ('*Heureux qui, comme Ulysse...*'), which Stevens had translated for his fiancée shortly before their marriage in 1909 (*L* 151); thereby evoking the importance of his Pennsylvanian roots at the very moment when he understood them to have been irrevocably severed – indeed, making acknowledgement of this severance the only possible means of preservation. It is in many ways appropriate that the first letter in Holly Stevens's edition of her father's correspondence should open with the 15-year-old Stevens announcing to his mother his intention of coming home early from the summer resort at Ephrata (*L* 5); and it is equally appropriate that, in the event, he stayed where he was: in many ways, for Stevens home was what one stayed away from.

In 1879 Garrett Stevens was a successful attorney in the city, where he had been nine years resident; he was a solid and respected citizen with some political inclinations, but his solidity permitted the anonymous publication of occasional verse in the local newspaper, as well as some verbal flights of fancy in letters to his second son. His business interests would expand to include a bicycle factory and a steel plant; but when he died, his will made plain that his estate fell far short of the inheritance he would have wished to bestow on his children. He considered himself to be a self-made man (see *L* 18); born on a large farm in Bucks County to a father who was a pillar of the local Dutch Reformed Church, he had left to take up schoolmastering before reading law and embarking on its practice (as boys, Wallace and his brothers had many opportunities to spend time on their grandparents' farm at Feasterville). In 1943, Stevens would remember his father as a solitary and even somewhat forbidding figure, who spent much time at his office and, when at home on Sundays, alone in his 'library'. Most commentators have noticed that Stevens's reminiscence of his father as a man desirous but starved of 'discreet affection', who wanted 'quiet' in which to create 'a life of his own' (*L* 454), seems also to describe Stevens's own emotional and domestic circumstances.

A later literary son of Reading, John Updike, born there a half-century after Stevens, observed in 1977 a city in decline, with its industries vanishing and a population that had fallen in every census since 1930; but in the closing quarter of the last century its had been a different story:

The natural landscape of Berks County, it may not be too fanciful to say, looks nurtured and used and, if not Arcadian, rather European to American eyes. The sky seldom lacks clouds, and the hills, with their shaggy crowns, do seem subdued giants. The frontier feels even more remote here than in New England, where an underlying austerity remembers it. Reading, its natives know, is a civilized place. Laid out on tidy English principles by Thomas Penn, an early center of American industry, populated by skilled craftsmen, and combining, in the words of the 1911 Encylopaedia Britannica, 'unusual business and industrial advantages' with a situation in a 'rich agricultural region', Reading had in the years when Stevens knew it best a proud sense of itself as a *place*.[4]

In his boyhood and youth Stevens grew accustomed to this landscape, through which he would take prodigious walks as a measurement of his animal vigour. A letter to his fiancée of January 1909 recalled an apparently idyllic succession of summers spent bicycling, rambling, and swimming, including what he referred to as a 'pirate period' amongst 'a really tough crowd', with whom he used to hop coal-trains up the Lebanon Valley to stone farmhouses and steal pumpkins (*L* 125). To my mind, these antisocial escapades evoke the world-view of Tom Sawyer rather than of Huckleberry Finn; but it was evidently of some importance to Stevens that he could pass as 'one of the roughs', in Whitman's phrase, and that he could explain to his betrothed that he had lost a world when he left Reading (*L* 98).

In the same letter describing his 'pirate period', Stevens wrote that he had taken *all* the prizes at school; this may have been an ironic boast, but the facts were otherwise (see *SP* 10–13), and there were a couple of unusual circumstances to his schooling. The first was that while still at primary school, Stevens spent a whole year living with the family of an uncle, Henry Strodach, in New York; Strodach, married to Stevens's Aunt Mary, was a Lutheran pastor in Brooklyn, and his nephew attended parochial school there. The episode left a sufficient emotional deposit for Stevens to revisit the school when, after university, he was trying to make his way as a newspaperman in New York (*SP* 76). The second unusual feature of his education was that at the end of his first year at Reading Boys' High School in 1893, his average was not high enough to permit him to pass into the next year, with the consequence that he was kept back and went through high school in the same class as his younger brother John – in academic rivalry with whom Stevens did not invariably prevail. It is not known why he was sent away for a year, nor why his first year's results were apparently so poor; but these disruptions modify to some degree the picture Stevens was painting of his boyhood in his letter of January 1909 (a darker tone still is added by the fact that Pastor Strodach committed suicide in Reading before the turn of the century; this seems to have played a part in Stevens's desire to see his school again).

Whatever lay behind Stevens's poor first year in secondary school, it clearly did not impede his subsequent performance there, and he left in the summer of 1897, having completed the school's classical course 'with merit'; whilst this did not signify the highest level of academic achievement, it was good enough to secure his admission to Harvard that autumn as a special student. His period at high school also saw his first publication: in December 1896 he had won the alumni medal for oration with his address on 'The Greatest Need of the Age', printed that month in the Reading *Eagle*, which had awarded him its essay prize earlier in the year. Although he was to deliver the commencement address on graduating from Reading School the following June (the *Eagle* reporting that his 'patriotic sentiments were rewarded with loud acclamation'), the essay prize more accurately predicted Stevens's future than the oration medal, and his days as a crowd-pleaser were drawing to their close.

His time at Harvard was decisive, although not perhaps in the way he might have wished; in his 1909 letter he saw that his first year away from home at Cambridge 'made an enormous difference in everything' (*L* 126). This touched on the sense of estrangement from Reading and, presumably, from his family, that going to Harvard inaugurated in him, and which was evidenced in the fact that his first year away was just that: he didn't go home (even at Christmas, despite his father's pleading) until the following summer. Stevens's status as a special student meant that he would spend three years at Harvard, rather than the four which were customary to complete a degree; because of this, his choice of courses was unrestricted. The reasons for his status were financial: although his elder brother Garrett Jr had dropped out of Yale after only four months he had then enrolled in law school in the autumn of 1896, and was still a charge on his father's purse at the time when both Wallace at Harvard and John (at the University of Pennsylvania) were also running up expenses; with two daughters to provide for as well, Garrett Stevens could not afford to do more for his second son. Although the need to be aware of economic realities forms a *leitmotiv* in his letters to Wallace, it was not until the end of the latter's period at Harvard that the financial pressures which were to drive the confident Garrett into nervous collapse became apparent.[5]

Despite the fact that Stevens would say he considered his practical side to have come from his father and his imagination from his mother (*SP* 8), on the evidence of the letters his father wrote to him at Harvard there was more to Garrett than this implies. With their directness and occasional humorous turns these letters, from one whom his son would recall forty years on as the least communicative of men (*L* 458), surely marked a real deepening of their acquaintance – in some way counteracting the sense of separation from home Stevens would remember in the letter to his fiancée. The correspondence certainly suggests that the father, like the son, found it much easier to relax on paper than in person. One of the first letters from Garrett (27 September 1897) asserted his belief that the useful should not always be preferred to the beautiful, and he was later able to applaud his son's election to the Signet Society and to the board of the *Harvard Advocate*; but at the same time he admonished him to remember the 'main purpose' of his being there, and – his concern doubtless sharpened by his eldest son's failure – he required constant reassurance that Wallace kept at his studies. The son's side of the correspondence is missing, but it is possible to infer some of it from the father's: whose stress on the need not to desire to do things (such as foreign travel) before one could well afford to undertake them, and whose relief that the composition of poetry was not so 'serious' as to impede 'real hard work' on his son's part (*L* 23), imply the nature of their dialogue.

It is possibly significant that Stevens had sent the poems provoking this comment to his mother; an earlier letter from Garrett (16 December 1898) refers to poetry Stevens had evidently sent *him*, adjudging that it ran 'prettily', but also emphasising the amount of prose in his own life, with just the slightest edge of reproach (presumably the poems were 'Who Lies Dead' and 'Vita Mea', the first of Stevens's poems published in the *Harvard Advocate*, in November and December 1898; *SP* 22–3). Garrett was no philistine; but Stevens's sense of a paternal resistance to poetry as a form of self-indulgence and – presumably – of a contrasting maternal receptivity, set the stage for his own wrestlings with the idea that writing poems was an inherently feminine activity, excluding its practiser from the fully masculine world of doing and money-making. By this stage Stevens was well aware of his father's exasperated disappointment with Garrett Jr (who had earlier that year over-committed himself to the masculine world of doing, by withdrawing from law-school to enlist as soldier in the Spanish–American war), and would have seen how all this heightened parental expectations and anxieties in his own regard. But although in the event his life turned out to embody perfectly the precepts of self-reliance his father had advocated, that parent died when his anxieties rather than his expectations in respect of Wallace's life seemed likelier to be justified. As Garrett Sr had written to Stevens to complain of his oldest son, so he wrote in 1907 to his daughter Elizabeth to apologise for his educational provision for her (no Vassar, as hoped), and blaming it, perhaps unfairly, on the wastrel tendencies of his two elder sons, 'as Romantic as Cinderella' (Bates, p. 10).

The father had been pleased when the son chose, in his first year at Harvard, to follow a course in 'Government' (*SP* 17); but although in each of his three years Stevens dutifully took a serious-sounding course ('Outlines of Economics' in 1898–9, and 'Constitutional and Political History of the United States, 1738–1865' in his final year), his other courses were preponderantly in English, French and German, with the emphasis falling – after the elementary courses of the first year – on literature (see *L* 17n., 23n., 33–4n.). The high school education Stevens underwent had been based on the old classical ideals; but Harvard, with its elective system instituted in the 1870s by President Eliot, represented a break from such beliefs, with modern languages considered to be as valuable for study as Latin and ancient Greek. Stevens's range of courses seems chosen to acquire a broad education in (principally) European culture – with a concentration on literature that might be thought particularly appropriate for an aspiring writer. For notwithstanding Garrett's aspersions on the seriousness of his son's literary ambitions, nor his expressed belief that going to Harvard meant the opportunity more quickly to advance oneself in the world, for Stevens, going to Harvard seems to have meant embarking on the road to becoming a writer. It may have been this fundamental (and necessarily disguised) divergence between their views of the matter that kept Stevens away from home for the whole of his first year.

Perhaps, too, he stayed up in affirmation of a desire that Harvard, rather than Reading, might be his truest home. As it turned out he regretted spending that first Christmas in Cambridge, for he grew lonely and depressed, and did not bother to attend the party given by Professor Charles Eliot Norton which had been his ostensible reason for remaining (*L* 575). The community of Harvard, whatever its intellectual stimulations, was not the warmest of surrogate families for a shy and essentially ungregarious young man; and as Milton Bates puts it, 'coming from a distant small town and educated in public schools, he was at a distinct social disadvantage' (p. 24). Although to a degree he made his way socially, achieving election to some societies and – in his final semester – presidency of the *Harvard Advocate*, he had neither the money nor the connections to penetrate the really exclusive clubs, and he spent his three years in the same lodgings on Garden Street, run by the Misses Parsons. These were genteel enough arrangements, but not to be compared with the luxurious accommodations available to members of the prestigious societies (it is possible that Stevens took his studies too seriously to conform to that Harvard type). The College was in a phase of growth when Stevens entered, as one of the more than 400 freshmen who constituted its largest intake to date; a whole set of gentlemanly conventions, based on the possibilities of acquaintanceship amongst students and between them and their teachers, was presumably changing toward a more impersonal system, as numbers continued to expand. Stevens's wish to stay away from home, together with his failure to attend the social event at Professor Norton's, seems aptly to express his ambivalence about belonging either to Reading or Harvard; we could speculate that he was 'in' both but fundamentally 'of' neither: susceptible to desires to lead the life of the mind, but not immune from paternal admonitions to make something of himself.

When eventually he did return to Reading in the summer of 1898 – which he possibly spent working for the local newspaper – it was noticed that he seemed to have put on Harvard airs and graces; judging from his journal and letters over the following years, he seemed also to have picked up the virus of anti-semitism. More beneficially, university encouraged in him habits of exhaustive and extensive reading (his own interesting expression was that he spent an afternoon reading 'violently'), and of mental speculation. This speculation concerned itself, as often as not, with

questions which were much in the air in the *fin de siècle*: what is the
true relation of art to life, between the ideal and the real? Two of
the figures at Harvard who were notable for their engagement in
these and associated debates were William James (brother of the
novelist Henry) and George Santayana. James's position was anti-
absolutist and anti-transcendental; he asserted that 'truth' is always
generated by context, rather than existing paradigmatically, and
that the search for truth was the expression of a human need rather
than an achievable goal. A religion, thus, would be true to the
degree it satisfied its adherent's will to believe; and, in such a
relativist rather than absolutist context, the value of any philosophy
or creed would be discernible in the conduct it inspired in the
adherent. In James's view, most human knowledge is based on an
interaction, usually unnoticed, of desiring mind and external
reality: the world we discover is the world for which we were
looking, and to that degree created. There is no evidence that
Stevens met James or was taught by him, but there is much
testimony to James's influence on the intellectual atmosphere of
Harvard during Stevens's time. James had taught Santayana, and
Santayana's assuredly *was* a personal influence on Stevens, who
seems to have been introduced to him during his second year there.

Santayana published his study *Interpretations of Poetry and
Religion* in 1900, and although he was to some degree estranged
from his former teacher James, he had in common with him an
element of pragmatism, in his consideration of the psychological
originations of aesthetic response. Although he asserted that the
imagination was 'the true realm of man's infinity', he remembered
that this faculty originated in matter, and was fastened to a dying
animal; his assertion that poetry and religion are essentially the
same thing is of obvious relevance to Stevens's mature verse and
the ideas behind it. However, what Santayana was exposed to was
Stevens's immature verse; for another virus that he had picked up
at Harvard was that of sonneteering; an infection that proved
equally difficult to conquer and, like anti-semitism, consisted in the
unreflective recycling of received ideas. Santayana, 16 years his
senior and remarkably tolerant of the poems the young Stevens
showed him (going so far as to compose a reply to one sonnet: see
L 482, 637), may well have seemed a more desirable father-figure
than the rather deflationary Garrett. His situation as something of
an outsider at Harvard, together with what he defined as the
'combination, not easily unified' in his own person, of elements

derived from his birth and early childhood in Spain, and from the Cambridge where he had come to study and then teach, offered parallels to the situation of his undergraduate visitor. Certainly, the position he adopted on the role of the poet and the use of his powers was remarkably predictive of what would be Stevens's views of the matter: in 'Understanding, Imagination, and Mysticism', the first essay in *Interpretations of Poetry and Religion*, he asserted that 'if the imagination merely alienates us from reality, without giving us either a model for its correction or a glimpse into its structure, it becomes the refuge of poetical selfishness'.[6] But if he was able to help point the way for Stevens, he was unable to offer a literary model in practice, for his verse displayed some of the features of derivative poeticality from which the younger man needed to disentangle his own writing.

Stevens acquired yet another, less pernicious, habit at Harvard: in his second year he started keeping a journal. It is fair to say that, notwithstanding the twenty-odd poems – together with some prose (including editorials) – that Stevens contributed to the *Harvard Advocate* (and to a lesser extent to its rival the *Harvard Visitor*), his most important creative writing during his Harvard years, as well as the early years in New York that followed, was in his journal. To say this is to recognise that it was here, rather than in those poems, that he began to forge his identity as a writer: and this way of putting it is particularly appropriate to the strenuous and self-conscious process involved. For quite a few years he was in the habit of reading over earlier entries, commenting censoriously, altering and even excising passages (a procedure which, after his death, his widow would also enact on the journals and letters); and the material in these pages was the psychic source for a good many of his mature poems, however radically modified. Late on in his extended and largely epistolary courtship of Elsie Moll, Stevens referred to a 'Book of Doubts and Fears', which was probably imaginary but may have referred to the very letters he was writing her; in fact this would not have been an inappropriate title for his journal: for although that contains some exuberant descriptions of his energetic country hikes around Reading and New York, it is also notable for recounting the uncertainties he felt at the outset of his careers.

These uncertainties were both specific and general. At their most specific they manifested themselves as his father, who had consistently preached the need that economic self-sufficiency should precede commitment to the muse (as in his letter of 1 November 1898: 'Young America understands that the question is – "Starting with nothing, how shall I sustain myself and perhaps a wife and family – and send my boys to College and live comfortably in my old age[?]" Young fellows must all come to that question...' *SP* 71), and who had as consistently blocked any proposals Stevens made that Garrett should finance his literary *wanderjahr* (see, for the clearest example, the journal entries for 11 and 12 March 1901). Stevens had gone up to Harvard in order to become a poet, but he left still unconfirmed in his literary vocation, to become first a journalist and then a lawyer – each at his father's prompting. Behind the father (beset at this period by financial difficulties whose gravity the son seems not to have realised) was the more general problem of whether or not Stevens really had the gift necessary to become an American poet. In almost his last journal entry while at Harvard (2 June 1900), he contemplated the apparent conflict between the world of work and the world of writing, and tried to summon the resolve necessary to commit himself fully to one or the other: what he wished *not* to be involved in, in either sphere, was 'a petty struggle for existence – physical or literary' (*SP* 71); but exactly a fortnight later, translated to New York, his mood was considerably less buoyant:

> I spent the afternoon in my room, having a rather sad time with my thoughts. Have been wondering whether I am going into the right thing after all. Is literature really a profession? Can you single it out, or must you let it decide in you and for itself? I have determined upon one thing, and that is not to *try* to suit anybody except myself.
>
> (*SP* 74)

Such were the doubts and fears confronting the young Stevens, whose expectations in regard of a literary life can hardly have been made more sanguine by the experience, only twelve days after that last journal entry, of going to the sparsely-attended funeral of Stephen Crane (1871–1900) in a small church on Seventh Avenue. 'The whole thing was frightful' he confided to his journal (*SP* 78), drawing from the meagre attendance the moral that the age afforded few hero-worshippers, and therefore few heroes. Yet there were other conclusions Stevens might have drawn from the facts of this short life. Crane had perished from tuberculosis, not from literary neglect; at the age of only 24 he had won celebrity on both sides of the Atlantic for his novella *The Red Badge of Courage* (1895), a minor classic which some see as pivotal in the transition from nineteenth- to twentieth-century American writing: so there were grounds for regarding him as a success, despite his premature end. But Stevens may have had his reasons for dwelling on the unachieved aspects of Crane's life and career, in order to obviate a potentially awkward comparison: Crane had embarked on the first version of *Red Badge* when still only 21, Stevens's own age in 1900; yet what had Stevens to show at this stage, apart from a small collection of conventional undergraduate verses? Moreover, Crane's brief life had included precisely that element of knocking about the world that Stevens desired for himself, with forays to Mexico, Cuba, and Europe; yet that Christmas he would record in his journal how his father effectively discouraged him from going to Arizona or Mexico; and, as he wryly noted, for him Europe was 'still on the other side of the ocean' (*SP* 94) - where it would remain for the rest of his life. I am put in mind of the speaker of Robert Frost's poem 'The Sound of Trees' (1914), determined to 'make the reckless choice' and 'set forth for somewhere', but knowing in his heart that he will only absent himself by dying.[7] Stevens may have had cause to be grateful to Garrett (as later, perhaps, to his own wife), for acting as the visible impediment to such schemes: thereby preventing him from having to confront the fact that, in this respect, he had not courage equal to desire.

What were the prospects for a would-be American poet, fresh out of Harvard at the turn of the century? Before the Civil War, Washington Irving had written of the predicament of the American writer in the following terms: 'Unqualified for business in a nation where everyone is busy; devoted to literature where literary leisure is confounded with idleness, the man of letters is almost an insulated being, with few to understand, less to value, and scarcely any to encourage his pursuits'.[8] For much of the nineteenth century, the phrase 'American literature' had had the force of an oxymoron, despite the efforts toward cultural independence made by some of the writers who are now canonical; in the same period as Irving, in England the clergyman and celebrated wit Sydney Smith had famously inquired, 'Who reads an American book?', without expecting to hear that anybody did. The case of Irving himself, who in his lifetime achieved a significant reputation in Britain and continental Europe, would in fact have answered the doubting Smith; and although an American sense of cultural inferiority would persist into the next century, in mid-nineteenth-century America there was a widely disseminated culture of the book, supporting a substantial publishers' market whose value had risen twenty-fivefold between 1820 and 1860.[9] Although this market was to a high degree penetrated by the Old World product, with pirated editions alike outraging American authors who felt themselves neglected and British authors who felt themselves defrauded, there was also evidence that the demand for and supply of domestic writing were buoyant – if not precisely healthy.

Reservations about the healthiness of the situation rise from the quality of the goods consumed, although their quantity is not in doubt. Improved transport systems (principally the railway) meant that whereas in 1826 James Fenimore Cooper's *Last of the Mohicans* was a best-seller at 5750 copies, in 1853 *Fern Leaves from Fanny's Portfolio* ('Fanny Fern' was the pen-name of Sara Payson Willis) quickly sold 80 000 copies throughout the settled states. Accustomed as we have grown to the notion that women writers were suppressed by patriarchal nineteenth-century literary culture in America, such sales are surprising, and imply a level of 'suppression' that Melville would have welcomed for *Moby-Dick* (1851), which sold 2300 copies in 18 months. Even Nathaniel Hawthorne – whose *The Scarlet Letter* (1850) had sold 5000 copies within six months (possibly due to its lurid title) – vented his spleen against the 'd[amne]d mob of scribbling women' who monopolised the public taste with 'trash' that sold by the hundred thousand. Ann Douglas notes that the combined total sales of Hawthorne, Melville, Thoreau, and Whitman in the 1850s were exceeded by the sales of just one of these best-selling domestic novels. Although the phenomenon of massive sales was more a feature of fiction than of poetry, there was also evidence of considerable demand for the latter. Rufus Griswold, best known today for his calumniation of Poe, compiled *Poets and Poetry of America* (1842), which sold well, and then used this as the basis for his *Female Poets of America* six years later, which went through multiple editions, including revision (by another hand) and enlargement in 1869. Thomas Buchanan Read's *The Female Poets of America* (1849) had run through nine editions by 1866. What this shows is the increasing importance of editors and anthologists as

cultural mediators and market-makers in the expanding book
trade; and it also suggests the extent to which commercial imperatives were likely to influence what was published: for one of the
most important facts about the market for literature in nineteenth-
century America was that the great majority of consumers were
women. This led to what Douglas has defined as the
'feminization' of American culture:

> [American women] comprised the bulk of educated churchgoers and
> the vast majority of the dependable reading public; in ever greater
> numbers, they edited magazines and wrote books for women like
> themselves. They were becoming the prime consumers of American
> culture. As such they exerted an enormous influence on the chief male
> purveyors of that culture, the liberal, literate ministers and popular
> writers who were being read while Melville and Thoreau were being
> ignored.[10]

Explicit in the activity of anthologisers such as Griswold was the
desire to establish the reality of an American literature; but the
success of his enterprise, from our perspective, is very much
compromised by the fact that so few of the poets selected have
withstood the test of time. The defining taste for which his (and
similar) compilations catered was one which desired to be soothed
or diverted by the predictable, not galvanised by the shock of the
new. Thomas Wentworth Higginson, the man of letters to whom
Emily Dickinson applied for advice about her poems, has attracted
scorn for his responses to her highly individual talent; but
whatever may be said about his literary judgement, his advice –
essentially, that she make her poetry more anodyne and more
uplifting – cannot be faulted as an analysis of what would have
been most likely to make its way commercially. His failure lay in
not appreciating how different Dickinson was from the average
'female poet of America', and how her practice quite explicitly
repudiated such an ideal; but the extent to which that type
governed conceptions and receptions of poetry was considerable.
Paradoxically, although the sales figures show that *belles lettres* in
America was big business, its 'feminisation' meant that culturally
it was situated outside the male preserve of working and money-
making, and to a large degree was seen as antithetical to it: poetry
became a kind of spiritual luxury item, commodified like other
non-essentials both as an affirmation of status ('I have leisure and

elevated tastes') and as consolation for the typical consumer's exclusion from political or economic power.

Stevens himself was certainly implicated in this perceptual alignment, as when he attributed his imagination to his mother and his practicality to his father. It was his mother, appropriately, who gave him the Riverside edition of Emerson for Christmas in 1898; later it was his wife-to-be whom he instituted as the keeper of his flame, dedicating little private booklets of his verses to her in a culturally sanctioned compact of femininities. That edition of Emerson, however, was itself evidence of the extent to which American writing was achieving solidity and respectability in the later nineteenth century, a process further seen in the *American Men of Letters* series of critical biographies under the general editorship of Charles Dudley Warren, which grew to 22 volumes between 1881 and 1904 (the 'men' of the series title was generic, since it included Higginson's study of Margaret Fuller). Despite their predominance in the mass market, women were not the only best-sellers in the field; for in 1900 the most commercially attractive role-model for the young man contemplating a career in poetry would beyond question have been Henry Wadsworth Longfellow (1807–82), who like Irving and Cooper before him was known as an American man of letters outside as well as inside the USA. In 1855 the long poem by which he is probably best remembered in our own times, *The Song of Hiawatha*, sold 30 000 copies in six months; in the same year Walt Whitman arranged for the private and virtually anonymous publication of *Leaves of Grass*, containing the long poem he would later entitle 'Song of Myself': most of the 800 copies remained unsold. Longfellow lived comfortably on the proceeds of his writing, and his popularity exceeded even that of Tennyson; he was introduced to Queen Victoria and is commemorated in Poets' Corner of Westminster Abbey. This was fame indeed; nevertheless, when near the turn of the century Stevens considered the issue of 'Poetry and Manhood', Longfellow was not one of his exemplars.

In this journal entry (23 May 1899), Stevens addressed himself directly to the issue of poetry and gender:

> Those who say poetry is now the peculiar province of women say so because ideas about poetry are effeminate. Homer, Dante, Shakespeare, Milton, Keats, Browning, much of Tennyson – they are your man-poets. Silly verse is always the work of silly men. Poetry itself is unchanged.

(SP 40)

In spite of his confident closing assertion, the entry touches on a source of considerable anxiety, which can be represented in the form of an approximate syllogism. As Washington Irving had diagnosed, literary leisure was confused with idleness; idleness, in the sense of abstention from remunerated employment, was the doubtful privilege of women (a form of 'conspicuous consumption' in Thorstein Veblen's sense); literature was therefore the speciality of women, and poetry their 'peculiar province' because the prevalent understanding of poetry was as improving verse, consumed as a kind of moral tonic by a readership that consisted either of actual or honorary women (like the ministers who – as Douglas shows – had been increasingly bereft of status in the developing nation). Small wonder that Whitman, starting 'Song of Myself' by stressing his possession of leisure ('I lean and loafe at my ease…'), should feel the need also to stress his possession of an erectable phallus ('firm masculine coulter, it shall be you [I worship]'): as if to counter in advance imputations of effeminate degeneracy that might attach to a disputably male poet. For Stevens, the era which had seen in England the trial and imprisonment of Oscar Wilde (1895), the era in which the word 'homosexual' first became current to denote a condition morally and sexually pathological, was also one in which a preoccupation with matters aesthetic could be conflated with a shameful vice.

Something of this view of poetry writing as a habit reprehensible in a man is apparent in him. Writing to his fiancée at the end of January 1909, having enclosed a sonnet, he alluded to a newspaper review which argued the writing of poetry in the present time to be an exercise of vanity (that is, a form of narcissistic display); Stevens partly admitted the charge, but also asserted the 'pure delight' involved, confessing that, having nothing to read, 'I am going to be at it again soon' (*L* 131). After their marriage (when frequent absences of one or other partner from home necessitated letters), we find him in August 1913 coyly admitting to his wife that he had been trying to assemble a little collection of verses during the lonely evenings. 'Keep all this a great secret', he admonished her, 'there is something absurd about all this writing of verses; but the truth is, it elates and satisfies me to do it. It is an all-round exercise quite superior to ordinary reading. So that, you see, my habits are positively lady-like' (*L* 180). The defensiveness about the possible lack of moral hygiene in what he had been up to, and the implicit appeal for absolution to the matrimonial cult of the feminine, are interestingly intermingled here. But being lady-like was justification only if one were a lady; and although up to this point Stevens's guilty poetic proclivities had been indulged within the sanctifying contexts of their courtship and marriage (and, to a degree perhaps neither partner appreciated, seem to have been constitutive of the relationship), his desire to be a 'man-poet' meant that his wife's approbation could not be enough; such recognition could only be conferred outside the marriage.

A year later in 1914 Stevens would publish his first serious poems in a 'little magazine'; and if it seems far-fetched that in my discussion above I have emphasised the potential transposability of terminology between poetic and sexual activity, it should be borne in mind that the evidence suggests that Elsie Stevens received this publication as a serious infidelity on her husband's part. The story of their relationship, so far as it is relevant to this study, will be dealt with in due course; but here I am concerned to suggest the extent to which it embodied and enacted the drama of the cultural-historical forces which were affecting Stevens in his choice of vocation. Unfortunately, the very roles in which they had allowed themselves to represent their marriage were ones which had to be broken with if Stevens was to achieve his poetic potential; for these depended on the tacit understanding that poetry was something intensely private which husbands and wives did with each other: it was largely a woman's affair, but involved no compromise of manhood when, in a modern variant of *amour courtois*, poems were written as a lover's tribute. The woman's role was as a kind of moral arbiter who permitted the man to express feelings which in a wider context might represent a diminution of his manliness. It was the essential propriety of such transactions that Stevens stressed (even allowing for irony) in presenting his wife-to-be with his first 'Book of Verses' for her 22nd birthday in 1908: 'It would only be *proper* for you to have your own private book of verses', he wrote, 'even if it were very small and if the verses were very bad' (*SP* 190; my emphasis).

Thus, the stock Edwardian lover addressing his beloved. In the broader American cultural situation, as a reward for her exclusion from the centres of power, the idealised woman was enshrined as a guardian of conscience (the reality of her influence in that sphere is visible in the introduction of Prohibition between 1920 and 1933). In literature, necessarily she would read nothing that disgusted or offended her, and since she and those like her virtually constituted the mass market, this discouraged the production of work unfit for her consumption. Given that what she *would* read omitted a great deal of human experience and behaviour, her position as effective censor incurred the resentment of (often *soi-disant*) red-blooded males – and of some red-blooded females, as well. We have seen this resentment in Hawthorne's comments about women writers, and we have seen Whitman exposing himself. In Stevens's case, a reaction against constraining 'feminine' decorum can be observed in the aggression-against-prudery of 'A High-Toned Old Christian Woman', in the unpleasant female corpse in 'The Emperor of Ice-Cream', in the rather unconvincing orgiastic male dancers in stanza VII of 'Sunday Morning', and, generally, in all of the bawdiness of *Harmonium* (1923), his first published volume. Stevens's poetic rejections of Christianity often entailed an attack on some version or other of what his culture deemed 'lady-like' – and this on the part of one who had formerly given his fiancée a booklet of his poems almost as if it were a prayer-book.

The answer to the problem of 'effeminate' poetry raised in his journal was, evidently, to become a 'man-poet' (or, to use his later phrase, a 'virile poet'); but why did no American precursor come to his mind as a role-model? Whitman would seem to have been an obvious – even parodistic – possibility, and it is unlikely that in 1899 Stevens would not at least have known about his poetry; but perhaps his was too idiosyncratic or temperamentally inaccessible a star for Stevens to steer by. The male poets he certainly would have heard of, the grey eminences who had defined the role for much of the century, were the Fireside poets (so called, because latterly they appeared in Houghton Mifflin's 'household' editions, to be read by the comfort of one's blazing hearth): W.C. Bryant, O.W. Holmes, H.W. Longfellow, J.R. Lowell, and J.G. Whittier. None of these commands much space in current anthologies of American literature, compared to the pages allotted their little-known or little-read contemporaries Melville, Whitman or Dickinson; but as Frank Lentricchia asserts, for a significant period their position had been virtually unassailable, as the practitioners of serious verse in America:

> The Fireside poets were among the chief cultural powers of our nineteenth century: they stood for poetry. By their lives as well as by their practice as writers they defined, however conservatively, a

broad-ranging cultural (educative) function for the man of letters: they translated Homer and Dante; they held chairs in romance languages at Harvard; they edited influential newspapers; they were foreign diplomats; they gave well-noted and well-attended speeches on the controversial affairs of the day.[11]

In June 1904 Stevens noted this in his journal: '*a taste for style* in everything, a taste for the brilliant, the graceful, & that common-place the beautiful. Moral qualities are masculine; whimsicalities are feminine. That seems hardly just but I think it is exact' (*SP* 114). It is as if he was looking for a middle ground between the whimsical 'female poet of America' and the staidly moral Fireside group, who lacked brilliance. They represented the dead hand of the past, and he desired to move beyond their example even as the poetry of his novitiate did little to displace the gentility principle they embodied, other than by its occasional frivolity, pseudo-Preraphaelite elements, or aestheticism. Another deadening cultural influence of the time, which also disseminated the notion of poetry as a discreet source of moral improvement, and which Stevens actually possessed on his shelves, was Francis Palgrave's *Golden Treasury of the Best Songs and Lyrical Poems in the English Language*. This anthology and best-seller (during the 1860s it sold 300 000 in the USA alone) enforced a preference for the lyric to the exclusion of other poetic modes, and by its commercial success stimulated the production of various competitors, such as Jessie Belle Rittenhouse's *Little Book of Modern Verse* (1912), which 'featured a table of contents of American poets almost all now unknown [and] sold 100 000 copies in its first edition'.[12] In both Palgrave and his successors, the power of the anthologist to institutionalise taste and exploit a market is apparent, as are the conservative values inherent in the process: in England, later, Ezra Pound made little headway with his attempts to market an anthology of innovative verse. Anthologies of the experimental (i.e. conventionalisations of the unconventional) are a publishing paradox of our own era.

Stevens thus found himself contemplating a predicament familiar to any artist wishing to 'make it new' – and in the American context most forcibly expressed by Melville, in the letter he wrote to Hawthorne (June 1851) as his labours on *Moby-Dick* drew to their close: 'Dollars damn me; and the malicious Devil is forever grinning in upon me, holding the door ajar. My dear Sir, a

presentiment is upon me, – I shall at last be worn out and perish ....
What I feel most moved to write, that is damned, – it will not pay.
Yet, altogether, write the *other* way I cannot. So the product is a
final hash, and all my books are botches.' If the Fireside poets and
their best-selling female counterparts might have exemplified for
Stevens the wrong kinds of artistic compromise with the market-
place, the fate of Melville – working as a lowly official in the New
York docks for 20 years, his books forgotten – could, had he known
of it, have functioned as a dire portent of the petty struggle for
existence that might dominate the life of a writer too neglectful of
publishing's commercial realities. Was it possible to have dollars,
and yet not be damned?

Dollars were very much on Stevens's mind in the summer of 1900,
during his first months in New York where, he observed, everything
seemed to be for sale (*L* 38); the young gentleman from Harvard
experienced a frisson of disgust and resolved not to stay, grateful at
any rate that the clouds and the winds were not manufactured, and
could be enjoyed free of charge. He spent his first night in the city in
the comfort of the Astor House (a 'fashionable residence hotel'
according to Joan Richardson), but then moved out into a rented
room in a tenement neighbourhood (his own words), where his
education as to the nature of the America that was neither Reading
nor Harvard began. Frank Lentricchia has argued that Stevens's
introduction to New York faced him with 'the thinness of his
middle-class insulation'; and certainly, from having been one of the
select few with a Harvard education, his new accommodation set
him amidst the undifferentiated many: at this period nearly 88 per
cent of New York's housing units were rented. In his journal
Stevens described his new quarters, in ironic rhapsody, as 'this
Eden, ... this Paradise ringing with the bells of streetcars and the
bustle of fellow boarders heard through the thin partitions, ... this
Elysium of Elysiums' (*SP* 73); but whatever the contrast between
these thinly-insulated lodgings and the Misses Parsons' Cambridge
establishment, the change represented the start of his journey
toward perceiving that the imperfect *is* our only paradise (see part
III of 'The Poems of Our Climate', *CP* 194).

On the same day that he was recording his misgivings over his
choice of vocation (16 June 1900), Stevens paid New York the

backhanded compliment that it was the greatest place to be
'Americanised' in that he had ever seen or hoped to see. This was of
a piece with his complaint, a year earlier, about the 'Chicagoan' and
'unmeditative' aspects of modern life (1 August 1899), which at that
time were interfering with the various 'thoughts for sonnets' he
desired to bring to fruition; but in New York he himself was in the
process of being 'Americanised', as later he came to appreciate. At
first he resisted the city, with its restaurants whose unappetizing
smells evoked the basic instinct in our need to eat: he proposed to
counteract that view of the human condition by lunching on
successive days on strawberries, a pineapple, blackberries, and
bananas (19 June 1900: the concept is pure Stevens). In the same entry
he noted that he was planning to dine with a friend that evening at
the Harvard Club: perhaps evidence of the desire to look for what
was, where it used to be, that would take him three days later to
revisit the school in Brooklyn he had once attended; but just as there
he saw that the memory and the reality were divergent, so he came
to see that Harvard had its shortcomings. The next month he was
almost simultaneously recording how impressed he was by the
'impersonality of New York' (*SP* 80) and noting that Harvard
encouraged in its young men a 'subjectivity' that left them ill-
adjusted to a world that was in essence 'impersonal' (*SP* 82).

He was of course measuring his own ill-adjustment in this; but
the big city was helping him to take new bearings. On 4 July
Stevens was still toying with the last line of a sonnet, was
denouncing New York's 'infernal money-getting' and planning to
purchase Jowett's *Plato* as a lifebuoy (*SP* 79); but soon afterwards,
having perused Edmund Stedman's recently published *Victorian
Anthology*, he decried the sonnet form for its irrelevance to 'real life
where things are quick, unaccountable, responsive' (*SP* 80). The
entry following described an early-morning detour he had taken to
look at the trees in Washington Square; but his pastoral impulse
met with an unexpected sight:

> I was surprised to find the large number of people who were sleeping
> on the grass and on the benches. One or two of them with collars
> turned up & hands in their pockets shuffled off through the
> sulphurous air like crows in rainy weather. The rest lay about in
> various states of collapse. There must have been a good many aching
> bones when the sun rose.

(*SP* 80)

Instead of Elysian fields, he had a vision of a 'sulphurous' nether world whose dehumanised denizens suggested that what was truly infernal about New York might not be its money-getting, but the consequences of failing to. At this stage Stevens drew no personal inferences from such observations; his own finances were sound enough that he had spent a month in the city without needing to ask his father for help, and was even able to set a little money aside. He had arrived in New York with letters of introduction from his Harvard teachers, and was earning acceptable money working for the New York *Tribune*, on a commission basis; thus he could roam the city with something of a privileged eye. Looking back from the vantage point of April 1903, however, by which stage he had failed as a newspaperman and was nearing completion of his law degree, his vista was more democratic:

> When one has lived for twenty-five years with every reasonable wish granted + among the highest associations – starting at the bottom suddenly reveals millions of fellow-men struggling at the same point, of whom one previously had only an extremely vague conception. There was a time when I walked downtown in the morning almost oblivious of the thousands and thousands of people I passed; now I look at them with extraordinary interest as companions in the same fight that I am about to join. At first, I was overwhelmed...
>
> (*SP* 114)

It is perhaps ironic that this suggests Stevens would embark on the profession of law, having developed characteristics more appropriate to the journalist he had recently failed to be. As for the aspiring poet, although the sonnet virus would persist in his bloodstream for a few years yet, he had been shown a world to which his sonnets were irrelevant. Who, after all, were these people thronging the morning pavements, sleeping uncomfortably on park benches, or having fits of *delirium tremens* in the New York streets (*SP* 85)? Many of them would not speak English, or not well enough to make headway with a sonnet; for they were evidence of the accelerated population-expansion necessitated by the great growth of American industry, creating in its turn a need for labour. Between 1880 and 1914 more than thirteen million immigrants flooded into the USA, the greater part of them from southern and eastern Europe: the Italian family Stevens noticed selling home-made ice-cream on the street two days after he arrived in the city, the long-haired Jews and the 'fat Greek' whose proximity at a concert later irked him (*SP* 131), were probably part of the flood. The 1910 census showed that 75 per cent of the population of America's ten largest cities were either foreign-born or of immigrant parentage; and the 1920 census would reveal that the majority of Americans lived in cities, rather than in the country. These demographic alterations in 'Americanness' were matched by political and geographical expansions: the Spanish–American War of 1898, provoked by the unexplained sinking of the USS *Maine* in Havana harbour, led to the American invasion ('liberation') of Cuba, and the annexation of Hawaii and the Philippines. With the almost fatuously easy expulsion of Spanish interests, the USA emerged as the major power in the area, and as an active player on the world stage, where its pre-eminence would be made manifest when President Woodrow Wilson sent American forces to sort out the Great War in Europe (1917).

This era of national enlargement and redefinition, with its attendant upheavals, created what Stevens would much later describe as a pressure of reality; bound to be more keenly felt in the city, where the velocities of change were most measurable, whether in terms of metropolitan technology or the immigrant influx which was literally and figuratively changing the face of America. Unsurprisingly, Stevens's responses were ambivalent. The differences between the Reading he had grown up in and the New York where he lodged were in essence the differences between old and new America: he hankered after the heaven of an old home, although he saw the danger of too close attachment to the apron-strings (*SP* 81); he was simultaneously stimulated and 'overwhelmed' by what he described as the electric city of New York. Reading may have had, as John Updike suggests, a strong sense of itself as a place; but part of what attracted Stevens to his new environment was the precise opposite, its lack of locality: 'There are few places in the city – there is always something disintegrating, dislocating & nothing is distinct, defined' (*SP* 81). Such were his thoughts as he overcame his initial aversion to New York; and although these closely follow home-thoughts about the countryside around Reading, the balance was shifting in New York's favour: when he did take a brief vacation at home, he was driven to the reflection that 'everything was there as usual – excepting myself' (*SP* 85).

In Reading, too, he would over the coming years begin to notice a certain staleness in family (his father's financial troubles were coming to a head), and a certain complacent tameness in the lives of friends who had gone back there to live. Moreover, although New York might offer the challenge of starting at the bottom, Reading offered him a more sobering example of downward mobility. He was on friendly terms with the Wily sisters, whose family had declined from a prominent position in the early days of Pennsylvania to a situation that was marginal. The family let out rooms to supplement their income, and it appears that Stevens was a (presumably) paying guest for some of the summer of 1899. As if to emphasise their plight, one of the sisters showed him the volume of poems published in 1719 by an illustrious ancestor, and Stevens, characteristically, did his best to avoid engaging deeply with the human destitution the family now presented. He accompanied two of the daughters (whose father had recently and suddenly died) on a trip to what had once been the ancestral home:

> In the evening Rose, Kate and I took a drive to see their original family property granted to them by Wm. Penn. There was an old house on the place with curious shutters, front-door, exposed joists, huge fire-place, thin partitions. Also a bed in every room and a smell in every corner – these two latter being modern additions.
>
> (*SP* 55–6)

It is possible that elements of this memory resurfaced decades later to suggest the 'shuttered mansion-house' of 'A Postcard from the Volcano' (1936), Stevens's poignantly angry poem about what the future cannot inherit from the present and the indifference which will allow the desecration of once-loved places by modern additions. If this connection between poem and memory exists, it is made more keenly complex by the fact that Stevens's own feelings with regard to the Wily misfortunes were kept in a state of semi-suppression such that, when another calamity befell the family a few months later, he was at an impasse:

> At the Easter vacation I had a second though less personal loss [he had just recorded his paternal grandmother's death]. Kate Wily died of pneumonia. I don't know just how I felt about it. When I had come back to college I found the rose she had stuck in my hat still there. I did not dare to visit or to write to her sisters.
>
> (*SP* 71)

As this unexpected rose suggests, Stevens could be discomposed by unprovoked sensations, as distinct from those he cultivated. One of the functions of his journal was to enable him to relive – and, evidently, to edit – his past experience (*SP* 80); and implicit in this is the notion of life as a book, and the book as life. Clearly, he studied his nostalgias, shown by his visits to the school in Brooklyn in 1900 and (in 1904) to Ephrata, the summer resort of his boyhood, where he discovered his own initials carved into a bench and was caught unawares by what he felt: 'Memory is too much of a pyre. I think human bones may be among my ashes' (*SP* 149).

There may initially have been some wavering on Stevens's part between a future-as-the-future in New York and a future-as-the-past in Reading; he seems at least to have considered the possibility of returning there to work on the local paper run by his father's friend. Nothing came of this, however, and he persisted with his decreasingly stimulating job on the *Tribune*; Witter Bynner, who overlapped with Stevens's final year at Harvard and who despite his uneuphonious name would achieve some reputation as a poet, visited him in New York after graduating; and many years later suggested that the journalism had been 'a very good offset to the fastidious instruction we had been receiving at Cambridge' (*SP* 96). Whatever its benefits, however, journalism was not to be Stevens's career; we know that he made the most of what New York theatre offered, seeing the 56-year-old Sarah Bernhardt as Hamlet in December 1900, and Ethel Barrymore make her debut in Clyde Fitch's comedy *Captain Jinks of the Horse Marines* the following February; and we know that he was sufficiently stimulated by the latter (which he went to see thrice) to embark, with a novice's plagiaristic enthusiasm, on the preliminary composition of his own romantic comedy, 'Olivia'. But in March that project was interrupted, never to be resumed; and Stevens had an *éclaircissement* with his father.

He may have been liking New York more, but he was liking his work as a newspaperman a good deal less; and however much he enjoyed the city, he also wished to see the world. In December 1900 Garrett had blocked his son's vague projects of foreign travel, and three months later he was urging him to take up law; when Stevens (who had been further disillusioned by looking into job opportunities in publishing) countered with the proposal that he give up journalism in order to spend his time writing, that suggestion was, predictably, 'torn to pieces' (*SP* 101). After this journal entry for 12 March, there is one more, dated 14 March, concluding with his gruesome account of having seen a recently-born 'two-headed Hebrew child'; then, with regard to his journal, Stevens went off the air for more than a year, leaving the remaining pages of the notebook blank. In August 1902 he recommenced his journal in a new notebook; by which stage he had completed the first of two years in New York Law School, which he had entered on 1 October 1901 (*L* 57). That 16-month silence may be eloquent. We can infer that his father had made plain that he would only subsidise Stevens if he consented to study law; and although it is highly likely that law school kept him busy, it is improbable that, had he wished to, Stevens could not also have found time to keep a record of his doings and thinkings. Renouncing his journal, he may also have renounced his dream of a literary life: Stevens had cut off one of his two heads, and was to be a lawyer rather than a man of letters.

The head grew back, however. The young man who resumed the journal was energetic, taking storming walks on the Palisades and into New Jersey on his days off. Literature was still a source of solace: when a friend with whom he was to have had a weekend's walking failed to keep the appointment (perhaps divining that the walk would cover 40 miles!), Stevens went on alone, but took care to read Bacon's essay 'On Friendship' that evening (*SP* 105). Although nothing suggests he was other than single-minded in his determination to pursue the law, his New Year resolutions for 1903 included one to 'write something every night – be it no more than a line to sing or a page to read' (*SP* 112). He seems to have broken this, as he broke others to do with abstention from tobacco and alcohol; but in making it, he affirmed a sense of mission: 'there's gold there for the digging: j'en suis sur'. The 'gold' he hoped to mine by writing was metaphorical; real dollars, he well understood, would have to be earned by hard work at his chosen profession, and would elude him for some years to come; but rather than damning him, as they had Melville, once the dollars started to flow, so the poems did as well.

Stevens was very fortunate in the attorney, in whose office he served clerkships qualifying him for his law degree (June 1903) and, after a further year, admission to the New York Bar (June 1904). W.G. Peckham seems to have treated his clerk as an interesting human being rather than as an exploitable drudge, inviting him for social occasions at his house and at his holiday home in the Adirondacks. According to a letter Stevens wrote in 1950, Peckham had been a founder of the *Harvard Advocate*, which would doubtless have been one reason for his kindly interest in its former president – and one which also illustrates the usefulness of Harvard connections. Stevens's visits to Peckham's holiday home furnished the opportunity for social intercourse with a beautiful young woman called Sybil Gage he had distantly admired at Cambridge; she appears to have been the first female other than his mother to whom he ever sent a poem (in July 1902; see *SP* 102–3). But his employer's hospitality left a more momentous mark than this on him; Peckham provided Stevens with what was to be one of the most precious experiences of his life when, at the end of his first period of clerkship in 1903, he invited the young man to join him on a hunting trip in the Canadian Rockies.

The importance of this trip is attested by Stevens's daughter, who says that in the final weeks of his life (when he must have suspected he was dying) the poet frequently referred to it in conversations with her. The fact that she could not remember his ever having spoken of it previously amplifies the impression that this episode was fundamental to his sense of self – as well as suggesting something of the hidden nature of that self. The whole excursion lasted 7½ weeks, with Stevens leaving New York on 28 July and arriving back on 17 September. Several days' travelling was involved before reaching the point from which the hunting expedition proper commenced: it took three days by train to get from Montreal to Palliser, British Columbia; and on his return Stevens noted that nine days had elapsed between their breaking up camp, deep in the Canadian woods, and his arrival back in New York. In terms both of time and space, it was the longest journey Stevens had so far undertaken, and at each stage it unfolded marvels. 'I have seen cowboys; I have seen prairie dogs; hundreds of wild ducks, Indians in camp with smoke coming through their discolored tent-tops', he enthused, 'I have seen mountains swimming in clouds and basking in snow; and cascades, and gulches' (*SP* 118): and this was simply his account of the train-ride out from Montreal.

A sense of the frontier, absent from Reading and merely alluded to in New England (in Updike's view), was to be had in abundance in the foothills of the Rocky Mountains. The party – consisting basically of Peckham, Stevens, Hosea Locke (an 'Adirondack woodsman' brought along by Peckham), and Tommy the cook –

took some supplies along with them into the deep country toward the mountains, and could ride back to replenish essential provisions; but the idea was to live mainly by the trap, rod, and gun. In this they seem to have been successful, as the entry for 8 August suggests:

> Today Hosey shot a yearling doe and we are having venison fried in olive oil tonight. Last night we had, besides stewed grouse, a short-cake made out of bannock and wild strawberries. A long string of trout are being kept cool in the river for breakfast. The grouse are thick. I shot a cock this morning.
>
> (*SP* 120)

In other words, deer walked upon the mountains, grouse were spontaneously plentiful, and sweet berries ripened in the wilderness: Stevens's experiences in the Canadian Rockies surely informed the closing images of 'Sunday Morning' (1915), his best-known poem – which is more usually associated with the compound ghosts of Walter Pater and Matthew Arnold as mediated by Keats, than with the spirit of, say, Hemingway. The care Stevens took to keep his journal during the trip certainly suggests his intention to preserve the experiences for future use.

For he was the man of letters, even there: reading Ovid's *Art of Love* or Bossuet's *Lettres Spirituelles* in camp, as well as adventure stories by Stevenson and Rider Haggard. In doing so he was not anomalous, for Peckham seems to have been in the habit of translating Heine aloud by the camp-fire; he may, indeed, have set his clerk an example of how art could 'fit with other things', as well as democratic gentlemanliness and economic self-sufficiency. As in any tale by Hemingway or Faulkner, Stevens was blooded in the chase ('I fired into his brisket splitting his heart' *SP* 126), and came back to New York emptied of funds but full of high spirits; able, even as he relapsed into his city ways, to recall in April 1904 the 'physical hugeness' of the earth, that it was still 'a disparate monstrosity, full of solitudes & barrens & wilds' (*SP* 134). This experience of vastness, which he probably first felt crossing the Canadian prairies (they had a similar effect on T.E. Hulme), the sense of having travelled and encountered the wilderness, must have appeased to some degree the *wanderlust* he had been feeling. From our perspective, there is also an implicit ritual element to the holiday, of the young Stevens's initiation into true manliness and acceptance into its confraternity by proving his worth in something that all others understood: the hunt to the death.

He had experienced, in his own later way of putting it in 'Sunday Morning', the 'heavenly fellowship/ Of men that perish' (*CP* 70); and death is the informing presence in this poem (which has prompted comparisons between it and W.C. Bryant's 'Thanatopsis', 1821). 'Sunday Morning', almost certainly Stevens's most anthologised poem, is also one of the more curiously qualified declarations of independence in American writing, threnodic rather than rhapsodic in mode: evoking an apparent leisure, it is afflicted by the compulsions of necessity; asserting that there is no god and that we are unsponsored and free, it nevertheless tells us how we live in a state of 'dependency' that is 'inescapable'; advising us against giving our bounty to the dead, it shows how finally we have no choice in the matter, and shall sink down to darkness no matter how ambiguous our undulations in the interim. All of these have to do with the nature of the choice confronting Stevens in the first years of the new century, when he was obliged to renounce the life he thought he wanted to lead, and for which he had been secretly preparing, in favour of the soberer course outlined for him by a father who, he ruefully reflected, always seemed to have reason (understood principally as economic realism) on his side.

The closing lines of 'Sunday Morning' have often been compared to the closing lines of Keats's ode 'To Autumn', but the comparison really points the differences; for Keats's imagery and syntax relate the minor premises of observed phenomena to the major premise of an early-autumn evening, experienced by an implied onlooker centred in place and time. Stevens's vision, by contrast, is a good deal more austere: the items on his list, existing in a kind of isolation from each other and from 'us', seem like a disassembled whole, lacking unity of time or place. Deer may walk upon our mountains, but what have they to do with us, and above all how are these mountains 'ours' (especially if they are the Canadian Rockies observed by a US citizen)? Although the poem's closure is designed to give a sense of natural profusion, with deer, quail, berries and pigeons on display if not on offer, an inhibiting forlornness prevents any effect of bounty, such as that achieved by Whitman in his triumphalist catalogues. Just as 'Earthy Anecdote' may allude to vanished Americans, so 'Sunday Morning' may evoke a vanished America: the pigeons sinking toward their sure obliteration might have been passenger pigeons, which once existed in such quantities that flocks containing billions would darken the skies in their passage. Indiscriminately slaughtered, what had probably been the most numerous bird in the world at the time (say) of American Independence was in steep decline during Stevens's early life, with the last known specimen dying in September 1914; 'Sunday Morning' was written the following year.[13]

I am prepared for the reader to find this a far-fetched connection; but irrespective of which species they belong to, the pigeons at the end of 'Sunday Morning' are the image of a radically circumscribed freedom, running counter to traditional symbolism of birds in flight. For even in British Columbia, in surroundings which came closest of any he had yet encountered to the purely natural, Stevens found himself thinking of New York. At Harvard, he would recall, it had been fashionable to reflect that all thoughts had already been thought and all books already written: consequently what seemed original was really secondhand.[14] It may have been the sophisticated Harvard graduate in the Canadian wilderness who humorously observed that the mountains seemed to be posing for their photographs (*SP* 120), but underlying it was the inference he would develop in his later writing, that we know our own knowing, and that the mountains were 'things as seen' rather than 'things seen'.[15] As William James argued in *The Will to Believe*, 'we have no organ or faculty to appreciate the simply given order'; if, therefore, we have no access to a reality unmediated by our own perceiving, if percept is always answerable to concept, the encounter between self and 'the wild' never really takes place, because consciousness involves prefabrication even of deer walking on mountains. Stevens might formerly have opposed sonnets to 'real life' considered to be 'quick, unaccountable, responsive'; but increasingly he came to see the interactions between spontaneity and structure.

The young man was inclined to see the contrast in terms of the exotic (foreign travel, poetry) as opposed to the routine (working for a living and so forth). Yet Stevens's desire to travel the world and build up writerly experience was as conventional a concept as his father's opposing law that he should get a steady job – although at the time that seemed like the obtrusion of anti-inspirational prudentialism. Such a conflict may resurface in 'Anecdote of the Prince of Peacocks' (1923), where madness, in the form of relentless consciousness, sets its traps even in the principality of sleep (a tributary state of the kingdom of waking), and permits neither beauty nor innocence. Stevens did as his father wished because he had not the resources (in various senses) to do otherwise, but perhaps also because he was beginning to see how following Garrett's advice need not involve renunciation of the man he wished to be. Perceived in one light, then, the father simply blocked the son, springing his traps of reason in the midst of the latter's daydreams; but in another light, his challenge enabled the son to reconceive the choice before him not as an 'either/or' binarism, but as potentially inclusive of both 'work' and 'poetry': a choice: not 'between' but 'of' different possibilities, as Stevens was later to express it (*CP* 403).

If we cannot experience true spontaneity, we can experience surprise, which is a sort of liberation from the usual. The obstacular encounter between 'I' and 'Berserk' on the bushy plain in 'Anecdote of the Prince of Peacocks' leads to a dread-filled paralysis; but in Stevens's earlier and earthier 'anecdote', the bucks and the firecat inhabit an equally closed system in terms of their repertory of available behaviour, but one whose repeated oppositions have a dynamic, generative power: the bucks clatter and swerve, the firecat bristles and leaps (and sleeps, which may be important). Although the firecat seems the freer agent, as it elicits fearful symmetries from the stubbornly evasive bucks, stimulus and response are interactivated, and both constitute the poem. A firecat, unlike the bucks, is not to be found in the 'real' world, yet it as much as they is a creature of the poem – in which it becomes domesticated, changing from 'a' to 'the' and finally falling asleep like any hearthside tabby. Yet every time we reread the poem it is reborn in its bristling vigour, and the foreseeable contest is renewed, with its issue as the poem and our readerly experience. Predictable as is the outcome, the whole is an exercise in the paradoxical repeatability of surprise: a process which is made possible only by the operation of conventions governing the behaviour of bucks and firecat, readers and poem.

The point of alluding to these later poems is that their presentation of the self in a constricted field of action aptly dramatises the situation in which Stevens found himself. In yielding to his father's wishes by following in his footsteps to a career in law, he was failing to be his own man and to steer by his own lights (to select appropriate clichés); there is likely to have been some cost involved in this, to one whom Witter Bynner in

April 1904 noted as being possessed of a 'monumental' egotism.[16] But Bynner also observed that, 'through being much alone, he has gone daffy a little'; and the plaints about loneliness which Stevens entered in his journal (for example, on 9 August 1902) corroborate the testimony, as well as showing that he had reason to be sceptical about the powerful American/Romantic myth that there is an accessible unstructured self, independent of the social contexts which sustain it. Whereas in embarking on his journalistic career Stevens had resolved to write only what would suit himself (16 June 1900), not long afterwards he was better placed to see that such heroic aloofness from the market-place could only be maintained if he were not relying on his pen to live. Simplistically put, the freedom to be himself in the realm of the poem was purchased by the consent to be other than himself elsewhere.

A great deal of what is valuable in Stevens's poetry has to do with the ways in which behaviour becomes obedience to conventions which we weren't initially aware of; how the fresh becomes the stale and the living thing consents to die: one has one's jar and one's wilderness, and then something ominous seems to happen, as structure deadens the unaccountable in this coldest of pastorals.[17] Stevens's misgivings about behaviour-as-conformity are accompanied, however, by a perception that without convention is no form, without form nothing is interpretable, and without interpretation there is only the nothing that is not there. What he wanted, in poetry and in life, was the balance of opposites engendering change rather than inertia: such a responsiveness as found, for example, in 'Nomad Exquisite' (1923), the issue of whose 'beholding' is energetically different from that of 'The Snow Man'. Coming back from his memorable holiday in 1903, however, Stevens had not yet developed into the acute commentator on states of habituation that he would become; for he had not yet done everything that was expected of him, culturally and parentally: he had gone to Harvard, he had set aside his notions of writing for a living and was on the right track for making a career, he had gone into the woods and killed his deer; what was left? Early and late the connoisseur of the nothing that was there, he had noted in 1900 how he began 'to feel the vacuum that wives fill' (*SP* 81): convention dictated he must fall in love.

3

Strict Arrangements of Emptiness

Stevens's trip to the Canadian wilds took place after he had graduated from law school; he then spent a further year as clerk in Peckham's office, and was admitted to the New York Bar at the end of June 1904. Thereby he accomplished his transformation from would-be journalist to qualified lawyer, doubtless to his father's relief – although neither Garrett nor his son could know that there were several years of false starts and failure still to be endured in this new profession. That summer must have seemed to Stevens like a time of self-renewal, however; an atmosphere which probably enabled, and was in turn intensified by, the start of his relationship with Elsie Moll, through which was slotted into place the missing piece in his personal jigsaw, as man and woman met, and loved forthwith. I allude here to the seventh canto of *Notes toward a Supreme Fiction* (*CP* 386), because its tricky way of putting the matter seems especially appropriate to the coming together of these two unusual people; whose apparently mutual falling-in-love is as easily interpreted as a balance that was 'achieved', as one that 'happened'. Whatever the emotional realities of their early attachment, it can be seen that each was peculiarly equipped to remedy the absent things in the other's life: it is almost true to say of them, as of Fred Astaire's and Ginger Rogers's film partnership, that he gave her class-credibility, while she gave him sex-credibility.[1]

They met at a party given by a friend of Elsie's in Reading, some of whose male guests had asked if they could bring along a 'very fine poet' from New York (*SP* 138): by repute both bardic and metropolitan, then, Stevens was evidently preceded by some clouds of glory to that social gathering, where he encountered for the first time the prettiest girl in town (this was his own judgement, given many years later in answer to his daughter's far-from-rhetorical question why he had married her mother). He had come back home soon after completing his bar exams on 7 June, and his stay in Reading would last over two months, possibly because he was considering practising law there; but if so nothing came of the idea, and in September he returned to New York to try his luck – or what would turn out to be the lack of it. At this threshold in his life, it must have been of some reassurance to maintain a link to his home town through Elsie, as well as to be acknowledged as a poet at a time when he was more visibly becoming a lawyer. The younger men who had taken him to the party were not qualified to award Stevens his laurels, on the basis of his competently undistinguished Harvard poetry; but the even younger Elsie (whose abiding taste for Longfellow would later exasperate her husband) was not in a position to question their judgement. None could know that this inhabitant of New York had a few months previously been reflecting ruefully on his maladjustment to city life:

> Here am I, a descendant of the Dutch, at the age of twenty-five, without a cent to my name, in a huge town, knowing a half-dozen men & no women.

> (7 Feb 1904)

Nor could they know that, a week later, St Valentine's Day had found their very fine poet in a black hole of loneliness: 'I want to see somebody, hear somebody speak to me, look at somebody, speak to somebody in turn' (*SP* 128 *both*).

The somebody turned out to be Elsie Viola Moll (or Kachel); she was to fill the emptiness of which he had grown ever more importunately sensible. From our perspective it would seem that her chief qualification for the role, alongside an evident willingess and her personal beauty, lay in the fact that both literally and metaphorically she would look up to this suitor. At the time of their meeting she had just turned 18, and Stevens was more than seven years older; he was physically imposing, whereas the top of her head barely reached his shoulder; he had been through Harvard and law school, but she hadn't even completed one year of high school; he was the son of a local notable, respectably bourgeois, but her parentage was a source of deep anxiety to her, and she dwelt in an emphatically lower-class area of town; he had lived in Cambridge and New York, but her life had been bounded by Reading, where like him she had been born. We don't, of course, know what happened: Stevens edited his own journals, his widow made further excisions and seems to have severely censored the correspondence between them; our chief witness is the daughter, born 20 years after their first meeting, and clearly more indulgent of her father's parental limitations than her mother's. The picture Holly Stevens paints, however, is of a woman with a constitution whose real or imagined frailty soon established itself as a factor in the marriage; one whose girlhood had been marked by anxieties about having been conceived out of wedlock – a circumstance compounded by her actual father's death within a year of his marriage to Ida Bright Smith, before Elsie's first birthday. She had been eight when her mother married Mr Moll, who never formally adopted her, thereby introducing further ambiguities into her situation. She left school early because her sight was too poor to see the blackboard (her parents could not afford to buy glasses), and she contributed to family income by working in a local department store, selling sheet music which she played on the store piano. Her accomplishment as a pianist and her delicate good looks seem to have been her chief claims to gentility; and clearly there were pronounced differences between her own upbringing and that of the large but soft-speaking poet from New York.

She presumably supposed that his sophistication and education would help her attain the same qualities; and it must have been difficult (since Elsie seems to have had no trace of the self-assurance that can come with beauty) for her not to have seen Stevens as something of a 'catch': able to elevate her socially, and to fulfil the role of dependable male in a life hitherto poorly stocked with examples of the type. We can intuit her desire to change her life, from her submission – albeit with some protest – to the five-year courtship Stevens imposed on her; and we can intuit his own awareness of the power realities implicit in their relationship, from his willingness to do this. Lengthy engagements were more common then than now, but Stevens's excessive prudentialism cannot have strengthened the fragile self-esteem of a spiky and insecure young woman, already sufficiently alert to the disparities between his background and her own. These two, who were in obscure but real ways quite unconventional people, seem to have projected on each other a set of wholly conventionalised expectations which when thwarted led to what looks like mutual revenge, through their adoption of even more parodically hyper-conventional roles: he as the hard-working and remote head of household, she as the devoted observer of niceties of social and religious etiquette, exerting influence through ill-health and doing what she could to restrict her husband's consumption of tobacco and alcohol. Latterly, the only area of their lives in which there seems to have been any real mutuality was in their cultivation of the garden at their house on Westerly Terrace.

Discussing this would represent a tastelessly unnecessary intrusion, were it not that his marriage and the life it engendered formed the ground in which all of Stevens's worthwhile poetry grew; as Milton Bates has put it, 'this rather prim and conventional woman was Wallace Stevens'[s] muse and a pretext for his flights of imagination, both in the winning and in the losing' (Bates, p. 50). But to be a muse and a pretext for imagination was to be both more and less than a human being; and there are indications that Elsie's function as his one of fictive music could only be fulfilled if he overlooked many aspects of the woman she actually was: for example, they were not officially engaged until December 1908, and Joan Richardson shows that Stevens was somewhat insensitive to Elsie's social predicament in Reading, attached to a man residing in New York who had not made his intentions unambiguously clear, and the infrequency of whose visits did not suggest uncontrollable ardour. When he did notice her situation, it was to minimise it as a shared inconvenience, and to suggest that she learn to make her own life.[2] Whereas she was understandably keen to make public their relationship, he was anxious that it remain secret as long as possible – an ironic inversion of his later desire to publish poems that she wished had been kept secret.

Her capacity to show him affection made a welcome change from the undemonstrativeness of his family; and the written record in journal and surviving letters suggests that in its initial stages their love affair was not without physical spontaneity, with Elsie permitting her suitor her 'warm mouth' and close encounters on the sofa.[3] But as the period of unsubstantiated betrothal lengthened, her bemusement and belated regard for her own propriety led to episodes of withdrawal, in response to Stevens the indefatigable procrastinator (his own description, *SP* 154), who kept coming constantly so near without finally arriving at the point of firm proposal. His living in New York necessitated the composition of many letters, as a substitute for conversation, and although these gradually supplanted his journal there was no real loss involved, for the tone of his letters to Elsie is eerily continuous with that of his journal, written for himself; indeed, just as he revised and revisited his journal, so he told her he anticipated looking over their letters once married, and weeding out the 'bad ones'.[4] The element of performance was present even in words meant to come from the heart: for when Stevens looked into his heart and wrote, he was as likely as not to be looking simultaneously into a dictionary ('Le Monocle de Mon Oncle' is perhaps the clearest example of his combination of the confessional mode with verbal baroque).

The developing relationship with Elsie coincided with the downturn in his father's health and fortunes, so that her freshness contrasted with the staleness he increasingly diagnosed at home (*SP* 156). It seems to have been the case that his parents did not adjudge her a suitable match, and resented the fact that his visits to Reading were spent ever more exclusively in her company; in turn, Stevens resented their attitude toward his beloved (the more so, as it may have reflected his own uncertainties); whatever the precise chain of events, its result was a rift between the poet and his parents, which in the case of his father was never resolved. In the latter stages of his courtship he didn't even bother to visit his old home when in Reading, and there was no family representation when eventually he and Elsie were married there. Having fallen in with paternal wishes in the matter of his profession, it may be that Stevens felt it all the more important to contravene parental preference when choosing his wife. Unfortunately, time would justify their judgement rather than his own; and the episode would be gallingly replayed more than thirty years later, in the circumstances of his daughter's first marriage.

Stevens had once published a short story titled 'The Revelation' in the *Harvard Advocate* (November 1899); in this Hawthornesque fable, a young man takes a photograph of his beloved to be framed only to discover, when the job is done and he unwraps it, a portrait of himself. In following the epistolary courtship of Elsie by Wallace, the documentary interchangeability of letters and journal can provoke the question of how far Stevens writes to her, and how much for himself: in Bakhtin's terms, are these letters 'dialogic' or 'monologic' in intent? The basic indiscretion of reading another person's love letters is mitigated by the fact that we read only what Stevens's widow has permitted us to read (though in doing so we should remain aware of how our own love letters might appear to total strangers in some future); but allowing for that, Stevens's correspondence with his wife-to-be has its uncomfortable aspects, seeming to chart the 'real' Elsie's disappearance within the construct of functions envisaged for her. She was both infantilised and fetishised in the letters: identified by nursery-rhyme nicknames, requested to wear certain types of slipper and certain colour ribbons for their not-very-frequent trysts in Reading, and instructed never to grow old, always to be his 'little girl', and always to have 'pink cheeks and golden hair' (21 March 1907, *L* 97). This is the 'doll-wife', indeed; and I am tempted to observe that had Stevens been able to give Ibsen's *A Doll's House* (written in the year of his birth) the same degree of attention and emulation he had earlier given *Captain Jinks of the Horse Marines*, matters might have gone differently. Joan Richardson has argued that letters such as the one just quoted from had an additional function: that of suppressing Elsie's anxieties about their lengthy and apparently improgressive courtship. Being instructed to remain for ever young and fair might have been daunting in itself; implicit, however, was the message that the state of matrimony with its attendant cares would sound the death-knell for her youth and beauty. For all her felt inferiorities of social class, experience, and education, there was a tenacity in the young woman that led her to challenge her suitor (although the elderly widow's preservation of certain of these letters, whilst destroying others, suggests her unenlightened complicity with the role-playing: she was no Ibsen heroine). In March 1907 she had evidently been guarded toward Stevens, and told him she felt they were becoming 'all letters';[5] earlier letters from Stevens show him meeting a similar charge of insincerity, of being one person 'on paper' and another 'in reality'; his justification was, 'I know it is only [*sic*] because I command myself there' (*L* 80). In a rather coercive way he shared with her his love for 'paper men and paper women', and later went so far as to suggest that the two of them were truer to themselves when in that category:

> I [have] stumbled across the reason for our being easier in our letters than we are – when we are together. It must be because you are more perfectly yourself to me when I am writing to you, and that makes me more perfectly myself to you. You know that I do with you as I like in my thoughts: ... You are *my* Elsie there. – Yet it is the real Elsie, all the time. ... – Now have you seen into my heart? And haven't you seen your own eyes looking out at you – and laughing at you?
>
> (10 March 1907; *L* 96)

The issue here is that of control. When Stevens confided to his journal that on one visit Elsie had been virtually 'unmanageable' (*SP* 174), he therein implied his desire to manage her, to turn her into a category of imagination that he could 'command' as he did himself: she was 'Ariel' to his Prospero. When he more than once paid her the tribute of describing her as his 'second self', he was defining a need rather than seeing a person who was there; given the disparities between them, the young woman must have been flattered – without grasping the constricting surrogacy such a role entailed.[6] Without her, he declared, he himself would be 'terribly unreal' (*L* 131); and it was as if this woman consistently evoked for her ethereality must somehow also be his point of connection to things as they are – or must at least shield him from his own disconnection. Thus the signals she received were mixed: he approved and encouraged her decision to join a church, and then told her he had thrown away his bible; he confessed to saying his prayers, but claimed to be not in the least religious; he defined her as his *alter ego* and anchor in reality, whilst writing of their love as an enchanted faeryland excluding the gross world (*L* 79) – yet did not hesitate to invoke that gross world and its laws of economics as a reason for the continuous deferral of their marriage. By the time that took place, a good deal of the bloom had been rubbed off their relationship, and an intractable shaping of selves occurred, in which Elsie altered from having been his 'princess' to someone observers characterised as 'very hard', 'completely subdued', and 'completely dominated' (Brazeau, pp. 232, 250, 278), able to mount only occasional guerilla attacks against superior forces.

These forces were not simply externally imposed. It was as much her own doing that she changed, from someone pretty enough to model for the profile on US coinage to a premature old-maidishness; this was in part the emergence of the latent awkwardness some had noted in her before she ever met Stevens, and he may have been less responsible for her later alteration than he had been for her transfiguration from shop-girl into fairy princess. She certainly colluded in the make-believe world of their early romance, itself a conventional – if, as Ibsen showed, potentially dangerous – form of lovers' intercommunication. But entranced as she must in part have been by her lover's placing her at the centre of his world of words, it would come to be the case that the very tokens of their early interchanges, the poems he dedicated to her and the books he spoke of wanting to share with her, turned out to constitute the gulf between them. Since a shared life was in question, what can she have made of his (apparently early) declaration that he wanted to make a music of his own, a literature of his own, and should like to live his own life (*L* 79)? When, later, she was clearly fretful about the dominance of written exchanges over actual meetings, how soothed can she have been by his suggestion (9 April 1907), 'we must talk about books sometime when we are together', what must she have felt when a few days later he declared that if he had ardour left for anything at all, it was 'for books' (*SP* 176)? When in August 1909 he wrote that he had located the right apartment for them to commence their married life in, he mentioned that he would move his books in before she came (*L* 156), which may have indicated his order of priorities to her; and the following month he told her about having dusted and packed the books, and of how he intended to shelve them, also telling her that he had thrown away a lot of old papers, but had retained his diaries and his 'priceless poetical scribblings' (*L* 161). Finding a place for these things might have seemed to be more on his mind than her own imminent arrival in those rooms; at any rate, by the time they moved to Westerly Terrace, in 1932, she knew exactly what she thought: Stevens was not allowed to turn one of its eleven rooms into his library, and his book collection mostly remained in packing-cases on the third floor. In their different ways, however, they each lived by the book: he by those he read and wrote, and she by the Bible (which dictated that she should not labour on the sabbath), women's magazines, guides on domestic etiquette and, eventually, manuals of child-rearing.

The 'very fine poet' went back to make his way as a lawyer in New York, in September 1904, having fallen in love at the age of 25. It would be four years before he was set in his career as insurance lawyer, five years before he married, ten years before he published his first significant poems; beyond that, his first volume of poetry and the birth of his only child lay, respectively, 19 and 20 years in the future. But it is the ten years leading up to his first serious poems that I want to look at now: the period in which, at last, the various elements of his life as lawyer, as husband, and as poet became defined.

Any euphoria Stevens felt at having passed his bar exams and having at last acquired a girlfriend was quickly tempered by the speedy failure of his first venture, in partnership with Lyman Ward, a former Harvard contemporary. During the closing months of 1904 he reported himself in his journal as being so desperately poor that he could not always afford enough to eat, in spite of putting in hours of work at the office. Although this must have been a difficult period for him, it seems from his journal that the thought of Elsie and her letters was an important resource, as a focus beyond his immediate professional disappointments. At this time he was rooming with Arthur Clous, an acquaintance from his Reading schooldays, with whom he went for walks in the city's parks and visited exhibitions – so the loneliness of which he had previously complained was somewhat abated. After the failure of 'Stevens and Ward', Stevens spent the next two years (1905–7) living mostly in New Jersey, in the successive but not continuous employ of three law firms in New York; work which saw him in July 1905 take a week's business trip through Chicago, Kansas, Colorado, New Mexico, Nebraska, and Iowa; followed the next month by another to the South, which introduced him to Tennessee, Alabama, Mississippi, and Louisiana (including New Orleans, which he found 'dull'). These bouts of employment seem to have raised him above subsistence-level living, but his failure to establish himself suggests what business colleagues subsequently confirmed: that Stevens's personal qualities were not best suited to practising law. The decisive move into the field of insurance came in January 1908, when he joined the New York branch of the Baltimore-based American Bonding Company, rising to a junior management position by the next year, when he and Elsie became engaged. This firm was taken over in 1913, and Stevens was the 'law officer' of its New York branch before moving in February 1914 to become resident New York vice-president of another firm; a position he retained after yet another merger, which resulted in the establishment of the New England Equitable Insurance Company in July 1915. Clearly, he had placed himself in a rapidly expanding sector of the market.

Between the ages of 25 and 35 Stevens addressed a set of inter-connected problems, relating to the economic, social/emotional, intellectual/religious, and literary aspects of his life; and in the resolution he found – or failed to find – for each of them, he estab-lished to a high degree the patterns predominating in his last 40

years. Having acceded to his father, and in doing so having learnt
something about the powerlessness of a man who has visions but
no bankroll, he had embarked on a career whose purpose was to
render him invulnerable to any repetition of that nightmare of
dependency – in which he had resembled what he most despised,
one who was the weak victim of circumstances (*L* 129). The money
he earned would be his means of freedom and a source of power:
'as he riffled those dollars, one could see dominance there', an
associate would recall of the senior executive (Brazeau, p. 136). In
the main, however, such ostentation was uncharacteristic; for the
thrift and self-denial practised – albeit intermittently – in his
impecunious years proved hard to shake off, once he was comparatively wealthy. Moreover, the world in which he most desired to
make an impression was not, in any simple way, the business
world; as he wrote to his fiancée in January 1909, on the anniver-
sary of his employment with the American Bonding Company
(which had been his most successful year to date):

> I certainly do not exist from nine to six, when I am at the office.
> ... There is no every-day Wallace, apart from the one at work –
> and that one is tedious. – At night I strut my individual state
> once more.
>
> (*L* 121)

Stevens tended to present writing and work as opposed and
exclusive activities – and to some extent this would remain an
attitude expressed throughout his life. But even the sense of
opposition voiced in 1909 can be construed as interdependency, in
which the tedious everyday Wallace was contrapuntally
resurrected, more truly and more strange, in his after-hours guise.
What his literary life and his life as lawyer had in common, in their
inceptions, was the need for an audience, the need to have his
talent appreciated: once Stevens's exceptional skill in the field of
surety claims gained recognition, his career was secure and he
never looked back. But although he did not write good poetry until
he was well-set in his profession, which further suggests the
interconnection of his two selves, the process of his establishment
as a poet was less assured, the appreciation of his gift less evident.
Here is the point of intersection between his creative development
and what I have defined as the social/emotional sphere: for
although he required the financial security which would enable

him to risk pleasing no one but himself, he also, semi-
paradoxically, needed 'somebody' other than himself to be pleased
by his writing. This, initially, was Elsie's role; and however
unfitted as a soul-mate she turned out to be, for a short but
significant while she shared his writings, constituted his audience,
and confirmed him in his poetic identity.

A lady-love was indispensable for one whose model was the
passionate Keats, even if Stevens's truer avatars were Hawthorne
or Henry James, those connoisseurs of disinvolvement; and Elsie's
presence – although for the most part this amounted to her absence
– both masked for Stevens what had been a growing sense of his
own oddness and maladjustment, and licensed his composition of
verses to lay at her feet. The 20 poems in 'A Book of Verses'
offered for her birthday in 1908, and another 20 in 'The Little June
Book' presented for her 23rd birthday the following year, have no
serious claim on our attention, as poetry: except where Stevens
experimented with unrhymed shorter lines, they lack any daring in
either style or subject, and were it not for their author's age it
would be easier to define them as juvenilia than as apprentice-
work. But in the case of a writer for whom, as later became
abundantly clear, the very putting-together of a volume of verse
was a major step, the compilation even of these pamphlets had
psychological if not artistic significance: in them, Stevens was
declaring an allegiance to the world of verse rather than the world
of work, and was inviting his beloved (the hackneyed term is
appropriate) to ratify his delinquency by her complicity in the
evasion. Their love was a fine secret, their poems were a fine
secret: part of a lovers' conspiracy against the world, and of a piece
with the fairy-tales Stevens was also reading and composing for
her at this period.[7]

That this nexus of secrecies could only be a short-lived phase
must have been as clear to Stevens then as it is to us now. The
customary reason for preferring marriage to celibacy seems not to
have operated: when, shortly before the event, he wrote to her that
it was wonderful to think that 'you are coming – in a month'
(*L* 158), the exact ground for pleasure seems appropriately
ambiguous. By marrying and bringing their relations into the
public domain, they were trying to insert a shared irreality into the
everyday world, escape from which had been a major theme of
their intercourse and, it appears, an important part of their
emotional dynamic. Stevens seems to have desired to have enough

money to maintain Elsie in a state of sublime disconnection: he would go out to the office, and return to faeryland to strut his individual state with her. But aside from the fact that there would and could never be 'enough' for that, it was certainly not sufficient basis for her life: there is some evidence that she wished to have a child, but he did not (*SP* 247); and that her extended visits back to Reading, with no signs of pregnancy, were not unjustifiably taken by some to suggest that their marriage was going wrong. It may be fair to say that in the earliest years she could better fulfil his notions of what he would like his wife to be (*SP* 156) than he could answer to hers of a husband. She could protect him from his fears of unloved loneliness, and be a centring presence – as in the evocative fantasy he indulged in a letter only a few months before their marriage: 'There is an apartment house on the West Side of Washington Square, where I often imagine we live. You often sit in the window-seat about six o'clock and I can see you as I come home, reading some wicked novel, you were there tonight, and looked up, and I waved my hand, and you threw me a kiss –'.[8] This is in some ways touching, but it is also obscurely coercive: she is evoked (at a distance which is a function of her allure) as a tutelary spirit who awaits, indoors, her lover's return from his adventures in the fallen world of getting and spending – from which it is his duty to protect her, in her bookish sanctuary.

The poem 'Tea' (1915: *CP* 112) comes to my mind, in illustration of how such implicit attitudes might operate in the mental geography of Stevens's maturer verse. The normative reading of this poem supposes a break exactly in its middle, whereby the wintry external scene in the park contrasts with the lamplit warmth of 'your' room, whose satiny decor inaugurates the imaginative excursus through which, in the course of eight short lines, we have moved from frosty New York to Javanese umbrellas. Thus we have Stevens's reality/imagination contrast – albeit made subtler by the fact that there *is* no line-break, and that both the leaves running 'like rats' and the fancifully named elephant's-ear indicate the metamorphic mind, operating even in wintry deprivation. But in the context of my present discussion, I am more inclined to interrogate the state of subjection of the 'you' evoked through presumably-her warm room, as passive focus for the longing of the implicit speaker; who may or may not be on presumably-his way to visit, and who, even should he arrive, will reach his journey's end only when he is mentally 'in Java'. As for her, she will sit there serving tea to friends, like the forlornly immobilised hostess in Eliot's 'Portrait of a Lady'. Aged 35 when 'Tea' was published, Stevens would be in his seventies before, in 'The World as Meditation' (1952), he imagined what it would be like to be Penelope alone in her room, rather than her interminably adventuring husband.

'Tea' is relevant in other ways, since it was almost certainly one of the poems Stevens read at a soirée at Walter Arensberg's New York studio in December 1914, along with 'Cy Est Pourtraicte...', written around the same time. The evening had been arranged by Arensberg and by Carl Van Vechten, who many years later published a reminiscence of this event (designed to draw Stevens into their orbit, who now – in the period of writing 'Peter Quince at the Clavier' and 'Sunday Morning' – had a much more substantiated claim to the accolade of 'very fine poet'). Elsie Stevens was also invited, and advance preparations had been taken to minimise the visibility of elements she was known to disapprove of, such as cigarettes and alcohol. Van Vechten's memoir cannot be entirely trusted, but it is clear that the evening was an awkward one for her, in which she cannot have failed to measure the gulf between herself and the *avant-gardistes* around her (whose cigarettes had been restored to them at her husband's request). She obstinately clung, however, to her own judgements, and pronounced her dislike of his latest work, as too 'affected'. There will always be those who sympathise with her opinion, but the occasion was emblematic of the change taking place, as Stevens addressed himself to a different audience: at its twelfth level of meaning, 'Tea' may have been *about* Elsie, but it was no longer *for* her. Her obstinacy may have been due to the effort she was making to retain their old understanding, already shaken by his having in September 1914 published some of the poems composed for her birthday volumes in 1908 and 1909; but her husband was no longer satisfied to be a private poet, and the event at the Arensbergs' can only have accelerated the process by which, from having been the only person to whom he could confide his poetry, Elsie became the one person with whom he could not share it. Formerly, as a 'closet' poet, he had read his work to her; but now the figurative became the literal, and when he wished to recite his poetry aloud he was obliged to retreat into the large clothes-closets in their apartment – whose doors, at other times, his wife would slam in her anger (*SP* 247).

Unsophisticated in her tastes and provincial in her outlook, Elsie Stevens could hardly fail to show to disadvantage in a New York *salon*; her social awkwardness in that setting may have offered her husband an unwished-for opportunity to contrast the subversive vigour of his new poetry, admired by these others, with the emotional timidity that underlay his unequal marriage to the pretty younger woman who now declared herself unable to appreciate his latest work. During the preceding years he had been reading weightier things than Hans Christian Andersen and Kenneth Grahame; but although he had tried to keep Elsie abreast of his programme, her capacity to participate in his obscurer musings was necessarily limited, and as she sensed the threat posed by his paper world of books, being part of it was an effort that declined: three months before their marriage, Stevens reported having bought a volume of lectures delivered at Oxford, then broke off with 'but they wouldn't interest you, I imagine' (*L* 146). They had evidently interested him enough to make a trip uptown to buy the book; and this thirst for connection, shown in the desire to keep up with what was emanating from Oxford, was a feature of these years, and indeed of the rest of his life: by 1909 he was already in the habit of reading French and British periodicals. In an important earlier letter to her (17 January 1909), he tried to explain why books mattered so much to him: they were what counteracted the deadening office routine that didn't, in his view, amount to life, but which merely seemed like 'moving in a groove. – But books make up. They shatter the groove, as far as the mind is concerned' (*L* 123). His acquisition of books constituted a mental resistance to what he would later call the malady of the quotidian, by which he was obliged from nine to six o'clock to do what he would have preferred not to; which is a way of saying that they were a surrogate or a compensation for the life unlived. They were also, in a more directly Franklinesque respect, a means of self-education and self-improvement; and Stevens's reading suggests the development of what I have defined as his intellectual/religious concerns – by which he came to the composition of his earliest mature verse.

It is possible that the book of lectures was *The Springs of Helicon* (1909), a study of the progressive contributions to English verse of Chaucer, Spenser, and Milton by the current Professor of Poetry at Oxford, J.W. Mackail. He was primarily known as a distinguished classical scholar, and in 1907 Stevens had given his *Select Epigrams from the Greek Anthology* (1890) a careful reading, before moving on to *The Roman Poets of the Republic* by W.Y. Sellar (who had taught Mackail at Edinburgh). This historical progress through classical anthologies implied Stevens's desire to trace the origins of Western culture, seen also in the time he gave to reading his bible at this period, with particular emphasis on the New Testament and the life of Christ. He also devoted considerable attention to Mackail's professorial forerunner Matthew Arnold, whose notions of the contrasting but complementary influences of 'Hebraism' and 'Hellenism' had some personal relevance for him, as well as conducing to a cultural relativism that was reinforced from other sources, as the opening of Japan made accessible a different set of philosophical and artistic perspectives. Stevens was familiar with some of Lafcadio Hearn's writings about Japan, as with Kakuzo Okakura's *Ideals of the East*, and was clearly affected by the wave of enthusiasm for things oriental that swept Europe and the USA at this time: in 1909 he told Elsie about an exhibition of Japanese prints whose catalogue he 'would give last winter's hat for' (*SP* 235; he acquired the catalogue, but whether he paid by hat is not known). He also read and reread the essays of Paul Elmer More, and went so far as to insert unacknowledged quotations from them in some of his letters to Elsie. More was at the time another conduit by which philosophical and religious ideas from non-Western traditions were made available – as in his translations from the Sanskrit *A Century of Indian Epigrams* (1898), with which Stevens was familiar (*SP* 220).

Stevens was interested in the personalities behind the writing: he read Matthew Arnold's letters and Boswell's *Life of Johnson*, as well as a life of Jesus (possibly Renan's); he was typical of his time in his awareness of the fading explanatory authority of Christianity, and his Arnoldian search for a substitute seems also to have involved searching for an individual of sufficient stature to unify things disparate – which is what Jesus, historically considered, achieved. Not for nothing did he desire to have a photograph of Professor Mackail, whom he clearly admired; and his concern for the idea of a hero would last for much of his life. Also evident in these years – and equally persistent into his maturity – was Stevens's fascination with epigrams and aphorisms. In February 1906, having copied out a French quotation encountered in Arnold's *Notebooks*, he also noted in his journal having finished Leopardi's *Pensieri*, describing these as 'paragraphs on human nature, like Schopenhauer's psychological obser-vations, Pascal's *Pensées*, Rochefoucauld's *Maximes*, etc. How true they all are! I should like to have a library of such things' (*SP* 160). As his daughter observes, he did accumulate such a collection during his lifetime, as well as composing some of his own, his 'Adagia'. He asserted in a letter to his fiancée that a love of maxims was a mark of idealism rather than of priggishness:[9] idealism, presumably, that reaches after the kernel of truth, rather than priggishness seeking to reduce experience to permissible behaviour. The aphoristic mode can of course collapse into sententiousness – such a tone as heard in Dr Johnson when he nodded. But with Stevens, it was more an aspect of his modernity than of any intellectual archaism: Frost's definition of the poem as a 'momentary stay against confusion' rather than a 'great clarification, such as sects and cults are founded on' (in the introduction to his *Collected Poems*, 1939) comes to mind as an appropriate description of the value Stevens found in epigrams.

In *The Dry Salvages* (1941) Eliot refers to having an experience but missing its meaning; seen from a certain angle, Stevens's appetite for maxims, as with other aspects of his life, suggests a man who half-believed that 'meaning' could be separated from, and could in fact substitute for, 'experience'. This shows up in his particular forms of acquisitiveness, which superficially resembled conspicuous consumption: the *exotica* he later caused to be sent him from faraway countries – which he would unpack and display in his office before removing to his home – represented for him a kind of essence of place, just as an aphorism was a sort of intellectual portable property, that could be abstracted from the haphazardness of mere being. The catalogues of art exhibitions which for a while he avidly collected, the extensive record collection he amassed and which, together with classical music broadcasts on the radio (his daughter recalled), formed the basis of family activity at weekends, implicitly define a life lived at one remove from source. Explicit was the collector's appetite; after telling Elsie of an exhibition he had attended in the city (3 May 1909), he went on to write that he was always 'especially interested at these water-color shows in the pictures of flowers – bowls of roses and the like. It would be pleasant to make a collection of them' (*L* 140). Collecting can of course function as a means of management: those catalogues were in themselves methods of control by arrangement, just as the French and British periodicals Stevens subscribed to presented France and Britain in a form amenable to his consumption. A watercolour of a bowl of roses is, after all, the depiction of flowers doubly commodified: an aesthetic arrangement aesthetically rendered and – it is to be supposed – for sale.

Commonsensical distinctions between object and idea are perhaps beside the point; for in Stevens, roses always have the look of flowers that are looked at (see 'The Bouquet', for example). This is appropriate, in that centuries of commercial breeding and hybridisation (which Stevens knew about) have made the rose naturally artificial, or artificially natural – for where does nature end and (horti)culture begin? He would later imply that one sees the sun clearly in the idea of it (*CP* 380); and although the opposition in Tennessee between jar and the surrounding wilderness may seem straightforwardly that between man-made thing and state of nature, a moment's reflection tells us that 'wilderness' is not an uninflectedly descriptive term but an interpretative concept. For all its artificiality, the jar is more of an object, in the poem, and the wilderness is more of an idea; and as for any accessible state of nature, *that* is the 'nothing' that is not there, in the riddling negatives with which this 'anecdote' closes.

The conceptual legerdemain characteristic of his mature verse was not evident in the poetry Stevens wrote between 1904 and 1914; he had first to work through the derivative impulses that kept him in thrall to the Preraphaelites and to Keats. He was not alone in this: in 1909 the 25-year-old William Carlos Williams published a short book of poems at his own expense, consisting of sterile sub-Keatsian verses full of poetic diction (a good example is his sonnet 'The Uses of Poetry', dedicated to Hilda Doolittle who, as 'H.D.', would become one of the better-known Imagists); like Stevens, he had been impressed by *Endymion*, and needed to get beyond the influence – the poems T.S. Eliot was experimenting with at the same period were streets ahead in their development of a non-derivative voice, despite their debt to (principally) French Symbolist precursors.[10] When in 1914 Eliot paid his introductory visit to Pound, in London, following this up a few days later with the manuscript of 'The Love Song of J. Alfred Prufrock' (written three years earlier and unpublished), Pound – then very much the senior poet – was amazed by the fact that Eliot had 'modernised himself *on his own*'. In Stevens's case, it would be necessary for him to break out of his literary isolation in order to make the transition from the nineteenth to the twentieth century; he would require the sense of there being an artistic community in contemporary America; and one of the people who enabled him to feel that, was the very person to whom Pound made his excited observations about Eliot: Harriet Monroe.

Eliot and Pound had decided that there was no future for the poet in America, and headed for Europe; and, stagnant as Pound found the literary situation to be in London on his arrival there in 1908, the position in America was still less promising (although Gertrude Stein published her ground-breaking *Three Lives* in 1909, she did so at her own expense, and had been living in Paris since 1904). The Canadian Bliss Carman, together with Richard Hovey, had managed with their *Songs From Vagabondia* (1894) and its two sequels in 1896 and 1901 – which Stevens inscribed and presented to Elsie in 1907 – to enjoy a short-lived popularity (Hovey had died in 1900); but their success seems mostly ascribable to having found an opportune marketing niche.[11] Even E.C. Stedman (1833–1908), whose *Victorian Anthology* (1895) and *American Anthology* (1900) sold well, described the period as a 'twilight interval'; and in fact the last decade of the nineteenth and the first of the twentieth centuries were an especially inauspicious period for serious poetry in America. The genteel principles disseminated by influential men like Stedman discouraged innovation, and had the effect of ensuring that any notable engagement with contemporary American life would be undertaken in prose – as by the 'muckraking' school of journalism and fiction. For a would-be poet the situation was compounded by the virtual unavailability of publishing outlets for individualistic talents: 'the opportunity for younger American poets to achieve periodical publication was squeezed between the small group of established magazines which had led American genteel culture for decades and new mass magazines that had developed into vigorous commercial and cultural forces by the mid-1890s'.[12] The former wished not to disturb or alarm their public by printing anything extraordinary, while the latter group tended to regard poetry as effetely irrelevant to the concerns of an expanding industrial democracy. Even poets who could hardly be considered as experimental writers found it difficult to reach an audience: E.A. Robinson, ten years older than

Stevens and with two books of verse to his name (1897, 1902), succeeded in placing hardly more than a dozen poems in periodicals, in the ten years up to 1905; Robert Frost, although he later became the pre-eminent commercial success of his generation, left America in 1912 aged 38, and published his first two books in London (1913, 1914). The policing of Parnassus (Frank Lentricchia's metaphor) by the custodians of gentility produced a cultural desert for the aspiring poet; and when in the century's second decade the great change came about, America's avant-garde poets who published in the burgeoning literary magazines were all in their thirties or older. Seen in this context, Elsie Stevens's provision of an audience for his earlier work, whatever shortcomings it had as poetry and she had as reader, was a significant contribution to Stevens's self-definition as poet.

'To have great poets there must be great audiences too'; Walt Whitman's words were the motto for *Poetry: a Magazine of Verse*, issued in Chicago by Harriet Monroe in October 1912, having persuaded a hundred of that city's worthy wealthy of the benefits in being patrons of the art. The contribution made by her magazine to the advancement of contemporary poetry was significant, and its importance in the development of Stevens's career was considerable; but in indicating the existence of an audience and a sense of intellectual community in the enterprise of modern verse, *Poetry* was responding to the times as much as it was moulding them: scheduled to appear in November, its first publication was brought forward in order to establish prior rights to the name over a Boston magazine (which became the *Poetry Journal*; first edited by W.S. Braithwaite, it lasted six years). The editorial policy was flexible: in an introductory circular, Monroe told possible contributors that although she sought 'poems of modern significance', she would also accept 'the most classic subject' if its quality was high enough – which makes clear that her criteria were driven more by content than by form. In her autobiography (1937) she judged Vachel Lindsay to have been the 'most gifted and original' of *Poetry*'s poets (out of a list that also included Yeats, Eliot, Pound, and Stevens), and her lack of critical discrimination – shown also in her own mediocre poetry – is an easy target, contrasting as it so blatantly did with that of Pound, who functioned as the magazine's 'foreign correspondent' in its early years; but it is interesting to note that her editorial openness to both modern and traditional contributions was a strategy that

Eliot himself would follow when, ten years later, he founded the *Criterion* (1922–39).

Like the *Criterion*, which never attracted more than a thousand subscribers, by 1918 *Poetry*, appearing each month, had only managed to achieve slightly more than half of its target readership of 3000; which suggests the limited nature of the community of interest to which it addressed itself.[13] But by existing at all, by paying contributors $10 a page as well as by offering annual prizes, Monroe's venture (which was in part an effort to challenge the intellectual/artistic pre-eminence of Boston and New York) encouraged writers and galvanised interest; and the subsequent competition from other magazines for new writing – chiefly Margaret Anderson's *Little Review* (1914–29) and the reinvigorated *Dial*, especially under the editorships of Scofield Thayer and, from 1925, Marianne Moore – were a kind of tribute to her achievement, even as they reacted against the limitations which had led her in the first issue of *Poetry* to give pride of place to an utterly conventional poem by Arthur Davison Ficke, and later (in spite of Pound's expostulations) to sit on 'Prufrock' for nine months before hiding it away in the issue of June 1915. Her circumspection may not have been due entirely to her own defective taste (of which we shall see further evidence): for Monroe needed not to risk alienating any of the sponsors who underwrote her magazine – and here again, Eliot's somewhat vexed editorial relations with the *Criterion*'s patroness, Lady Rothermere, come to mind.

Stevens might have complained to Elsie in June 1909 that the 'modern conception of poetry is that it should be in the service of something' (*L* 147), rather than standing or falling by its own 'Beauty' (he had been reading Keats); but given his own awareness even then of the connections, both antagonistic and nutritive, between poetry and money, and given also his professional awareness of the business world, he would hardly have expected magazines of verse to be entirely free from fields of influence or extra-literary contexts. Indeed, it was his own inhabitation of a certain field of influence that enabled him not to be wholly dependent on *Poetry* for the publication of his verse; nor did that magazine provide his principal source of artistic community at the outset of his publishing career. Throughout his New York years, Stevens had dined intermittently at the Harvard Club; and in 1908 his father, forwarding an alumni notice, advised him to 'keep up with the boys'. Although Garrett doubtless had in mind the cultivation of professionally useful contacts, it was actually in furthering his literary career that Stevens found that advice most useful. In August 1905, shortly after his return from his business trip to the South, he noted having had lunch at the club with Walter Arensberg, whom he reported as a 'fellow of most excellent fancy' (*SP* 154); and while this inertly Shakespearian tribute might be appropriate to the Arensberg who would later devote a good deal of his mental and financial resources to arguing that 'Shakespeare' had really been Francis Bacon, it insufficiently represented the minor poet and significant collector of modern art, in whose New York salon on West 67th Street Stevens would for a few years experience the heavenly fellowship of men and women who were responsive to the newest developments in the arts.[14]

Arensberg and his wife Louise moved to New York from Boston in 1914, the year following the celebrated 'Armory Show' (so-called because it was held in the armoury of the 69th Infantry Regiment on Lexington Avenue), at which the latest European Post-Impressionist work was introduced to America. Arensberg knew Walter Pach, one of the show's organisers, whom Stevens got to know through him; and given Stevens's avid interest in art exhibitions it is almost unthinkable that he did not attend the show, which opened in February 1913 amid some notoriety – although there is no record of his having done so. Some of the works were acquired by Arensberg and displayed in his apartment (including a version of Marcel Duchamp's 'Nude Descending a Staircase'), so even had Stevens not attended, he would have been familiar with certain aspects. He was introduced to Duchamp by Arensberg in the summer of 1915, when the artist was using the apartment as his studio, but reported himself to Elsie as having been able to make very little of what he was shown of the work in progress (*L* 185). As with Stein's *Three Lives*, whose starting point had been Cézanne's 1881 portrait of his wife, the visual arts (along with music) were leading the way in their challenging innovativeness, and in so doing provided a powerful stimulus for practitioners in the verbal medium. In Stein's case, Cézanne's depicting his wife's face more as a mask than as a revelation of personality by means of a technique which drew attention to the very materiality of the oil-paint on his canvas, inaugurated her own experiments in the use of language as a non-referential opacity (Stevens's brief efforts, later, to create 'a theatre without action or characters' (*L* 203) suggests a similarly reductive extremism).

If the written word was catching up with contemporary painting and sculpture, those in their turn were catching up with science and technology. In the case of Stevens, disengaging from his thoughts for sonnets as the first flying-machines were taking to the air, the modern world was his before he was the modern world's. Robert Hughes has written in *The Shock of the New* that 'the speed at which culture reinvented itself through technology in the last quarter of the nineteenth century and the first decades of the twentieth, seems almost preternatural', going on to list a startling number of profoundly transformative discoveries and inventions occurring between 1875 and 1905.[15] Duchamp's 'Nude Descending...', which caught the American public's attention by being the object of press ridicule ('an explosion in a shingle factory'), was, Hughes notes, based on E-J Marey's sequential photographs; and the technological precedence is appropriate. The problems addressed, and caused, both by the painting and its painter are relevant here, irrespective of whether or not Stevens had any pronounced opinions about either. For Duchamp's 'Nude ...' shocked by its contravention of most of the conventions generically implicit in nude studies and the life class: it was as much abstract as representational, it lacked anatomical detail or sensuous pleasure (or disgust) even in its colours, its subject was uncertain. In fact, the picture can only 'work' in the antagonistic energy engendered between its modernist presentation and a viewer's classicising expectations.

The 'Nude...' may be an example of a subject being seen most clearly in the idea of it: the formal problem to which it offers a solution is how to depict motion in a static medium; but it is more a diagrammatic presentation of overlapping phases of movement than an attempt to render actual motion.[16] Yet its refusal to prioritise a single image of the body, and its explicit reduction of that body to a series of mechanised gestures, was a significant demotion of the human subject; which in his own person Duchamp took further. Unlike some theorists and practitioners of exploded humanism, apparently immune in their own lives and writings to the various forms of false consciousness they diagnose as the modern condition, Duchamp seems to have assented to the logic of his own perceptions. If the nude was obsolete as representation of an unique individual, so was the artist as originator: by producing series of works (there are at least three versions of the 'Nude...'), he subverted the notion of the sacralised uniqueness of the art-event, and of the artist's originality; a process which he took further in his 'Ready-Mades', *objets trouvés* which required little or no 'creative' intervention on his part, the most notorious of which was a urinal. Finally, by withdrawing altogether from the creation of 'art' in 1923 (at least publicly) and devoting himself thereafter to chess, Duchamp made his most eloquent statement about the disappearance of the artist.

Fascination with the mechanical and an associated glorification of the geometric over the organic was a feature of theory and practice in many of the arts at this time, most obviously seen in Futurism and Cubism; when Williams in 1944 asserted that there was 'nothing sentimental about a machine' and described a poem as 'a small (or large) machine made out of words' he was nailing his colours to the mast of a ship already under full sail.[17] When in November 1900 Stevens observed in his journal that the stars recently had been clear, golden, and geometrical, and immediately commented, 'I rather like that idea of geometrical – it's so confoundedly new!' (*SP* 90), he had a glimpse of something for which he would not find the words until more than twenty years later (in 'Stars at Tallapoosa'). Both Williams's image and Stevens's have in common the objectivist desire to represent the otherness of things too easily co-opted to a humanising vision; and when Stevens caught Williams indulging a moment's anthropomorphic sentimentalism in a poem about the morning-star, his response was to expand the theme in an inflationary parody which nevertheless acknowledged that seeing what is as 'other things' (*CP* 272) is bound up in being human and using language (see 'Nuances of a Theme by Williams', 1918). For although Stevens was as clear as any that a large part of the modern condition concerned awareness of the relativities of seeing – a lesson learnable both from the flat presentationalism of Japanese prints and from pictures like Duchamp's 'Nude...', and embodied in poems like 'Thirteen Ways of Looking at a Blackbird' (1917) and 'Metaphors of a Magnifico' (1918) – he was not persuaded that the necessary replacement of an obsolete unified worldview had to entail the disappearance of the unitary viewer (the virile poet or figure of capable imagination would be Stevens's later names for this; 'unitary' is Whitman's term from 'Song of Myself').

If the Victorian era in which Stevens had grown to manhood seemed so entirely dead by the century's second decade, this was because the certainties on which that age had sustained itself – as it appeared in retrospect – had been incapable of adjusting to the accelerations of history: the Victorian was the man whose mind was made up and who, therefore, died (*CP* 472). Of course, it had actually been the work of Victorian pioneers which paved the road to modernity: and the title of 'Nude Descending a Staircase' (in French, *nu descendant un escalier*) could be seen to allude to Charles Darwin's *The Descent of Man* (1871) in which, extending the epochal discoveries of *On the Origin of Species* (1859), the author argued that mankind had evolved from the higher primates. Duchamp's figure describes its declining arc from left to right, an unaccommodated man-machine enacting humanity's dethronement as the favourite creature of gods no longer to be found at the top of the stairs.[18] Resisting stasis by representing kinesis, Duchamp's picture could have suggested to Stevens a necessary strategy for the modern artist; in addition, its elements of humour (why is a man walking downstairs naked, and why doesn't he look like what he is supposed to be?), as well as the distance opened up between title and actual picture, offer points of comparison with the poems Stevens would write between 1914 and 1922. 'Nude Descending...' forcibly illustrates how the disestablishment of habituated ways of seeing – the shattering of the groove, in Stevens's terms – was a major endeavour of the modern movement. But useful as the picture has been to my discussion as an icon of the modern, the very nature of its canonicity (which is partly due to the publicity of its initial reception) highlights problems relevant to Stevens's thoughts about the artist's role.

The relation of art to life was a matter of permanent interest to him. Richardson quotes an unpublished part of a letter of 14 April 1907 in which he asked his fiancée, 'suppose on a summer day I quoted "Rest, and a world of leaves and stealing stream," I should be adding another day to the real one, don't you think?';[19] the context was Stevens's attempt to persuade Elsie of the riches they could share, were she to participate in his love of books. Such a process could, however, be expressed as the loss of the real day beneath a literary superimposition; much later he wrote 'The Poem that Took the Place of a Mountain' (1952): would this substitution be benign, or otherwise? As with Duchamp's 'Nude...' (which Williams, for example, would much later describe as having become hackneyed), masterful images can become inert once their anti-institutionalism has been institutionalised; and a force of liberation turns into its obverse, becoming potentially an obstacle to vision. I recently heard Jack Lang, former Minister of Culture in France, comment to the effect that he could never drive by Mont Ste-Victoire (the obsessive subject of many of Cézanne's late studies) without seeing it through the artist's eyes; that being so, one might legitimately wonder whether Cézanne had given him the mountain, or taken it away for ever. Cézanne, however, furnished Stevens with a model of how the artist could remain a unifying presence, without becoming canonically repressive: some time around 1937, he copied a paragraph from *The New Statesman* which stressed the relation between Cézanne's integrity and his refusal to become fixed in his art, instead pursuing 'new discoveries of technique' and 'new realisations of the motive'. Stevens added the gloss that these comments stressed the too-often overlooked reality of 'the artist, the presence of the determining personality' (*OP*1 xxxix); but whatever that might suggest of a disdainfully aloof supervisor, Cézanne's own comments in a letter to his son display the pragmatic humility that prevented any imperialist appropriation: 'The same subject seen from a different angle gives a motif of the highest interest, and so varied that I think I could be occupied for months without changing my place – simply bending a little more to the right or left'.[20] Earlier in the same letter (a few weeks before his death) he had written, 'here on the bank of the river the motifs multiply', and it is this capacity for renewed response which Stevens admired: 'This Solitude of Cataracts' (1948) starts with the line 'He never felt twice the same about the flecked river' (*CP* 424), and goes on to suggest that, however arduous the constant changingess might be, desire for permanence is a kind of death-wish.

It is therefore appropriate that the belated appearance of Stevens's first collection in 1923 coincided with Duchamp's virtual withdrawal from the practice of his art. For whereas Duchamp's work might be compared to the disruptively energetic humour that went into the making of *Harmonium* – and particularly to the sardonic reductivenesss of attitude detectible behind its paradoxically ornate language – the person and career of Cézanne suggest the flexible single-mindedness and seriousness of purpose that would sustain Stevens's poetry-writing from the mid-1930s to the end of his life. It has been customary to suppose that the silence which descended on him after his first volume was in large part due to its commercial failure; but without disputing this, it may also have been due to an artistic exhaustion which would have occurred, no matter what had been the book's reception. To pursue this analogy with French painters: post-*Harmonium* Stevens would need to progress beyond the technically striking but rather aggressive pessimism shown in Duchamp's 'Nude...' stepping downward to darkness; and this he would achieve by adjusting his stance in respect of things as they were, and by embracing the infinite resurrections made possible when the same subject was seen from different angles: a Cézannesque celebration of the inexhaustible 'metaphysical changes' and multiplication of motifs that are consequent upon our merely living as and where we live (the allusion here is to the end of 'Esthétique du Mal', 1944).

These are, at best, suggestive parallels; I am not proposing that Stevens was directly influenced in his own practice by either artist. For although the visual arts probably offer the clearest illustration of the changes taking place, both generally and personally, as Modernism became established, Stevens was first and foremost a writer, with limited time (and, some have suggested, limited talent) for the consideration of pictorial art. The writers whom he met at Walter Arensberg's gatherings were of more immediate consequence to his literary life; and in a recollection of this period written the year before he died, Stevens emphasised that his primary perception of Arensberg was of his interest in poetry: they had, after all, first met at Harvard, where Arensberg had the reputation of being an expert on Walter Pater, and was involved with the *Harvard Monthly* as Stevens worked on the *Advocate* (*L* 821). But although it is true to say, as Glen Macleod does, that 'while Stevens was writing the poems of *Harmonium*, he was more closely involved with other writers and artists than ever before or since', the nature of that closeness and its direct effects on the poems are open to question.[21] When Hi Simons, an early commentator, implied that something tantamount to intellectual collaboration with Arensberg and with Pitts Sanborn had taken place during his Greenwich Village years, Stevens assured him that the sort of literary discussions envisaged were 'the last thing in the world that I should be likely to engage in except casually. I am not a good talker and don't particularly enjoy exchanging ideas with other people in talk' (8 July 1941; *L* 391). Although frequently willing to engage in correspondence about such matters, there is evidence that Stevens strongly discouraged those who attempted to talk about his poetry with him, were they Alfred Kreymborg or even his own daughter; and a picture consistently painted is of a man who needed a fair amount of alcohol to overcome his natural reticence in situations where (unlike in business meetings) his presence was not a direct function of his authority. We know that he showed drafts of some poems to Arensberg, and to William Carlos Williams who also frequented the salon; and we know that he responded to their suggestions; but nothing indicates the creative interchanges one imagines Pound and Eliot had over *The Waste Land*.

The founding of *Poetry* in 1912 and the Armory Show the following year are habitually taken as landmark inaugurations of American Modernism. Each had its effect on Stevens, but at the outset of his literary career, the effect of his having been at Harvard is more immediately traceable. In 1914 Pitts Sanborn, who was a good friend of Arensberg and had known Stevens at Harvard, joined the staff of *Trend* magazine, and solicited contributions from his literary acquaintances; Stevens responded to his request with 'Carnet de Voyage', a group of eight poems, five of which had been in the 'Little June Book' presented to Elsie in 1909. On 13 August 1914 he wrote to her that he was awaiting their appearance with mixed feelings, but had been disappointed not to find them in that month's issue (*L* 165–6). They appeared in the September number, which as Bates notes featured the work of seven Harvard alumni, including Arensberg and Witter Bynner – another university acquaintance whom Stevens had taken on to the *Advocate*, and with whom he had kept in contact. At this stage Bynner was much further advanced on a poetic career, with a published collection to his name and a good number of poems appearing in established magazines, and the title of his volume *An Ode to Harvard* (1907) underscores the significance of the network.[22] Richardson has speculated that it may have been Bynner who caused Harriet Monroe to take an interest in the first poems his old friend submitted to *Poetry* (the submissions were meant to have been anonymous): she selected four out of the eleven, which were published as 'Phases' in the 'Poems of War' issue (November 1914). The same month saw Stevens's second appearance in *Trend* with two poems, one of which ('Home Again') had been included in the 'Book of Verses' presented to Elsie in 1908.

None of the verse Stevens published in 1914 would be admitted to his first volume or collected works; but it marked the decisive beginning of a public career that would see him publish nearly a hundred poems in little magazines, in the period leading up to *Harmonium*. Given that both Arensberg (whose *Poems* came out in Boston early in 1914) and Bynner had already published collections of verse, it is remarkable that Stevens, whose reputation must have been based only on his 14-year-old Harvard poetry (some of which had been included in subsequent Harvard anthologies), was in the position of being solicited for contributions at this stage. His decision to use poems from his gift-books to Elsie suggests, first, that the compilation of those had been a real enough expression of poetic aspiration and, second, that he had not written very much since then. The invitation to write and the discovery that he could be taken seriously – together with expanding publishing opportunities and the quickening cultural atmosphere – operated as a strong incentive to composition; as would be the case, later, when he emerged from his post-*Harmonium* silence.

Other factors likely to have played a part in his delayed flowering ('thawing out so beautifully at forty', as Williams put it), were the progress of his professional career and the deaths of his parents: his father in 1911 and his mother almost exactly a year later. Although not finally settled, Stevens by 1914 had begun to establish his career, and was engaged in the pursuits appropriate to his position: learning golf and encouraging his wife to do the same during the stays at summer resorts, to which he was proud to have the money to send her. According to Richardson, Elsie's long periods away during the New York summers seem quite quickly to have become something her husband actively desired and prolonged where possible, as part of the emotional economy of a marriage in which it appeared they could share less and less: theatre-going was an important resource for them – light theatre and heavy cooking, along with the piano he acquired for her, representing the dwindling reserves of their common currency. Stevens's progress as lawyer and as poet in this period was halting; but perhaps the real unbroken narrative of 1904–14 lies in the rising and then sadly falling arc of his relationship with Elsie, who started as his imaginative and emotional cynosure, but who finished confronting her diminishing importance, compared with Arensberg and Harriet Monroe and what they stood for. Her anger at the appropriation of 'her' poems at the beginning of his career is more explicable if we see the theft as symptomatic of a deeper offence; but whatever the truth might be, Stevens became more visible as poet as she became less visible as wife: and none of her rages could alter his course. Some words he wrote to her shortly before their wedding, describing the cleansed apppearance of his old bachelor quarters, are eerily predictive of the kind of balance they would achieve in their marriage: 'Yesterday's disorder has turned into the strict arrangements of emptiness'.[23]

4

1914–23: Accents of Deviation

Elsie's separation from her husband's poetry was a gradual process rather than an absolute withdrawal: at the end of August 1915 he wrote to her of his dissatisfaction with what he had managed to compose during her summer absence from the city (*L* 186), and there are other such references in the correspondence at this period. His desire to share with her was still in evidence, then; but also evident was the implication that both sharing and composition were made easier by her not being physically present in their apartment. Whereas his wife might hanker after a home in Reading, Stevens, after a long period in which he had felt like a neglected outsider in New York, found himself part of expanding circles of attention, in respect both of his poetry and his profession; indeed, there was competition for his work. One door opened another: the group of poems which he had sent to his friend Sanborn the previous summer, published as 'Carnet de Voyage' in the September *Trend*, caught the notice of Carl Van Vechten, who was to be temporary editor; he asked Stevens for more, and duly published 'From a Junk' and 'Home Again' in the November issue – in which he also described Stevens as 'one of the most gifted of the younger American poets'. These poems hardly justified his accolade, although the subsequent work would; but it suggests that there was something about Stevens which compelled attention: for Harriet Monroe would recall having noticed his unsolicited manuscript of the 'Phases' poems (submitted under the *nom de plume* 'Peter Parasol'), and how – having scrawled 'jewel' on the top page of his submission – she had inserted four of them into the November 'Poems of War' issue of *Poetry*, despite the fact that her magazine was already in proof.

While working on the *New York Times* in 1913, Van Vechten had met Allen Norton and Donald Evans, who also shared his dissatisfaction there and like him were determined to stir things up; all were involved with *Trend*. Evans had published two volumes of verse by the time Stevens met him, *Discords* (1912) and *Sonnets from the Patagonian* (1914), and after his suicide in 1921 was remembered by Alfred Kreymborg for the 'exquisite masks of cynicism' by which he had offered a 'graceful defiance of society' – a description which may suggest why some felt him to have influenced Stevens (who regretted the death of a great ironist and 'pure *littérateur*').[1] Evans (who had founded the Claire Marie Press to publish 'belles-lettres for exotic tastes'), Van Vechten, Norton and his wife Louise formed a loose group centred on the Nortons' Greenwich Village apartment that germinated a small magazine, *Rogue* (March 1915 to September 1915), which was '*chic, if not precious*'.[2] In literary terms the group's principal roots lay in 1890s decadence, although they were also open to experimentalist writing; there was thus a natural overlap with the Arensberg circle. They attended the evening at the Arensbergs' apartment when Stevens read his poems, which led to a request from Norton, early in 1915, that he be permitted to publish 'Cy Est Pourtraicte...' – the 'poem connected with radishes', as he called it – in the forthcoming first issue of *Rogue*. This could hardly have been more opportune, given that Harriet Monroe had recently (27 January) rejected Stevens's latest offerings to *Poetry*, objecting as she did to their 'gargoyle grin' and 'Aubrey Beardsleyish' qualities. 'Cy Est Pourtraicte... ' and 'Tea' duly appeared in the first number of *Rogue* (15 March 1915), alongside prose by Gertrude Stein; the other Stevens poem to be published (in September) would be 'Disillusionment of Ten O'Clock'; *Rogue* also published poetry by Arensberg and Mina Loy.

In his memoir *Troubadour* (1925), Alfred Kreymborg recalled how he had first met Stevens at the Nortons' in 1915, and had been surprised by the sheer size of the poet, whom he abortively attempted to engage in conversation about 'Tea'; Allen Norton intervened, explaining that 'cornering Wallace about his own work' wasn't done. Kreymborg (subsequently nick-named the patron saint of American little magazines) had in September 1913 started the *Glebe*, which ran for little more than a year, its most notable achievement having perhaps lain in publishing Pound's anthology of *Des Imagistes* (consisting principally of poems by Richard Aldington, H.D., and Pound, with additional contributions from – to name the most relevant – Williams, F.S. Flint, and Amy Lowell). Kreymborg's presence at that evening was a sign of imminent changes, for the meeting had been convened to discuss the future of *Rogue*.[3] He and Arensberg talked about the need for a successor to Norton's magazine which would be 'more imagistic than the Imagists', and this conversation was renewed a few days later at Arensberg's studio, when the two men talked through the night, Kreymborg agreeing with his host that *Rogue* 'would never do', and that what was needed was 'a poetry magazine, not like *Poetry* in Chicago, which admitted too many compromises, but a paper dedicating its energies to experiment throughout'.[4] Out of their discussions came the plan for the magazine *Others*; Arensberg like Kreymborg deciding that it was essential for success that they should secure contributions from Mina Loy and Wallace Stevens. Loy was featured in the magazine's first number alongside Kreymborg himself and Orrick Johns, and Stevens was represented the next month in its second issue (August 1915) by 'Peter Quince at the Clavier' and 'The Silver Plough-Boy'; the September issue contained Eliot's 'Portrait of a Lady'. Remembering Arensberg in the 1950s Stevens would recall his boyish enthusiasm, and *Others* seems to have been a case in point, since he quickly lost his desire to be involved editorially; but he held to his agreement to underwrite its costs for a year, and gave Kreymborg a free hand.

Literary factions, with their unstable ideological compounds and resultant associations and dissociations of sensibilities, are difficult to map reliably. *Others* was conceived as the superior successor to *Rogue*, with which it overlapped for three months; and several of the *Rogue* writers contributed to Kreymborg's magazine. The amalgamation of the two groups seems not to have been acrimonious; but it is clear from Stevens's letter about having been introduced by Arensberg to Duchamp, that there had been a falling-out between them and Van Vechten (3 August 1915; *L* 185), and possibly this was connected with the poet's new alignment. There was a good deal of competitive jockeying for position at this period, particularly visible in the disputes about what 'Imagism' was, who had discovered it, and who owned the mining-rights. Pound's sense of himself as the onlie begetter and sponsor of the movement was resented – by Flint, for example, who attributed much more to T.E. Hulme. In his turn, Pound was affronted by Amy Lowell's appropriation of the tag, as also by the fact that her successive anthologies *Some Imagist Poets* (1915, 1916, 1917) easily outsold *Des Imagistes* (1914). Since March 1913, when *Poetry* had published Flint's 'Imagisme' and Pound's 'A Few Don'ts by an Imagiste' (as well as poems by Aldington in November 1912 and H.D. in January 1913, identifying both as imagists), Harriet Monroe had regarded herself as having certain rights in the matter, and took Kreymborg to task for reproducing in *Des Imagistes* poems which by that stage had already appeared in *Poetry*.

'Imagism', loosely understood as a commitment to *vers libre* and precision of expression, was for a few years conceived to be the essence of the modern movement in poetry; and s/he who held the standard led an army, or so it seemed. Being the standard bearer was much easier if one had editorial control of a publishing outlet: this led to Pound's repeated efforts to establish himself, and to the – much wealthier – Lowell's equally unsuccessful attempts to buy a controlling interest in *Poetry* and the *Little Review*.

This context of various camps and coteries vying for centre-stage was surprisingly beneficial for the establishment of Stevens's reputation; in part because he was not exclusively identified with a particular sect. He was evidently held in high esteem: to be wooed (by the party at Arensberg's, to coax him into the ambit of *Rogue*), to be cosseted (Norton's instructing Kreymborg not to 'corner' him), and regarded as one of the two poets essential to the early definition of the avant-garde identity of *Others* (whose title came from its manifesto that 'the old expressions are with us always, and there are always others'). As well as with the *Rogue* group, the Arensberg circle partly overlapped with that of Alfred Stieglitz – the 'intellectual conspirator' whose gallery on 291 Fifth Avenue was both a conduit for the latest ideas from Europe and a centre for American artists such as Charles Demuth and Marsden Hartley, and would play its part in New York Dada.[5] At this period, therefore, Stevens's acquaintances potentially included most of the significant figures in the New York literary and artistic scenes, although how many of them he actually met remains uncertain. There is no indication that he knew Mina Loy, despite being bracketed with her by Kreymborg; but he did meet Williams at this time, and Williams tells us of at least one of the colourful Bohemian types he also encountered, the Baroness Elsa von Freytag-Loringhoven, who pursued both men – and several others – with some vigour. Just what degree of sympathy can have existed between Stevens and the wilder elements is questionable; after the intense repressions of the Victorian era, in these circles this was what Baudelaire might have called an '*époque nue*', with a talent for actual and virtual self-exposure. The pronounced eroticism of Mina Loy's verse was matched by such challenges to conventional propriety as her having once shared Marcel Duchamp's bed with Duchamp, Demuth, and two other women; the Baroness (some of whose verse would be published in *The Little Review*) was happy to model in the nude and didn't always need an artist to justify the activity (she later starred in the film by Duchamp and Man Ray, self-explanatorily titled 'Elsa, Baroness von Freytag-Loringhoven, Shaves Her Pubic Hair'); in 1917 Stieglitz embarked on his 20-year series of photographic nude studies of the painter Georgia O'Keefe, whom he married. It is unlikely that the relentlessly-clothed Stevens would have felt much in common with such goings-on: the nearest he came was in the unconvincing naked dancers of 'Sunday Morning' (1915); throughout his poetry, nakedness is a metaphysical rather than a physical state.[6]

The prudentialism which, particularly at the outset of his career, made Stevens sensitive to the need not to acquire a reputation for bohemianism that might hamper his professional advancement, together with his attested lack of ease in social situations – not helped, presumably, by the fact that he was deaf in one ear – make it improbable that he surrendered to the avant-garde in the way that some others did, except philosophically. In this he resembled Arensberg, whose own poetry, apart from some later Dadaist pieces, was very much less experimental than the work of the artists he collected (and Stevens, in whose *oeuvre* the iambic pentameter retains its old ascendancy, seems the obverse of Eliot, whose practice was radical but whose theory was pronouncedly traditionalist). The degree of personal closeness between Stevens and Arensberg is also difficult to gauge; there was certainly enough friendship and personal regard to have kept them in contact beyond Harvard; but although Stevens owned copies of both Arensberg's 1912 volume and his last book of verse *Idols* (1916), neither was signed by the author, unlike the volumes by Williams or Marianne Moore in his library. Their friendship was glacially terminated shortly before the Arensbergs left New York for California in 1921, and could not be resuscitated even by Van Vechten's presumably well-meant strategy to effect a reconciliation (see *L* 850). The fact that Stevens went on writing poetry after the dissolution of the Arensberg salon demonstrates his independence of it; and it may have been the case that Arensberg, whose great wealth came from the family steel business, too much represented to Stevens the kind of life he knew himself debarred from living, for complete openness between the two men.

It may also be that his more relaxed relations with Harriet Monroe were due, at least in part, to the fact that he did not at the most important level consider her to be his equal, and could therefore expose himself to her judgement with greater equanimity. The undiscerning editorial policy felt to be characteristic of *Poetry* caused dissenters to found magazines intended to be more selective and more radical, such as *Others* and *The Little Review* (especially after its move to New York in 1917), which defined itself as 'A Magazine of the Arts Making No Compromise with the Public Taste'. Monroe's literary discrimination was not held in high regard by many of her contemporaries, as Stevens would have been well aware; which makes it even more remarkable that in June 1915 he should have assented to her proposal that 'Sunday Morning' needed cutting down. Initially he was prepared to countenance a 50 per cent reduction to four stanzas, merely stipulating the order as I, VIII, IV and V, but she evidently suggested that room might be found at the end for stanza VII; and it was in this form that Stevens's best-known poem was first published, in *Poetry*, November 1915 – with an additional adjustment to the wording of stanza V (*L* 183). Her rearrangements effected a fundamental alteration in the mood of the poem, which thus moved from the morose languor of the woman's meditations to the neo-paganism of its assertively male dancers: a much more upbeat closure than the dying fall of the original. She also diminished the pronounced agnosticism, whether out of deference to her magazine's financial backers or in recognition of the context of the Great War raging in Europe, where Christian values were being bloodily defended by combatants on both sides of the conflict.

This was one of the occasions when the editorial policy of *Poetry* seemed not just undiscriminating, but to embody actively bad judgement. Stevens's consent to this form of censorship, by an editor who had earlier that year rejected poems which were welcomed in more adventurous magazines, is difficult to explain: the more so, as a concern with wholeness and a dislike of the fragmentary would become evident in his attitude to his own writing. Monroe treated 'Sunday Morning' with the high-handedness Pound would later show toward *The Waste Land*; but with much less justification, either in terms of the poem it was or her own powers of discernment. At the time of Stevens's negotiations with Monroe, the first issue of *Others* had not yet appeared, and the attention it would command was uncertain (it attracted some hostile notice in the New York press, and was nicknamed the 'little yellow dog': so it made an impact). Given the fact of *Poetry*'s establishment, and that even in her January rejection Monroe had encouraged him to 'send more', Stevens probably felt that she needed to be cultivated; and he could hardly have sent her a poem more steeped in nineteenth-century resemblances than 'Sunday Morning' was. If he seems not to have taken offence at her emendations, this must have been because he felt the sacrifice was worth the opportunity to publish; in the years to come he would charm her into greater acquiescence, in part by playing hard to get: for none of his poems was published in her magazine between 'Sunday Morning' in November 1915 and 'Lettres d'un Soldat' in May 1918 (his playlets 'Three Travelers Watch a Sunrise' (1916) and 'Carlos Among the Candles' (1917) did, however, appear in *Poetry*).

There is obviously no reason to suppose that in the summer of 1915 Stevens would have been as certain of the merits of 'Sunday Morning' as its subsequent reputation entitles us to be, over eighty years later. The following year he adopted the emendation Williams proposed for 'The Worms at Heaven's Gate', which was published in the issue of *Others* (July 1916) that Williams guest-edited; so Stevens was open to suggestions – and it continued to be characteristic of him, even when submitting poems at the request of editors, to be self-deprecating and prepared to have the manuscript rejected. However, for nearly three years he sent no poems to *Poetry*; and this has been taken as an implicit reproach to Monroe at a period when the pre-eminence of her magazine as showcase for contemporary verse was under some threat.[7] In 1922 he would assert to her that he sent *Poetry* what he liked most (*L* 230); but he can hardly have disliked poems such as 'Peter Quince....' (1915), 'Domination of Black' (1916), 'Thirteen Ways of Looking at a Blackbird' (1917), 'Earthy Anecdote' and 'Le Monocle de Mon Oncle' (both 1918) – to list only the obvious jewels that he sent to *Others*. It was certainly the case that to be associated with the 'little yellow dog' was to be perceived as avant-garde and, just as Stevens had been named at its inception as one of the poets the magazine needed to attract, he was associated with *Others* even after its demise. In its early days (while Arensberg's funding permitted regular publication) *Others* could display talent more effectively than *Poetry* did: in his first appearance in the second number, for example, Stevens featured alongside Amy Lowell and Williams. Yet even when the magazine was virtually on its last legs, he still could think it worth his while to give *Others* a poem as substantial as 'Le Monocle... '.

He may have been 'punishing' Monroe in denying her such poems; but perhaps the cause also lay in his sense of the different function of *Poetry*. 'Le Monocle…', for all its verbal bravura, has an intensely personal core, which Stevens may at first have wished to give a more restricted exposure: thus the poem's own dissimulations would be further masked by the experimentalist slant of *Others*. The first poems he had published in *Poetry*, 'Phases', were a response to the war engulfing Europe; the next, 'Sunday Morning', addressed the crisis of faith and the meaning of life, using an imagined female protagonist; he then let *Poetry* publish his two short plays, before returning to the fold in May 1918 with 'Lettres d'un Soldat' – a set of poems which itself returned to the topic of the European war (which by that stage included America). The distinction cannot be drawn absolutely, but it is fair to say that the poems he placed elsewhere during this period were to some degree different in kind; the subtitle for the special issue of *Others* (December 1917) in which 'Thirteen Ways…' appeared with four other poems best captures the difference: 'A number for the mind's eye/ Not to be read aloud'. For most of the poems published in *Rogue, Others*, and sundry little magazines were more inward-focusing: uttered by a self-identifying 'I' or implying a more intimate relation either between poem and reader, or between poem and writer; whereas the pieces in *Poetry* seem more evidently public in intent – as was obviously the case with the plays which, whatever their pre-Beckettian exiguousness, were written for an audience. The ten poems published as 'Primordia' in *Soil* (January 1917) form a slight exception; but Robert Coady's New York-based magazine, which ran from December 1916 to July 1917, was dedicated to the expression of an exclusively American aesthetic, and Stevens's regional miniatures, inspired by his business travels in the north-west and the south of the country, were appropriately targeted (only 'In the Carolinas', 'Indian River', and 'To the Roaring Wind' would appear in *Harmonium*; the second not until the 1931 edition).

Poetry was the most important publishing outlet for Stevens between 1914 and 1923, and was identified as such on the acknowledgements page of *Harmonium*, where Harriet Monroe was mentioned by name. Of the 74 poems in the first edition, 64 had been previously published in little magazines (scrupulously if unsystematically listed on the same page); 25 of these had first appeared in *Poetry*. Of the 110 poems published in the period to

December 1923 ('Earthy Anecdote' was published twice), the 40 Monroe printed greatly exceeded the tally of her nearest rival, *Others* (18).[8] If, however, the years 1914–18 are analysed (the first five of Stevens's serious publishing), 61 of his poems appeared in little magazines, 14 of them in *Poetry* – of which only one ('Sunday Morning' in its expanded form) would be preserved in *Harmonium* (1923). The strike-rate of the other magazines was collectively much better: 23 *Harmonium* poems out of 47 overall, with *Others* doing best in matching quantity with quality, by publishing 16 poems, of which 10 were included in the first edition. The correspondence shows that Stevens kept on friendly terms with Monroe, but Newcomb may well be right in his suggestion that her advocacy in securing Stevens's play 'Three Travelers Watch a Sunrise' the $100 first prize in the competition for which the staff of *Poetry* were judges (she overrode the objections of a fellow-judge), may have been intended to secure his loyalty to her magazine. He sent her the manuscript of 'Lettres d'un Soldat' in September 1917, and in March 1918 they met to weed out the bad ones (*L* 205) – omitting four of the 13 poems submitted (of which one, 'Lunar Paraphrase', later appeared in the second edition of *Harmonium*). It would be the summer of 1919 before *Poetry* had another chance to consider poems by Stevens (he wrote of his intention to send items on 22 March that year, but was anticipating a lengthy business trip). By that time, however, the editor had learnt her lesson, and accepted more of the poems he sent than he had supposed she would: in a letter of August 1919 (*L* 214) he requested that she substitute three of the group already in her hands by new poems he enclosed ('The Weeping Burgher', 'Banal Sojourn', and 'Anecdote of the Jar'), and he also enclosed a 'trifle' ('The Indigo Glass in the Grass'); she printed all of the new work he sent, but removed only one of the poems he had condemned. The October 1919 number of *Poetry* contained 14 poems by Stevens, collectively entitled 'Pecksniffiana', given pride of place in the magazine's first eleven pages. The following year it was announced that 'Pecksniffiana' had been awarded the magazine's Levinson Prize: it seemed as if *Poetry* was wooing Stevens. Twelve of those 14 poems would appear in *Harmonium*, and in October 1921 *Poetry* again devoted its first nine pages to his writing: 12 poems with the obscurely rebarbative collective title 'Sur Ma Guzzla Gracile', which certain readers thought were 'hideous ghosts of [himself]' (*L* 223). 'The Snow Man' was one of the group, but others – such as

'Tea at the Palaz of Hoon', 'Of (*sic*) the Manner of Addressing Clouds' and 'Of Heaven Considered as a Tomb' – might well be thought to display some of the Aubrey Beardsleyishness or gargoylism, that had provoked Monroe's dislike six years earlier.

After the demise of *Others*, although Stevens contributed to *Broom* (Kreymborg's next venture) and, in 1922, to the reinvigorated *Dial*, as well as to other little magazines, *Poetry* mattered most to him. Yet the significance of his earlier association persisted so that, as Newcomb observes, 'even in reviews of *Harmonium* in 1923–24, with *Others* four years dead, Stevens was remembered as a primary member of the group' (p. 39); and until the publication of his second volume in 1935, three of the four poems by which he was most readily identified in critical discussion ('Sunday Morning'; 'Peter Quince...'; 'Thirteen Ways...'; 'Le Monocle...') had been published in *Others*. Magazines like the *Measure* and Gorham Munson's *Secession*, to which he also contributed, had been founded specifically to counteract the 'Chicago School' poets promoted by *Poetry*; yet even as his work graced their pages, Stevens could share his doubts about the worthiness of her rivals in letters to Monroe (see *L* 222, 223). In some cases, he sent work as a favour to a friend who was editor; as with Williams of *Contact*, Carl Zigrosser (met through Walter Pach) of the *Modern School*, or Pitts Sanborn on *Measure*. If one fact seems to emerge from a consideration of Stevens's establishment as a poet between 1914 and 1923, it is that he avoided becoming dependent on any particular outlet for his verse, and took care not to have any greater need of people than they might have of him. Whatever benefits he derived from his association with the Arensberg circle, he did not require the oxygen of being in the avant-garde to the extent that Williams, who felt his isolation in New Jersey, did.

Stevens's appearances in little magazines formed the occasion for the first critical remarks on his work: in February 1916 some lines from 'Phases' were cited in a strenuously hostile review of the War Number of *Poetry* ('nauseating'); in October 1917 both the *New York Times* and *Tribune* gave unfavourable notice to the Wisconsin Players' production of 'Carlos Among the Candles'.[9] More significant in the forming of his reputation in these years, however, was the inclusion of certain poems in anthologies, which by their nature were more durable and reached a potentially wider readership. W.S. Braithwaite included 'Peter Quince...' in his

Anthology of Magazine Verse for 1915, issued at the end of November that year (presumably with the Christmas market in mind); in March the following year Alfred Knopf published Kreymborg's first *Others: an Anthology of the New Verse* (1916), reprinting nine poems in a group that started with 'Peter Quince...' and finished with 'Domination of Black'. In 1917 Stevens's poetry appeared in two anthologies: *The New Poetry*, edited by Monroe and her associate editor Alice C. Henderson, contained 'Peter Quince...', one of the 'Phases' group, and the shortened 'Sunday Morning', and came out in an edition of 4000 in February from Macmillan; and on 31 October Knopf issued the second *Others* anthology, with ten Stevens poems, chief amongst them 'Cy Est Pourtraicte...' and 'Thirteen Ways...', and publishing three (including 'The Plot Against the Giant') for the first time anywhere. Stevens next appeared in *Others for 1919* (1920), represented by 'Le Monocle...' and most of 'Pecksniffiana'; and thereafter in Braithwaite's Anthologies for 1921, 1922, and 1923 (he tended to select poems not published in *Others* or *Poetry*). The year of *Harmonium*, 1923, also saw in May an enlargement of the 1917 Monroe/Henderson anthology from 404 to 640 pages, which added 16 Stevens poems to the original three, most notable amongst them 'The Snow Man' and 'Le Monocle...'.

What can be seen from this is that virtually all of the poems by which *Harmonium* would be characterised had been published at least twice before the book's appearance – 'The Comedian as the Letter C' was its most striking unpublished item. Because of the anthologists' choices, a canonical process was under way, in which 'Peter Quince...' (four appearances) stands out, with 'Sunday Morning' and 'Le Monocle...' (two each) making a claim. There are also indications of Stevens's growing stature: it is difficult to believe that 'Cortège for Rosenbloom', chosen by Braithwaite for his 1921 anthology, really justified its place on literary merit; but presumably it was desirable that Stevens should be represented, and therefore the editor had to take what was available.[10] After its first appearance in Braithwaite (1915), 'Peter Quince...' was singled out for mention in a review by George Soule in the *New Republic* (25 March 1916), and in 1919 Conrad Aiken, reviewing the second *Others* anthology, looked back to 'Peter Quince...' – alongside Eliot's 'Portrait of a Lady' – as typifying the kind of excellence present in the first collection but missing from this one, although he allowed that Eliot's 'Preludes' and 'Rhapsody on a Windy

Night', along with 'Thirteen Ways...', caused 'admiration and delight' as no other contributions did. But if an anthologist like Braithwaite felt that Stevens was a necessary poet, there was one more influential who felt the opposite. That same year Aiken (an early advocate of Eliot as well as admirer of Stevens) had an exchange of views in the pages of the *New Republic* with Louis Untermeyer (who preferred Frost) in which some of the battlelines of emergent American Modernism were demarcated.

Aiken had reviewed Untermeyer's *The New Era in American Poetry* (1919), a critical companion to his anthology *Modern American Poetry* (1919) which, through successive editions, would establish itself as one of the most influential classroom texts of American poetry. Untermeyer excluded Eliot, Stevens, and Williams, and marginalised Pound (Lentricchia sees this anthology as a bridge between the earlier genteel anthologies like Stedman's or Jessie Belle Rittenhouse's, and the modern era); instead he championed the cause of an 'unflinchingly masculine' American poetics, a native strain derived from nineteenth-century precursors such as Whitman, and free from the disabling taint of Euro-literary association. Modern poets whom Untermeyer took to exemplify the desired qualities were Frost, Robinson, Vachel Lindsay, Edgar Lee Masters, and Sandburg (the last three were principal figures in the 'Chicago School'). Aiken's critique accused Untermeyer of a chauvinism that dismissed as decadent any poetry that implied an undemocratic concern with literary experimentalism, presuming it irrelevant in an American context. In his retort, Untermeyer took Aiken to be a defender of the aesthetic absolutism of 'art for art's sake', which he saw as leading 'inevitably to the Yellow Book, to the mere verbal legerdemain of the Pound-Stevens-Arensberg-Others'.[11] Here, as Lentricchia argues, is the visible opening of the chasm between the high Modernism of formalist innovation, esoterically responsive to Eliot's diagnosis that contemporary poetry had to be 'difficult', and the low Modernism of Frost and the Chicago School, apparently rough hewn and all-American. Untermeyer's exclusion of Stevens until the 1930 edition of his anthology must have had a small adverse effect on the poet's forming reputation; but at least his critique of Stevens's devotion to an 'absolute' poetry had some basis in reality; whereas Williams, also omitted, was the proponent of an ideology that was both experimental and American-demotic. It would turn out, however, that Stevens's reputation would outlast a whole range of poets who came to earlier prominence than he did: Aiken, Bynner, Arthur Davison Ficke, John Gould Fletcher, Lindsay, Amy Lowell, Masters, and Sandburg were all better known than he was, yet all have either vanished, or have dwindled in significance to a particular epoch or region.

Stevens had advanced from being the writer of whom in 1914 *Poetry* could report that he was 'as yet unknown to the editor', to become the poet whose allegiance editors competed for, and whose work, regularly anthologised, could provoke strong opinions in its readers. His professional career also showed the gradual establishment of his reputation: when, in February 1916, the New England Equitable Insurance Company suddenly failed, his standing was such that a phone-call to his former colleague James Kearney secured him a position, the following month, on the home office staff of the Hartford Accident and Indemnity Company. This necessitated a move out of New York, and in May Stevens and his wife settled permanently in Connecticut, living from 1917 until 1932 at addresses on Farmington Avenue, Hartford. Although in later years his job would evidently leave him time and opportunity for poetry, in these years of the company's pioneering expansion he was working under greater pressure. Whilst he might manage to devote evenings in hotel rooms to polishing his verses – as he did with some of 'Pecksniffiana' – one reason he published nothing during 1920 was because of the demands made by several insurance cases, described to Elsie that May as 'by far' the most difficult and dangerous he had handled for the Hartford. He was intent, he told her, on managing matters as nearly perfectly as possible; and his letter (from Erie, PA) gave a rare glimpse of the kinds of business that could crowd out poetry as he '[floated] on a Gulf Stream of talk with lawyers, contractors, dealers in cement, lumber and so on. I have not had a poem in my head for a month, poor Yorick. This long absence upsets life at home abominably but it cannot be helped' (*L* 219).

Evidently, both as poet and surety claims attorney Stevens was a perfectionist ('the grindingest guy they had there in executive row', Brazeau, p. 20), and each activity presumably called forth obsessive aspects of his temperament, as well as providing the satisfactions involved in conjuring forms of order out of disorderly situations. The move to Hartford seems to have eased some of the pressures in his marriage, although the difficulties there were chronic, and would remain so (Joan Richardson speculates that the long absence of 1920 marked a crisis in the relationship).[12] Elsie preferred it to New York, and Stevens felt easier about her being on her own there during the extended absences his job demanded, and which characterised the first five years of his work for the Hartford (when the company moved into its newly constructed Head Office in November 1921, he hired an assistant). The distance from New York offered an excuse for Elsie's not accompanying his visits to the Arensberg salon, in their earliest Hartford years; and it seems that for a while they were able to simulate the social behaviour of other married couples, entertaining literary acquaintances such as Harriet Monroe, Amy Lowell, Genevieve Taggard and even Carl Sandburg with his guitar at their home, on separate occasions. But if at first Stevens kept up his social and cultural associations with New York, there came a stage when these diminished: first came the dissolution of his friendship with Arensberg, and then in early 1922 he donated his carefully collected art catalogues to Hartford's Wadsworth Atheneum, comprising a 'virtually complete record' of the significant exhibitions in New York for the previous decade.[13] If Stevens was renouncing New York by this farewell to arts, it was not because of any immersion in what Hartford had to offer him: he held himself aloof from the various groups of writers in the city (which was not without a literary tradition), perhaps because he retained from his New York years a metropolitan disdain for provincial doings. He later rebuffed the approach of a local press ('I'm not that poor a poet that I have to look around for local publishers'), and the citizens of Hartford returned the compliment by preferring to buy the poems of Edna St Vincent Millay at the city's bookshops (Brazeau, pp. 116, 117, 118n., 120).

The peremptoriness which could often characterise Stevens's behaviour was born of shyness, coupled with authority. It was an attitude easily mistaken for conceit, yet seems really to have been more complex, having much to do with the desire to be *safe* – seen for example in his perfectionism. The speaker of Frost's 'Two Tramps in Mud Time' (1934) declares it to be his 'object in living' to unite his avocation (what he loves to do) with his vocation (what he needs to do).[14] A good deal of the logic of Stevens's living, however, lay precisely in separating avocation (poetry) from vocation (law), as a survival strategy that not only ensured the bills would be paid (which had essentially been Williams's reason for going into medicine) but which enabled one life to offset the other. His increasingly ample salary enabled him to be entirely independent of the commercial fate of his writing; and this was itself a form of indifference to its potential readership. Stevens knew that he could not be a self-publicist along the lines of Lindsay, Lowell, or Sandburg, with their money-making poetry readings and lecture tours; but if he envied more obviously successful poets (or, more probably, suppressed the envy), then at least he had the consolation that none was as successful in an entirely unconnected sphere as he was; and although it seems that his colleagues on the Hartford's 'executive row' included some intellectually distinguished men, none was as notable a writer as he was. Although he tended to express the relation as a matter of his poetry representing his nocturnal or weekend escape from the tedious everyday self, the everyday could also offer its own consolations: as when he retreated into the pursuit of his career and the opportunities of fatherhood, after the sales failure of *Harmonium*.

If he was to alter his priorities after *Harmonium*, there seems also to have been at least one change of direction, and perhaps two, in the period preceding its publication. His different job and place of residence in 1916 coincided for him with other aspects of the new: that April he visited Florida for the first time, and he experimented with writing drama. On his return the next month he learnt that his one-act verse play 'Three Travelers Watch a Sunrise' had taken the $100 first prize offered by the Players' Producing Company and awarded on the adjudication of the staff of *Poetry*. Writing to Monroe on 22 May, he explained his intention as having been to create, with a minimum of narration, a poetic atmosphere; she published his playlet that July, but it would be another four years before a performance was attempted – by which time Stevens had lost all interest in drama (*L* 216). For a while, however, he gave it considerable attention, encouraged as he had been by receiving the prize; in a high-spirited letter to his wife from Minnesota in June 1916, he identified himself as an 'eminent vers libriste' and 'playwright and barrister' (*L* 196). Joking aside, to identify himself with *vers libre* in 1916 was to claim his place amongst the avant-garde (it would be the following year before Pound and Eliot in London would mount their attack upon the 'floppiness' of bad free

verse); and it is clear from his comments and the plays he went on
to write ('Carlos among the Candles', performed once in October
1917 and published in *Poetry* that December and 'Bowl, Cat, and
Broomstick' (1917), not published in his lifetime) that – unlike the
derivative 'Olivia', much earlier – his new dramatic work was
intended to be innovative, pushing the resources of the theatrical
to a sort of minimalist limit. These plays suggest a degree of
ambition: the leaps with which Carlos enters and exits, for
example, and his balletic movements generally, doubtless took
inspiration from Nijinsky's famous performances for the Russian
Ballet (which had played New York in 1916); but the play's failure,
despite the efforts taken by author and set-designer, certainly
showed Stevens the gap between conception and embodiment; he
would much later confess that he would probably have been more
interested in the theatre if his early experiments had not given him
the horrors (*L* 290).

The set-back was significant, illustrating for him as it did the
problems he would have establishing an audience, and probably
undercutting some of the confidence imparted by his prize. For her
part, Monroe continued to encourage him; and the announcement
of the Levinson Prize in the November 1920 *Poetry* (which reprinted
four of 'Pecksniffiana') must have been helpful in keeping him in
the public view despite his having published nothing new that year
(although the *Others* anthology for 1919, in which he featured, had
come out in April). In a letter written on 4 March, Stevens told her
of having recently received a copy of Eliot's *Ara Vus Prec* (1920), as
a subscriber to John Rodker's Ovid Press in England, commenting
that he did not think the volume contained anything he had not
already seen (*L* 217). Stevens may or may not have cut the pages of
this book, issued the previous month (*somebody* did; his later
practice with Eliot material was to leave books in the condition as
acquired); whichever way, he may have been suppressing
consciousness of the fact that its first item was the previously
unpublished 'Gerontion', a significant poem whose forceful
rhetoric engaged with historical perspectives in a manner that his
own poems about the Great War had failed to do. Even the
relatively unproductive and younger Eliot, then, had brought out a
book (published by Knopf in the USA, late February); coinciding
with his own year of silence, and not easily dismissed as a
miscellany, Stevens might have found it expedient to avert his gaze
from *Ara Vus Prec* (as from Pound's *Hugh Selwyn Mauberley*, which

he also received that year). But unlike Eliot with his recurrent periods of writer's block, Stevens stopped and started writing in response to more conscious processes: because he was too busy, or because there was a prize to compete for. The announcement in *Poetry* (December 1921) of the new Blindman Prize offered by the Poetry Society of South Carolina, for which poems had to be submitted by the new year, provoked him to a frenzy of composition (as he told Monroe, *L* 224), whose issue was the first long poem he had attempted, 'From the Journal of Crispin' which, further enlarged and revised, would appear as 'The Comedian as the Letter C' in *Harmonium*. I believe this represented a further shift in Stevens's sense of poetic self: for whereas the plays and poems of 1915 to 1919 seem consciously aligned with the avant-garde, the Crispin poems – with their pronounced narrative element – seem as consciously to depart from it.

By a happy and hilarious accident we are able to compare the two versions. From 1924 Stevens, Elsie and their daughter lived in an apartment at 735 Farmington Avenue, Hartford, alongside their landlord Mr Gay, and his family. These knew that their tenant was a poet, and Mrs Gay was in the habit of going through the Stevens dustbin in search of his *rejectamenta* (we suddenly find ourselves in the world of Nabokov's *Pale Fire*). According to her son (who donated the manuscripts to the Beinecke Library in 1974), one day she found a 19-page typescript and some carbon sheets, which constituted the poem Stevens had submitted for the Blindman Prize some years previously.[15] 'From the Journal of Crispin' had received first honourable mention, but the prize – of which Amy Lowell had been sole judge – was awarded by her to Grace Hazard Conkling, who was on the faculty of Smith College, had already published two collections of her own verse, and was about to publish the second collection of poems by her daughter Hilda (born in 1910, Hilda had been 'lisping in numbers' since the age of four, with her mother recording the results). Stevens was gentlemanly in defeat (see *L* 226); but given the intensity of his effort, it is likely to have been a real enough disappointment. He seems to have accepted Lowell's verdict to the degree of deciding his poem needed revision (he had possibly been obliged by the competition deadline to send it before he really felt it to be finished); and late in September he told Monroe, who had expressed an interest in acquiring it for *Poetry*, that he had rewritten and retitled the 'Crispin' poem, now identified as 'The Comedian as the Letter C' (*L* 229–30).

Stevens's revision of his Blindman entry coincided with his yielding to persuasion that he publish his first collection of verse (as well he might, in the year that saw the 12-year-old Hilda Conkling exude her second volume). This therefore represents a decisive stage in his self-enunciation as a poet, worth examining in some detail. The two versions resemble each other to the extent that the four sections constituting the earlier (I – 'The World without Imagination'; II – 'Concerning the Thunderstorms of Yucatan'; III – 'Approaching Carolina'; IV – 'The Idea of a Colony') were retained in the later; in revision Stevens added two further sections (V – 'A Nice Shady Home'; VI – 'And Daughters with Curls') and changed the overall title. The superficial resemblance masks considerable differences, however; 128 lines were excised from the four original sections, and many others were altered in detail. As the first title implied, the idea of a journal, of documentary self-disclosure, played an important part in the conception; and 'From the Journal of Crispin' ended in anticipation of 'the book/ That will contain him', whose function must be to 'discourse of himself alone' (*OP*2 59). The last lines from the 'Journal' that survive in 'The Comedian... ' underline the stipulated preference for 'text' (the thing itself) over 'gloss' (ideas about it):

> Trinket pasticcio, flaunting skyey sheets,
> With Crispin as the tiptoe cozener?
> No, no: veracious page on page, exact.
> (*CP* 40)

The title as revised, however, stressed the comic element, and linked it to the different sonic consequences of recurrent uses of the letter 'c' (see *L* 351–2). To recognise this, however, is at once to see how, even in these lines with which part IV of the published version closes, tenor (the need to achieve honesty by avoidance of pastiche or over-elevated language) and vehicle (language characterised by consonantal riot and quasi-euphuism) seem to have parted company: excess runs counter to exactitude. These effects were present in the earlier version, but were amplified in its successor which – whilst following the geographical and philosophical stages of Crispin's voyage of discovery from the Old World to the New, and toward an aesthetic *credo* appropriate to what he learns and wishes to write – added deflationary force to the fable by transposing the narrative from present into predominant past tense, and by becalming the questing proto-American hero amid feminine domesticity at the end. 'So may the relation of each man be clipped' runs the isolated final line, perhaps presenting Crispin as a sort of shorn wether, but also enacting an ironic contrast between this laconic utterance and the narrative profligacy of the preceding 572 lines.

From the energy which he put into its initial composition and subsequent revision, it is clear this was an important project for Stevens, even if after revising it he anticipated a time when it might not seem to have been worth the effort. It was the first of several long poems he would compose during his career, but is unlike the others in its narrative continuity and the sustained foregrounding of its rhetoric; in his letter to Monroe of 23 September 1922 he wrote of the pleasures that 'prolonged attention to a single subject' afforded (*L* 230), and the next month, writing of the dissatisfaction he had felt with putting *Harmonium* together, he wished he could find time to put everything else aside and 'amuse [himself] on a large scale for a while. One never gets anywhere in writing or thinking or observing unless one can do large stretches at a time. Often I have to let go, in the most insignificant poem, which scarcely serves to remind me of it, the most skyey of skyey sheets' (*L* 231). Here, in contrast to the lines from 'Comedian...' quoted above, the phrase 'skyey sheets' denoted something desirable rather than something overinflated; and the wish to find his power by extending and expanding his range is of a piece with comments he made to Williams about the sterility of incessant new beginnings. The stories told by underlings at the Hartford of Stevens's anger when his concentration was disturbed, remind us of related aspects of the man who liked 'large stretches' – whether in walking, working, or composing.

This is very different from the momentariness which, according to Williams, characterised his own opportunities for writing poetry during surgery hours, when he would raise or lower his typewriter on its hinged flap, between consultations. Famously described by Kenneth Burke (in 1922) as engaged in finding 'the shortest route between object and subject', Williams's epistemological economy could in many ways be contrasted to Stevens's, who often sought (and found) the longest routes, and knew of at least 13 ways of looking at his blackbird. Yet for all that, it may be that a Williams poem played its part in provoking 'The Comedian...': 'The Wanderer', first published in the *Egoist* in 1914, but familiar to

Stevens (who made marginal notes in his copy) from *Al Que Quiere!*, was a poetic testament of a kind that Stevens's long poem would be – and behind both distantly lay the idea of a long poem as enkindled in them by Keats's *Endymion*. 'The Wanderer' extended over several pages, and as his 'first "long" poem' was later seen by Williams as the germination of what would become *Paterson*; it is a first-person narrative, telling of the narrator's encounter with an old woman/muse (inspired by the poet's grandmother), who will instruct him in the answer to the question he had been pondering, 'How shall I be a mirror to this modernity?' This she achieves by baptising him in the polluted waters of the 'filthy Passaic' (the river which flows through the heavily industrialised parts of New Jersey), in an obvious allegory of the poet's necessary immersion in the uncompromising actualities of America. Williams's poem was (defensively) subtitled 'A Rococo Study', and this seems a much more appropriate way of describing the pseudo-scholarly over-ornamentation and self-generative stylistic excess of 'The Comedian as the Letter C' – which also tells the story of a wanderer whose adventures allegorise the growth of a poet's mind. Louis Martz has argued that 'From the Journal of Crispin' stressed 'Stevens's alliance with the other writers who had … , as Williams reports, sought to create American art and literature through cultivation of the "local"'.[16] 'The Comedian… ', however, by closing the narrative down to what *has* happened and by presenting his 'grand pronunciamento' as an actual retreat from grand designing, presents Crispin as a kind of anti-hero – far from the youth who, at the end of 'The Wanderer', is potentially afoot with his vision.

In Stevens's poem the real hero is the language itself, obtrusive and assertive, full of pseudo-Shakespearian locutions in its resonant extravaganza. Although Crispin embraces the everyday as 'The Wanderer' does, his tale does not embrace the demotic with it, but is a wild celebration of the linguisticity of being, in which the story of a man's accommodation to the ordinary universe is told in extraordinary words. If, then, there is a relationship between 'The Comedian… ' and 'The Wanderer' (itself revised by Williams for his book), it is similar to that between Stevens's 'Nuances of a Theme by Williams' and Williams's 'El Hombre' which provoked it, where Stevens's variations on Williams's theme amount to an almost explicit critique of the view that perception rooted in language can ever escape from the figurative, or from anthropocentric constructivism. That being so, it is a delusion to suppose that forms of language cleansed of more obvious rhetorical adornment are inherently closer to 'the' truth – which was an article of faith for Williams, as for the Imagists (although as with all faiths there could be gaps between profession and practice). In his first long poem, Stevens confronted the same question posed by Williams in his, of how to reflect modernity; but his answer was radically different, and recognised that one could be American without rejecting Europe, contemporary without rejecting the past, and human only by exploiting to the full one's linguistic inheritance – which involved acknowledging that your relation to words could never be Adamically unpreconditioned by their previous usage. Thus, of all Stevens's poems 'The Comedian… ' is probably the least related to any colloquial tradition, the least productive of any imaginable 'voice', his most extravagant embodiment of 'style'.

This poem was indeed the accomplishment of an extremist in the exercise, an act almost of aesthetic terrorism in a society whose post-puritan recrudescence had recently (1919) introduced Prohibition. It was also, as I have tried to suggest, a repudiation of several of the precious tenets of literary Modernism, in its unorthodoxy with regard to location and locution – no wonder Stevens and Hemingway later came to blows! Although the heightened consciousness of the materiality of his linguistic medium might link Stevens's poem to radical experimenters such as Stein, the willed anachronism of its lexicon, and the old-fashionedness of its blank verse and basic narrative shape, suggest a more traditionalist poetics. It is almost as if the poem had been expressly designed to appeal to nobody at all: certainly, it was a very radical performance indeed, full of good humoured aggression toward potential readers. 'Good humoured', because unlike *The Waste Land* (1922) – which Eliot with Pound's assistance brought to its final shape the month after Stevens wrote 'From the Journal of Crispin' – recourse to the past (even in the earlier version) is celebratory rather than elegiac: the blank verse and archaic diction denote resources still accessible, unlike the parodic heroic couplets Pound savaged in Eliot's drafts; and the biographical narrative bespeaks a confidence in the possibilities of wholeness, unlike the procedural fragmentariness characterising what Pound announced as the 'longest poem in the English langwidge'.

The Waste Land, of course, eclipsed whatever notice Stevens might have anticipated for his first volume, issued the following year; his magnificent measures contravened the sumptuary regulations coming into force, whereby poetry, if not direct and masculine, should be the vehicle of spiritual bleakness and express the despair of a generation. In 'The Comedian...', the high style expounding a low life at inordinate length contravened the privileged elevation of the lyric moment. His 'verbal legerdemain' was heretically negligent of the need for an exact gearing between word and thing, and therefore was dismissed as aesthetic absolutism by those who did not notice that he had in his own way learned a style from a despair (in Empson's phrase), and that his excesses were linked to a vision of poverty rather than of plenty. The jocular linguistic procreations of 'The Comedian...' described – Stevens claimed – the sort of life that millions lived (*L* 294), whose point lay in its very ordinariness (when in the 1950s Renato Poggioli proposed translating the poem, Stevens drew his attention to the need to be aware of the contrast between the 'plainness' of Crispin and the 'plush' of his setting; *L* 778); in a darker way, shorter poems such as 'Of the Manner of Addressing Clouds' (1921) and 'The Emperor of Ice-Cream' (1922) exemplified a similar technique of disproportion, embodying in their magniloquence assertions of transitoriness and inevitable death. Even evil, as he later saw, has its aesthetics; and the inverse relation between words and facts was set forth in 'Esthétique du Mal' (1944):

> Natives of poverty, children of malheur,
> The gaiety of language is our seigneur.
> (*CP* 322)

Carl Van Vechten had written in July 1922 urging Stevens to issue a collection; he replied that he was 'frightfully uncertain about a book' (*L* 228), but the two met in New York and Van Vechten obviously prevailed, for on 24 August Stevens told Monroe, in confidence, that he had reached outline agreement with Alfred Knopf and that the manuscript was due for delivery by 1 November. For Stevens, putting his book together turned out not only to be a 'damned serious affair' but also a slightly dispiriting one; acknowledging *Poetry*'s 'honourable mention' of four of his poems from 'Sur Ma Guzzla Gracile' in its announcement of awards (November 1922), he confided to Monroe that he had been depressed by the process: 'all my earlier things seem like horrid cocoons from which later abortive insects have sprung' (*L* 231). In part, it seems as though to issue a collection was an infringement of the spirit of independence animating his writing: in his previous letter to Monroe (23 September), explaining his disinclination to write much poetry, he had told her he knew that people judged a poet in terms of quantity, however, 'having elected to regard poetry as a form of retreat, the judgment of people is neither here nor there. The desire to write a long poem or two is not obsequiousness to the judgment of people' (*L* 230). Publishing a book might well expose him to the judgement of people, and for a man who was nervous even when he met his friends (see letters to Monroe, *L* 223, 228), exposing his poems to the kindness of strangers may well have constituted an ordeal. But by the third week of November he had made his selection and prepared the typescript, which he delivered in person to Van Vechten in New York; by the end of the year Knopf had it and the contract had been signed; Stevens told Monroe that he had been as fastidious as possible in his choice, but had not felt himself over-supplied with first-rate material (*L* 232).

In some ways what happened to his first volume bore out the misgivings he expressed as he was assembling its contents. Whilst it could be argued that his dissatisfaction with *Harmonium* was an exercise in pre-emptive damage limitation, I think it more likely that he was being sincere rather than disingenuous in his criticisms. The fact that it took him so long to issue his first collection of verse, after he had started publishing in little magazines, possibly indicated a degree of self-uncertainty; but I think the real cause for the delay was in the seriousness of his poetic intentions and the scope of his poetic ambitions – neither of which was adequately reflected (nor, perhaps, ever could have been) in the book he was eventually persuaded to publish. But to suggest this is not to underestimate the doubts which Stevens did have about his poetry, nor the defensive strategies he put in place in its regard; both ambition and defensiveness were visible in the title he considered using for this collection, 'The Grand Poem: Preliminary Minutiae' (*L* 237) – which grounded the major intention in self-deprecatingly minor evidence. Two months later he sent Knopf a telegram restoring 'Harmonium', but even that title is potentially two-toned: in its upper register indicating a world brought 'round' (as the Blue Guitarist tries to do), a tribute to what Stevens later called the complicate and amassing harmony (*CP* 403); but in its lower, denoting a slightly old-fashioned miniature organ, suggestive of faded Victorian parlours or churches too humble to afford the full-scale instrument.[17] Possibly there was also an additional resonance, in the distinction noted by Webster's Dictionary between a harmonium (which blows air out) and an 'American organ' (which sucks air in): perhaps intended to demarcate his difference from the masculine inflations of Untermeyer's favoured poets: the last poem in the volume (all editions) was entitled 'To the Roaring Wind'.

Stevens was always alert to the beginnings and endings of his volumes: it is far from accidental that the last words in the *Collected Poems* (1954) should be 'new knowledge of reality' (*CP* 534) – denoting the epistemological enlargement he wanted his poetry to bring about. He was alert, also, to the whole construction of books of poetry; in 1953 he confessed himself shocked by the poor proofreading and lack of care exhibited in his young friend Richard Eberhart's newly published *Undercliff*, which he condemned as a 'miscellany without an axis' (*L* 804). His own care over starts and finishes and his abhorrence of the miscellaneous were as evident at the outset of his publishing career, as at its close: commenting on 'Pecksniffiana' to Harriet Monroe in October 1919, he declared himself partly satisfied, but noted that it lay 'under the curse of miscellany' (*L* 215); in May 1922, writing to the editor of the *Dial* about the six poems which would be published as 'Revue' in its July number, he was relaxed about the order, but stipulated 'Bantams in Pine-Woods' as first and 'The Emperor of Ice-Cream' as the last of the group, in his desire to make 'a good beginning and a good end' (*L* 227). The clearest indication of the seriousness with which he viewed such matters came even earlier, when responding to Williams having sent him a copy of *Al Que Quiere!* (1917), in a letter which he confessed to be 'quarrelsomely full of my own ideas of discipline'.[18] Stevens was struck by the 'casual character' of the poems gathered, commenting that personally he had 'a distaste for miscellany. It is one of the reasons I do not bother about a book myself.' He went on:

> My idea is that in order to carry a thing to the extreme necess[ary] to convey it one has to stick to it; ... Given a fixed point of view, realistic,

imagistic or what you will, everything adjusts itself to that point of view; the process of adjustment is a world in flux, as it should be for a poet. But to fidget with points of view leads always to new beginnings and incessant new beginnings lead to sterility.

Whether or not Stevens's comments were just criticism of Williams's volume (and this would not be the only occasion when he needled him), quarrelsomely or otherwise they illustrated his own concerns, seen in his admonitory observation, 'Well a book of poems is a damned serious affair'. Yet if by implication he was reproaching his friend for having fallen short in that respect, his own verse hardly suggested any sustained reaching after a post-Arnoldian high seriousness, characterised as it was by quirkily dissociated titles that seemed deliberately to court the charge of flippancy. What, after all, did he mean by linking a set of poems *Poetry* would deem worthy of its Levinson Prize, with the unctuously malignant hypocrite in Dickens's *Martin Chuzzlewit*? And in the year that would see publication of 'Thirteen Ways of Looking at a Blackbird', was its author best placed to reproach a fellow-writer for fidgeting with points of view? Pound would later criticise Stevens's 'damnd laisser aller attitude RE/ *his* writing', with the implication that (as by associating his poetry with Pecksniff) Stevens simultaneously dared his readers to like it and made it obvious why they wouldn't. Yet appearances could be deceptive, and even the titles of poems – which would exasperate some hostile critics – were not dismissive or defensive afterthoughts: we know, for example, that it took eight attempts to arrive at 'To the One of Fictive Music'.[19]

Harmonium, dedicated to his wife, was just under 150 pages long. None of the 'war' poems printed in *Poetry* in either 1914 or 1918 passed the selection process, but 'Nomad Exquisite', mailed to Monroe on a postcard from Florida in January 1919 and previously unpublished, was included; 'The Man whose Pharynx was Bad' (1921) was inexplicably excluded (and only entered the 1931 edition after suffering mutilation).[20] 'Earthy Anecdote' gave its decisive start to the volume, but was, curiously, followed by 'Invective against Swans' (1921), whose pronounced oratory and uncharacteristic use of rhyme offered an awkward contrast (as was perhaps intended: Stevens wishing to alert his reader straight away to the different shapes a firecat could assume); the American tonality was re-established by 'In the Carolinas'. Stevens told Monroe that he appreciated the South because he felt that there he came into contact with the 'early and undefiled American thing' (*L* 229); but celebration of the South, or of what America in general offers to the beholder, is not a simply sustained element in the volume. Assuming that for the most part poems were written close to their dates of first publication, it is very clear that, in arranging *Harmonium*, Stevens either wished to obscure the chronology of composition, or followed organising principles that prevented its demonstration. *Harmonium* contained all six poems published in 1915, with the earliest placed, 'Cy Est Pourtraicte...', preceded by 14 poems written later; the last placed, 'Tea' (which had been published alongside it in *Rogue*) was the penultimate poem – and clearly felt by Stevens to be part of the ending, since he stipulated for the 1931 edition that it retain this position. He deliberately separated poems from the groupings in which they had initially appeared, and in the rare instance where four of the 14 'Pecksniffiana' poems were permitted to remain together ('The Place of the Solitaires' through 'Banal Sojourn'), their original order in *Poetry* was altered. 'The Comedian as the Letter C', given its own internal title page, came after only 30 pages of text, in a prominent position that stamped its character on the whole book.

Whatever thematic considerations may or may not have operated, Stevens was presumably concerned to disrupt any familiarity a reader might bring to poems, some of which had been in the public domain for the best part of a decade. He was finalising the order of his volume as *The Waste Land* was published in the *Criterion* (October) and the *Dial* (November), and it is possible he relished the opportunity of offering 'The Comedian...' as his buoyantly sustained antidote to what may have struck him as that poem's neurasthenic pessimism; in any case, he would have wished 'The Comedian...' to have made due impact on a reader, as the major previously unpublished piece in the collection. Nevertheless, the note of dissatisfaction with *Harmonium* sounded to Monroe may not have been purely conventional self-deprecation: perhaps there *was* something missing he had wished to be there, perhaps the grand poem *was* falsified by these minutiae? Much later, in 1940, he would write two poems ('Man and Bottle' and 'Of Modern Poetry') which made it clear that poetry had to be adequate to war, and his important association with *Poetry* had been formed on that basis; yet in 1922 none of his published war poems satisfied him enough to merit inclusion, and nothing he had written (he must have been aware) accrued the authority accorded to the historical representativeness of poems like 'Gerontion' or *The Waste Land* – which already in the *Dial* of

December 1922 was hailed by Edmund Wilson for voicing the 'starvation of a whole generation'. There is an irony in the fact that Stevens, with his horror of miscellanies and his desire to craft a serious whole, should find his long-delayed first volume overshadowed by a poem offering a heap of broken images and assembled by a committee of two; but so it was. For his own part, as its rejected title suggested, Stevens may have felt that his book did not adequately order the 'dreadful sundry' of the world (*CP* 47): the slightly mocking injunction in its last poem, that this big noise blowing in should form itself into the clarity of speech, may intimate that the whole of *Harmonium* was as yet unrealised. In a strangely incoherent letter written to Elsie after their engagement, Stevens had confessed that there was 'a great sleepy jumble in me seeking to be arranged, to be set in order, and then to be spoken' (6 January 1909, *L* 115); perhaps the positioning of 'To the Roaring Wind' at the end of his first collection made a similar confession.

Having got the typescript of *Harmonium* off his hands and (via Van Vechten) into Knopf's, Stevens started 1923 with a long trip south that confirmed his good spirits; in early February he wrote to Elsie from Long Key, Florida, that it had been one of the most agreeable trips he had undertaken. He appreciated Florida's sunshine, and he appreciated the moonshine available in the circles in which his business contact and friend Judge Arthur Powell moved (Stevens had already noted in May the previous year how useful it was to have acquaintances in places where liquor could be obtained, *L* 227). Powell, from Atlanta, was a lawyer retained by the Hartford, and seems to have been a 'good old boy' very much in the Southern mould, courtly in bearing and trenchant in expression (the in-your-face title 'Like Decorations in a Nigger Cemetery' derives from one of his phrases); he knew the benefits of play after hard work, and took Stevens on offshore fishing trips after their business was concluded. The first weekend in February Stevens spent by himself in Havana, having taken the ship across from Key West; in Cuba he saw buildings older than he had ever seen, and was surprised how foreign 'beyond belief' (as he put it on a postcard home) things could be in Uncle Sam's backyard: he approached a 'nigger policeman' in Havana for directions, but the 'poor thing' could not even understand English (*L* 234). A week later he was in Greensboro, North Carolina, where he observed more disconcerting types in the public places:

> At the railroad stations and on the trains one surely sees an uncommon number of people who quite obviously just eke out an existence, people brought up in dirt and ignorance with not a thing in the world to look forward to. Possibly that is a good deal truer of the rural sections of South Carolina than of North Carolina for North Carolina is making very rapid progress in every direction. She is one of the great states or will be.
>
> (*L* 237)

This was a new sort of poverty for Stevens, afflicting as it did not Jewish or Italian immigrants or the black population, whose ethnic otherness tempered perceptual consequences and rendered any political deductions less urgent. With the exception of figures like Bonnie and Josie – who may be black anyway – in 'Life is Motion' (1919), the poems he had recently given to Knopf paid very little heed to Americans such as these he noticed on his travels. But although in his letter he quickly moved from their unAmerican hopelessness to the more edifying progress of the state of North Carolina, his next book of poetry would be more attentive to such fellow-citizens.

These comments in his letter followed from his observations of the greater power and presence of the church in the southern states; he attributed this to the bleak life led by its poorer denizens, who needed something to console them. For Stevens, speculations such as these led inevitably to his consideration of the role of the poet, for – as he later explained to Hi Simons – it was a habit of mind with him to think of some substitute for religion (*L* 348). It was possibly his sense of there being a vital spiritual function for the poet to fulfil, that he wished he had more successfully communicated in *Harmonium* (thus the wind invoked at its end would be secularly pentecostal, but had not yet made its visitation); it was a sense more visible in the longer poem he went on to write, initially entitled 'Discourse in a Cantina in Havana' (1923), subsequently as 'Academic Discourse at Havana' (*CP* 142). The genesis of this poem is obscure; in September 1922 he had told Monroe that, having revised 'The Comedian...', he was contemplating writing another long poem on his return from a trip to the South that October; but the title makes it likelier that it was composed after his weekend in Cuba, the following February –

notwithstanding that Stevens's poetry often refers to places he had never visited. Fifteen years later, he would recall for Simons that the poem had been intended as his contribution to an abortive project to issue new work by several poets; then, in a revised and shortened form, he offered it to Kreymborg's *Broom* (*L* 335), where it appeared in November under the earlier title (and in 1929, having forgotten that, he let Richard Blackmur publish it in *Hound and Horn*). He had been struck by the old churches in Havana, many of which he had visited; and the poem's central image of life as a ruined casino is presumably an ironic allusion to Pascal's argument (in the *Pensées*) that belief in God was a sure winning bet.[21] In *Harmonium*, poems like 'Sunday Morning' (politely) and 'The Worms at Heaven's Gate', 'Of Heaven Considered as a Tomb' and 'A High-Toned Old Christian Woman' (more aggressively) had made the point about a *deus absconditus*; but what was offered instead was a sort of pagan bawdiness. 'Discourse in a Cantina… ' was the poem in which Stevens first made explicit – even programmatic – his concern that the poet should fill the gap left by the disappearance of Christianity as a serious force in the modern world (up until the end of his life, he took it as axiomatic that Christianity *had* disappeared); and if I am right that he started on it soon after his return, then its commencement would exactly coincide with his doubts about the title of his first collection.

In October 1900 he had commented in his journal that New York was so large a battle could be fought on one side of the city, and poets could 'meditate sonnets' on the other (*SP* 89); part of his development would involve reducing the intervening distance, just as it would also involve perceiving how a book about the self should also be a book about the world. The process was still incomplete at the time of *Harmonium*; early 1923 saw the publication of two poems also included in the book: 'Last Look at the Lilacs' in the January *Secession*, and 'Floral Decorations for Bananas' given to Sanborn for the April *Measure* (along with 'New England Verses' and what would be retitled as 'Public Square', both in *Harmonium* 1931).[22] The same month saw his first original publication in England in Harold Monro's *Chapbook* (which had previously reprinted four stanzas of 'Sunday Morning'); and if he had wished to alienate a British audience, he could hardly have chosen a better poem than the provocatively flippant 'Mandolin and Liqueurs'. On 7 September, 1500 copies of his book were issued, and four days later he sent a copy to Van Vechten with an appreciative note; Stevens was pleased with its appearance – and he was a man who noticed such things. No author can fail to be excited by his first book; and Stevens, successfully settled in his career and now promisingly embarked as published poet, must have felt that life was going well as he and Elsie sailed out of New York on 18 October for a 15-day cruise to California via the Panama Canal, returning overland through New Mexico and calling in on Witter Bynner. It was their first long holiday together since their marriage, and involved nearly two months' absence from home and office so that, by accident or design, Stevens had no inkling until his return of the critical and commercial reception of *Harmonium*.

5

1923–37: From the Edge to the Centre

A bibliophile with a time-machine could do worse than set its clock to Christmas 1924 and head for Boston where and when, in the sale at Filene's bookstore, remaindered copies of *Harmonium* were selling at roughly a twentieth of their original retail price of two dollars; Conrad Aiken and R.P. Blackmur, the critic who would play an important part in the re-establishment of Stevens's reputation, bought them to send as Christmas cards to friends. Within a year of publication Stevens's book was suffering a fate which differed markedly from that of *The Waste Land* which – published as a book by Boni and Liveright in December 1922 – had quickly sold out its first edition of 1000 copies, necessitating a second impression of another 1000 early the next year. Stevens may have wished to present a sharp contrast to Eliot (letters between him and Robert McAlmon of *Contact* suggested as much), but not in terms of commercial failure; and *The Waste Land* is relevant because its reception demonstrated, first, that there was a market for difficult contemporary poetry in America, and second, that Eliot had pretty much cornered it. Stevens could not achieve the 'high' Modernist market penetration of Eliot, just as he could not emulate the more populist 'low' Modernism of Lindsay, Sandburg, or Frost. To be sure, the appearance of *The Waste Land* had been a carefully orchestrated affair; but Stevens, too, had influential friends in the opinion-forming circles, who had gone to some lengths to help him achieve the necessary exposure. The market research, such as it was, had seemed auspicious. Given the various prizes and honourable mentions he had accrued in the years leading up to *Harmonium*, as well as the fact that editors of little magazines were usually keen to secure contributions from him, he had every right to be surprised (as they were) when his book did so badly: it turned out to be the Ford Edsel of poetry publishing – although unlike that ill-starred car, *Harmonium* proved to be resurrectable.

He and Elsie had returned from their holiday in a positive frame of mind, one infers, because the dates suggest that during it they had conceived their daughter Holly, born 10 August 1924; and in

111

doing so had – in their own marital context – achieved an unusual degree of closeness and community of purpose. If Holly was to be the physical evidence, the mental evidence was 'Sea Surface Full of Clouds' (*CP* 98), published in the *Dial* the month before her birth, which is a spousal verse secretively full of mingled guilt and jubilation; its repetitious structure and thematics seem designed to prevent 'the good minute' from going (my allusion here is to Browning's 'Two in the Campagna'), but rather than achieving a new knowledge of reality, the effect seems hallucinatory rather than celebratory, an eerily suspended animation where objects and states persist as in a dream that claustrophobically mimics the waking state. The poem commemorated the illicit achievement of summer in November (Stevens falsified the date to emphasise this, since they actually passed Tehuantepec in late October; see *L* 241); but the complications attendant on the bearing of a child by a mother of 37 (an 'elderly primogravida' in medical parlance) not noted for her physical endurance, and to a father of 44, must also have been apparent to the parents. If 'Sea Surface...' marked matrimonial harmony, this seems to have been short-lived, for 'Red Loves Kit' (*OP2* 63), published in *Measure* in the month of Holly's birth, manifestly dealt with discord. It would be nearly six years before Stevens published a new poem.

In 1929 the endlessly energetic Alfred Kreymborg expressed his frustration at what he took to be Stevens's final removal from the literary scene:

> Formerly, it was impossible to get him to publish a book; now it is impossible to get him to publish a poem. Write him, wire him, or visit him, one always receives the same answer: he has written nothing for years.[1]

Would this silence have happened irrespective of its possible external causes, in the wretched sales of his long-delayed book and the distractions of his longer-delayed fatherhood? Certainly, Stevens spent several years after his book was published fending off requests for poems or reviews: from Monroe (1924, 1925), from Marianne Moore of the *Dial* (1925, 1926, 1927), from Untermeyer (1925, 1926), from Pound (via Williams, in 1927), and (1930, 1931) from Lincoln Kirstein of *Hound and Horn*, the magazine which was aiming to take the place of the recently-folded *Dial*. Evidently Kreymborg had also attempted to prise something from him, but to no avail. Stevens was selecting his own society, and, as Kreymborg went on to complain, had closed the valves of his attention to the degree that he ceased even writing letters (although he was friendly enough, if unforthcoming in literary terms, with a chosen few correspondents, such as Monroe, Moore, and Williams). In the letters he did write, there is the distinct impression of a life shutting itself down: replying to Monroe probably in July 1924, parrying her request for a poem he explained that he had been doing a lot of reading; he would be in Hartford over summer, didn't anticipate visiting Chicago, hardly ever went to New York. Noting the presence of acquaintances in Europe and Peking, his own plan for travel was the sarcastic proposal that he charter a boat to take his friends round the world, using his unprincely royalties from *Harmonium*: $6.70 for the half-year (*L* 243). With the birth of Holly, things changed further: he was moved into the attic of their apartment to be out of the way (*L* 245), he was no longer reading very much, and if there was no disillusionment at ten o'clock, that was because the entire household went to bed an hour earlier.[2]

Why that last measure should have been necessary, when by his own account the baby slept well and he himself occupied separate sleeping-quarters, is unclear. Some of the reasons he offered for being unable to write poetry are distinctly fatuous: he was too busy listening to the radio, or trying to locate laundresses to undertake the baby's washing; one does not have to be sceptical about the compulsive quality of a new invention or the onerousness of nappy-washing (in pre-disposable days), to doubt the strict veracity of such explanations. It is highly likely that the ultra-cautious Stevens responded to the financial consequences of parenthood by closer attention to the sources of his income – doubtless sharpened by the absence of income from his book. Nor was the renunciation of poetry unprecedented for him: in a letter of May 1937 he recalled once having given up writing poetry because he wished not to be 'bedeviled (*sic*) all the time about money', so instead he went to work like everybody else and 'kept at it for a good many years' (*L* 320). This memory, presumably of the period when he had switched from journalism to law, also offers a possible reason for his virtual disappearance from the literary scene in the later 1920s – such that in 1928 the poetry editor of one of the Hartford newspapers could write enthusiastically to Monroe about poetic activity in Hartford, without showing any awareness of Stevens ('the Poetry Club of Hartford meets at Mitchell's and the poetry center here is really at that shop'). Monroe loftily corrected him as to where the poetry centre in his city 'really' was (quoted *L* 255n.); but her former prize-winning contributor gave her and other supporters precious little ammunition to fight with on his behalf.

As Richardson shows in her biography, the mid-1920s were also a time of worries about health for Stevens: eye-problems led him to consult a doctor, who found that he was overweight, out of condition, incipiently diabetic, and with a very high blood-pressure. He had already been told that he might be dead by 40 (*L* 398), but whatever his satisfaction at having passed that fateful threshold, his was the ironic situation of being an insurance man whose health was too uncertain for him to be an acceptable risk for a life insurance company. The immediate consequences were a strict diet, which produced results highly satisfactory to his doctors; the change in his appearance is visible in the top photograph facing p. 310 in the *Letters*, showing a lean and hungry Stevens in front of his daughter's snowman, in the winter of 1928–9; on the same page, two or three years later, abating worries have restored his resemblance to W.C. Fields. He later told the woman who was working on his family tree that his policy of going to bed early had been part of the attempt to control his blood-pressure (*L* 470); it is also possible that eyesight worries led him to cut down on his out-of-office reading and writing. Whilst all this doubtless contributed to his period of creative abstinence, the principal reasons are likely to be bound up with his own reactions to *Harmonium*, and those of its readers. Some evidence for this is provided by the fact that, according to Holly Stevens (*L* 242), in the year of her birth her parents moved to 735 Farmington Avenue from their apartment further down the same road, to have more room for her; since it was at that address that the ms. of 'From the Journal of Crispin' was found in his dustbin, it follows that at some stage after transporting the material there, Stevens decided to throw it out – possibly in the same spirit that had earlier led him to get rid of his collection of art catalogues (which similarly signalled a temporary abstinence).

The Hartford writers enumerated to Monroe by the literary journalist were not bohemian types, although younger than Stevens; two would go on to win Pulitzer prizes, and two would become senior officials in the state of Connecticut. But Stevens did not know them, nor they, apparently, him. His letter to Monroe alluding to the meagre sales of his first volume informed her of several things he was unlikely to do; its tone may have been due to the enervatingly hot weather, but seems also to enact withdrawal, in its choked-off sentences. His refusal to find time even to review books by friends suggests something more than being busily preoccupied by work or paternal duties (or the radio!) – after all, he found time for a yachting trip of several weeks, up the west coast of Florida at the beginning of 1926 (*L* 247). The impression is rather more of someone who wished to withdraw from a particular context. The failure of *Harmonium* must have disappointed him, interrupting what had seemed his rising trajectory; persuaded, against his instincts, to publish a volume, in doing so he had exposed himself to public judgement in a way that humiliatingly illustrated not its hostility, but its indifference, to what he held most dear. He had broken faith with his desire to regard poetry as a form of retreat, and had been rewarded with a vision of his own irrelevance, that also underscored the difference between recognition in the coterie world of little magazines and broader acceptance. For one who was also developing his ideas about the importance of poetry in the modern world, this can only have been an ungratifying revelation. A letter written to Hi Simons in January 1940 – in which he discussed his position on the spectrum of political right/political left, and then offered (in response to Simons's essay) some comments of his own on 'The Comedian as the Letter C' – has an interesting postscript, in which, prompted by having thought about that poem and its significance, Stevens gave an explanation of what happened to him after *Harmonium*. It was a time when he was looking for a 'new romanticism' (glossed earlier in the letter as a new system of belief); but the search involved him in a revisionary critique of his own position: 'I began to feel that I was on the edge: that I wanted to get to the center: that I was isolated, and that I wanted to share the common life' (*L* 352).

Stevens's sympathies toward or understanding of 'the common life' may be debatable: in 1934, replying to a questionnaire sent out by *New Verse* in London, he had responded to the question of what he thought distinguished him as a poet from 'an ordinary man', by affirming his 'inability to see much point to the life of an ordinary man' (*OP*2 307); adding for good measure that he didn't suppose the ordinary man could see much point to it either. Although the brevity of his replies, as well as their content, seem intended to *épater les Anglais* by his apparent disavowal of the socialist-realist programme then fashionable, it is worth remarking that this final answer is self-undermining: for if the ordinary man as well as the poet sees little point to his life, the perception becomes a ground of commonality rather than of difference between them, and indeed opens the way for the poet to provide the satisfactions of belief, in his measure and his style.[3] That he had failed to accomplish this in *Harmonium* had been hinted to him by his own revulsion on reading the proofs for that volume (*L* 251), and would have been further underlined by the reviews it received, which can hardly have portrayed him in the light by which he most wished to be viewed.

The first notice was Mark Van Doren's in the *Nation*, which came out in the month following publication. Considering the book alongside volumes by Robert Graves and Alfred Kreymborg, Van Doren mentioned 'Peter Quince...' as Stevens's 'most famous poem', and whilst not wholly unappreciative of the quirky line of wit in which he felt the poetry to stand, he described Stevens as straining 'every nerve every moment to be unlike anyone else who ever wrote', and aimiably predicted that he would 'never be much read'. Matthew Josephson's more appreciative comments in *Broom* the month after nevertheless intimated the limitations of the poet's particular 'strangeness', and by implication hoped that a future volume would outgrow this. The review in *Poetry* that December was by Marjorie Allen Seiffert, Monroe having decided that to review the book herself would be to risk accusations of partiality; she attended to the new 'Comedian...', and alerted readers to the 'brilliant country' of Stevens's verse, whilst asserting that it concealed a 'rocky substratum of reality'. This was, as he might well have expected, a basically friendly notice, but one which gave no sense of *Harmonium*'s amounting to a whole. The same month, John Gould Fletcher in the *Freeman* considered the book alongside several others (Aiken, Kreymborg, *et alii*), as part of the 'revival of estheticism', and praised Stevens for being an 'honest' aesthete; he acknowledged the accomplishment of the writing, but made a bold prediction that either Stevens would have to 'expand his range to take in more of human experience', or give up writing; in his opinion the book was 'a sublimation that does not permit of a sequel'.[4]

The most appreciative and perceptive review of *Harmonium*, which still reads well today, was that of Marianne Moore in the *Dial* for January 1924, entitled 'Well Moused, Lion'. She was completely unafraid of what she found in the volume, to whose hidden ferocities she was alert – at the same time that she took Stevens to task for his unnecessary aggression, his 'deliberate bearishness'; she celebrated the power of his imagination, and showed herself familiar enough with his writing to bemoan his exclusion of 'The Death of a Soldier' and 'The Man whose Pharynx was Bad' (which Stevens duly incorporated in the second edition; there, perhaps angered by the attention reviewers had paid to the rather-too-programmatic poem 'Architecture', he omitted it). A poet of the younger generation, Allen Tate, considered Stevens in the *Nashville Tennessean* the next month, alongside Edith Sitwell and Edna St Vincent Millay (to whom he gave most space); his brief comments noted Stevens's 'freshness', but defined him as an 'explorer of the exotic'. In March, Harriet Monroe offered some comments in *Poetry*, noting Stevens's indifference to the fate of his poems once written, and stressing his humour; but the same month, Edmund Wilson in *New Republic*, reviewing Stevens and E.E. Cummings, contrasted the richness suggested by reading a few of Stevens's poems, with the 'sort of aridity' imparted by the volume as a whole. By July 1924 it was already clear that the book was not doing well, so the first essay entirely on Stevens, by Llewellyn Powys in that month's *Dial*, would have made little difference to sales; it started off citing Aubrey Beardsley, and went floridly on in a similar vein, striking a note that Stevens doubtless wished had been left unstruck, but which he had done little to modify by providing the highly mannered 'Sea Surface...' as the poem to accompany Powys's article. In October 1924, in the *Yale Review*, it was to be expected that Louis Untermeyer should prefer the poems of Robert Frost to those of Stevens, whom he berated for obscurity, and found wanting: 'For all its word-painting, there is little of the human voice in these glittering lines, and so, lacking the spell of any emotion, *Harmonium* loses both itself and its audience'.

Untermeyer was right about the effects if not necessarily about their causes; shortly after his remarks appeared the book was being remaindered – in contrast to Frost's *New Hampshire*, published the same year and awarded a Pulitzer prize. In 1939, replying to another questionnaire, Stevens would observe that 'much of the criticism one receives is a good deal keener than people who have not been subjected to the same thing can know' (*OP2* 310) – where the keenness seems to imply pain as well as insight. That he reacted (even over-reacted) to criticism was illustrated by his response to Stanley Burnshaw's comments on *Ideas of Order* (1935); but it is likely that the critics of *Harmonium* may have harped his own fears all too accurately, and shown that he had, in contemporary jargon, a severe image-problem. This was compounded (and perhaps clarified for him) in 1925, where a tiresomely over-written commentary in Paul Rosenfeld's *Men Seen – Twenty-Four Modern Authors*, published by the Dial Press in New York, presented him as a latter-day pierrot – and therefore an anachronism: 'the characteristic note of the 1890s was not outworn for us ten years ago; and yet, today, ... we have transcended it'. More influentially still, Gorham Munson wrote in the *Dial* (November 1925) of 'The Dandyism of Wallace Stevens'; stressing his wit (as Van Doren had) and reticence (also noted by Untermeyer), Munson – whose essay was included in his 1928 volume *Destinations – A Canvass of American Literature Since 1900 –* diagnosed in his subject the 'well-fed and well-booted dandyism of contentment', postulating a connection between the 'sensible discriminations and comfortable tranquillity' of his poetry and 'the America that owns baronial estates'. Although Stevens acknowledged the notice in a friendly enough way (*L* 246), the comments, even if they kept him in the public consciousness at a time when his book had failed and he was writing nothing, marginalised him as a curio.

The number of reviews *Harmonium* received confirm that its appearance was regarded as a significant literary event; none was so negative that it would have quenched any prospective reader's desire to explore Stevens's book – whose failure, in the light of such attention, is a reminder of the unpredictable nature of the market-place.[5] He had speculated to Monroe that the book might teach him something; and what he now learnt was that he had virtually no audience; along with this perception, the reviews themselves must also have been instrumental in showing him just how far out 'on the edge' he was seen to be. The story of his poetry writing, from the pamphlets dedicated to Elsie through his tentative first and more confident subsequent appearances in little magazines, had been a narrative of the expansion of his sense of an audience – whether conceived as passive or antagonistic readers. It must, therefore, have been chastening to discover that he was, figuratively, still reading his poems aloud to himself in a closet. Viewed in the retrospect of his triumphant resumption of poetry-writing from the mid-1930s to the end of his life, his withdrawal seems evidently to have been a case of *reculer pour mieux sauter*; but it is open to question whether at the time his intention to resume publication was as clear-cut as that implies. Several factors may have operated, some of them quasi-paradoxes. I would guess that the publication and poor reception of his first volume compromised his sense of poetry as his 'piety' and his 'retreat', and damaged the spirit of independence and self-command he felt in it; by trying to sell copies of his book he had forgotten the first, foremost law his father had enjoined him to respect: that poems and market-place or money-making do not mix. It was no accident that his next collection would turn out to be a non-profit-making limited edition published by a private press. If his spirit of independence had been compromised, it could most effectively be restored by being practised, more radically, as an independence of the need to publish poems; a refusal to write letters to a world that never wrote to him. But at the same time that he so intensified his already-noted indifference, he was also aware of the centre to which he wanted to have access: and perhaps the radio, to which he listened so assiduously in those years, was teaching him about precisely those human voices which some had felt to be conspicuous by their absence from his poems. He wanted to learn how to address an audience, of which it was essential that he felt himself to have no need.

As one of the indications of mass-cultural transformation – more even than the cinema, which can be seen, less epochally, as a technological extension of theatre – the radio became a potent symbol for the democratic accessibility apparently neglected by the author of *Harmonium*. The first commercial broadcasting started in Pittsburgh in 1920, and by the time of the first television broadcast (in 1928, the same year as the first full-length feature film with sound) 13 million radio sets were in use in the USA; ten years later, the power of the medium was famously demonstrated when Orson Welles's modernised version of his namesake H.G.'s *War of the Worlds* caused widespread panic. A radio switched on in 1920 and kept tuned to the signals of America throughout that decade would have received indications of a society in considerable tension between its past and its future, consequent upon the rapid post-war expansion. In 1919 Prohibition had begun, the following year women achieved the vote: one piece of legislation seems to hark back to God-fearing origins of America, the other to acknowledge what the future must bring (both pieces of legislation, in fact, indicated the influence of women within the political system, as well as the limitations of their power). The 1920 census showed for the first time that the urban population exceeded the rural, and there were signs of America's fear of what it was becoming: the 'Red Scare' of that year led to mass arrests of labour agitators, and the following year saw the introduction of immigration quotas (extended in 1924). The trial of the anarchists Sacco and Vanzetti the same year (they were executed in 1927) became the American equivalent of the Dreyfus case in France, polarising opinion round a *cause célèbre* that seemed to demonstrate an institutionalised fearfulness of the immigrant population – mirrored, below the Mason-Dixon line, in the increasing membership of the Ku Klux Klan: three million by mid-decade (however, the 1919 race riots in Chicago showed the problem not to be exclusively southern). In 1923 *Harmonium* was published, and flopped; the magazines *Time* and *Reader's Digest* were started up, and flourished. Despite the standardisation of time, intellectually people inhabited different epochs: the State of Tennessee outlawed the teaching of evolutionary theory in 1925, and two years later Lindbergh flew across the Atlantic.

In the essay devoted to Williams in his survey of American writing, *Destinations...* (1928), Gorham Munson declared that 'an outstanding feature of the last decade in American letters has been the working of a nationalistic impulse'; but he had started the essay with the observation that several of the writers most obviously straining to express such an impulse had manifestly failed to develop their art – citing Sandburg, Lindsay, Masters, Sherwood Anderson, and Theodore Dreiser as examples. The first edition of H.L. Mencken's *The American Language* (much admired by Williams) had appeared in 1919; 1925 would see a various harvest of Americanist definitions: Williams's *In the American Grain* (which Stevens declined to review), Dos Passos's *Manhattan Transfer*, Dreiser's *American Tragedy*, Fitzgerald's *The Great Gatsby*, Stein's *The Making of Americans*. Writers in the Harlem Renaissance – most signifcantly Jean Toomer, Langston Hughes, and (slightly later) Zora Neale Hurston – were in their different ways attempting to enlarge American self-perceptions; Van Vechten performed for Hughes the same office he had previously undertaken for Stevens, in recommending that Knopf publish his first volume *The Weary Blues* (1926). In a different way and a different region, the little magazine the *Fugitive* (1922–5), published out of Nashville, attempted both to dissociate itself from clichéd stereotypes of the Old South, as well as to refute the cultural slurs laid on the region by Mencken; the most significant of the 'fugitives' (John Crowe Ransom, Allen Tate, Robert Penn Warren) contributed to the polemical volume *I'll Take My Stand* (1930), offering a recrudescent Southern agrarianism as a corrective to the metropolitan industrialism of the North (which, with the stock market crash of October 1929 inaugurating the Great Depression, looked less evidently sustainable than during the earlier boom years). The scholarly journal *American Literature* was started in 1929, and D.H. Lawrence's seminal *Studies in Classic American Literature* had appeared in 1923.

Impressionistically speaking, these are the sorts of thing that Stevens might have heard about on his radio; these were the messages at large in the cultural airwaves. Like the *chinoiseries* he had Harriet Monroe's sister send him from Peking, the radio could offer manageable versions of experiences he had not easy opportunity to have at first-hand: at worst a form of arrogant commodification and complacent cultural sampling, but at best a means of self-education and of identification with the wider world. Although we can be certain that Stevens knew what was happening – given his habits of newspaper-reading and subscription to journals – we do not so clearly know what his reactions were; for most of the 1920s he remained silent. It may have been an introspective exile, akin to the actual expatriations of some of his contemporaries; but still one is inclined to ask (borrowing from 'Metaphors of a Magnifico') of what was it he was thinking, in these years? There is no strong evidence that his routines were profoundly disrupted by the birth of his daughter, whose upbringing fell mainly to her mother; although at weekends Holly was taken on walks and well-provided picnics in her father's beloved Elizabeth Park (through which he would walk on his way to work), on their first holiday in Atlantic City in 1929, his room was in a separate wing of the hotel. It seems to have been such a rare occurrence for Holly to have close physical contact with her father, that she remembered specific occasions when he actually carried her.[6] At the Hartford, by the late 1920s he had given up hopes of further advancement within the company (so Richardson reports), and was apparently noted for his indifference to such matters. His specialism must, however, have placed him in a 'win-win' situation: in the boom years, expanding business presumably contained its usual proportion of projects which ran into trouble and required his skills; and after the crash, although the volume of business presumably decreased, the number of surety claims as a proportion of the total would have increased sharply.

Despite Munson's association of *Harmonium* with 'baronial' America, Stevens contributed virtually nothing to the 'nationalistic impulse' in literature during the years of apparent plenty. He began to revive as a poet in the catastrophically lean years after October 1929, with a poetry for the most part lacking in the sumptuousness of his first volume, seemingly keen not to present itself as any kind of luxury item of the spirit. If this was the outcome of his conscious desire to move closer to the common life (and there seems to be in *Ideas of Order* an energy of repudiation directed at his earlier book), the fact is that in the year of publication Stevens was, in material terms, further away from the prevailing conditions of most people's lives than he had ever been or would ever be again. In the depths of the Depression (1932–3), national income had almost halved from its pre-slump level, and nearly a quarter of the labour force was unemployed; Stevens, on the other hand, in 1932 bought his substantial house on Westerly Terrace, and although he had taken a salary cut, still earned an amount that made him, relative to the majority, very well-off. The poet of *Harmonium* had lived in rented rooms; the poet of *Ideas of Order* verged on the baronial (and had in 1934 been promoted to the position of vice-president at the Hartford).

The persistence of the attention Stevens received during these years of silence is noteworthy; people kept on reminding him he was a poet, in spite of his own forgetfulness – which was such that he offered 'Academic Discourse in Havana' to *Hound and Horn* (where it was published in the Fall 1929 number), without recalling its earlier appearance in *Broom* (November 1923). He had presumably been approached on the suggestion of Blackmur, who joined the magazine in the summer of 1928 and had been influential in remodelling it along the lines of Eliot's *Criterion* rather than, as initially, the defunct *Harvard Monthly*; Blackmur wrote introducing himself to Stevens in April 1929. Stevens's poem, with its prevailing imagery of the ruined casino and lean times succeeding former plenty, took on an unforeseen relevance to current affairs in the light of that October's crash – as well as fitting in with the discussion undertaken in the magazine throughout 1929 until its third number the next year, of 'new humanism's efforts to articulate a conservative alternative to contemporary social unrest'.[7] His appearance in *Hound and Horn* was his first publication for five years; but earlier than that Stevens had found himself in correspondence with L.W. Payne, who had in 1927 sent the poet a copy of his annotated selections from American writers (see *L* 249n.); on 31 March 1928, after a delay that probably indicated his reluctance, he offered comments on some of his *Harmonium* poems, and on Payne's understanding of them (*L* 250–2); and although he was less revelatory than he imagined, and disliked the whole process – 'no more explanations' were his closing words – the letter was part of a slow and perhaps uncomfortable revival. The first poems that we know he composed were enclosed in letters that June to Harriet Monroe ('Metropolitan Melancholy', composed the previous day and not offered for publication; see *L* 252, *OP*2 64), and 'Annual Gaiety' (*OP*2 65), sent to Untermeyer and included along with six *Harmonium* poems in the fourth revised edition of his anthology of modern American poetry (1930).

When Stevens really broke his silence, in 1930, with 'The Sun this March' (*CP* 133) in the *New Republic* (April), the utterance seemed confessional – and, interestingly, played on notions of turning and returning, similar to the first poem in Eliot's simultaneously published *Ash-Wednesday*, also intimately in the first person. Was he renouncing his previously rich vision, to embrace a colder contemporary world? Yet the other magazine publication from this year, 'The Cattle Kings of Florida' (*OP*2 209), a prose piece published in the *Atlanta Journal* for December 1930, seems rather more nostalgic for old days and old pioneering ways, free of the curse of money: it told of the great cattle-drovers of the late nineteenth century, who exported their stock to then-Spanish Cuba and were paid in gold coinage that they carelessly but safely – such was the code of honour – secreted in saddle-bags or common kitchen utensils. Any nostalgia for the unfenced free-range days was, however, pragmatically banished by his closing affirmation of the future adaptability of the Florida cattle industry. This short essay probably owed itself to Stevens's affection for Florida, and his experiences as an officer of the Hartford Live Stock Insurance Company; quite possibly the time he spent composing it was time that – as he confessed to Lincoln Kirstein in July 1930 – he should have been devoting to writing poetry (*L* 258). Something else to which, like his reply to Payne's enquiries or the writing of poetry, he might have given a higher priority, was his publisher's proposal in the spring of 1930 that a second edition of *Harmonium* might be contemplated – to which he responded in mid-October (*L* 259–60). Newcomb is drily apposite: 'after seven years during which Stevens published exactly three poems, Knopf was willing to reissue *Harmonium* as if the whole enterprise had been quite satisfactory to everyone' (p. 81).

Whether Stevens's delay in replying was due to any self-doubt as a poet (also evidenced, perhaps, in his having neglected to send Harriet Monroe a card that Christmas) is unclear; by the time he replied, he had given the project enough thought to have decided on which (three) poems he wanted to drop, and which new material to include at which point in the volume. His decisions in those areas are interesting: 'The Silver Plough-Boy' (1915; *OP*2 17) may have seemed too complacently slight, 'Architecture' (1918; *OP*2 37) too clumsy, and 'Exposition of the Contents of a Cab' (1919; *OP*2 41) too near the knuckle, with its 'negress' imagined *à la* Jospehine Baker; but why he chose to include 'New England Verses' (rejected by *New Republic* in 1922, taken by Pitts Sanborn in *Measure* the next year) as preferable, is obscure.[8] He stipulated the new material should be inserted *en bloc*, and his order bore no relation to dates of composition; he may have started with 'The Man whose Pharynx was Bad' (1921) and 'The Death of a Soldier' (1918) because Moore had regretted their omission from the first edition, and he thought of them first; he may have chosen to finish with 'Indian River' (1917) because it was nearest in time to the period of composition of 'Tea' – which he referred to in his memo to Knopf as 'A Tea' – and 'To the Roaring Wind', which ended the book, as before.

The effect of his insertions was that the buoyant affirmations of 'Nomad Exquisite' were followed by the depressive tones of '...Pharynx...' – which poem was further darkened by the omission from its original publication in *New Republic* of lines evoking obsidian oceans and 'midsummer blaze', which were possibly cut because they indicated an imaginative energy Stevens now felt to be inapposite. Clearly, as the first of the 'new' poems, it could be read as Stevens's account of his own recent silence, pent too dumbly in his being; and the following 'Death of a Soldier [Death of a Poet?]' could, then, almost be read as a valediction forbidding mourning. The next poem inserted, 'Negation' (1918), had also formerly been one of the same group of war poems; but in its new context, also deprived of the quotations from the French soldier's letters home as published in *Poetry* (see *OP*2 29–36), it could be taken as an adverse commentary on *Harmonium* (1923), repudiating the vague idealism which had too single-mindedly sought an 'harmonious whole' (*CP* 97). With the exception of 'Sea Surface Full of Clouds' (1924) – itself a poem containing colder cross-currents – none of the 14 new poems (only five of them previously unpublished) was jubilant or affirmative. It is as if Stevens wanted to emphasise the minor key: even though he now included consecutively three of the poems from the sequence 'Lettres d'un Soldat' (also retrieving 'Lunar Paraphrase' which had been 'weeded out' from the batch submitted to *Poetry*; but separating this from the others), he reversed their order and removed all evidence of their originations as 'war poems' intended to address a major issue. His retention of 'To the Roaring Wind' as last poem possibly underlined his continuing sense of the volume's unfulfilment: he would have been alerted to that construction of its placing by Edmund Wilson's review of the first edition.

The most interesting omission from the new edition of *Harmonium* is 'Academic Discourse at Havana' (1923). Although it had apparently taken Stevens only six years to forget about its appearance in *Broom*, it is implausible to suppose that, the poem having been published in *Hound and Horn* the previous autumn, he had forgotten about it by the time he was compiling his list of new material to send to Knopf. He must, therefore, have deliberately excluded it; and the decision cannot have been based on grounds of any presumed inferiority, since subsequently he included it in *Ideas of Order* (1935). If I am right in my earlier suggestion that 'Academic Discourse...' gave a foretaste of the direction in which Stevens wished to go after *Harmonium*, then its incorporation in his second book rather than the revised edition of his first made good sense. This also implies that Stevens thought no better of *Harmonium* with the passage of time, since such modifications as he introduced operated to diminish its high-spiritedness, and even hinted at a disapproving commentary on his first effort. The second edition was published on 24 July 1931, priced at $2.50; as before, 1500 copies were printed. He cannot have thought entirely negatively of a volume whose dedication he extended ('To My Wife and Holly'); but what seems to be inferrable from the absence of 'Academic Discourse...' – which would surely have been a stronger poem to include than some of his additions – is that he was more concerned that his book retain its integrity as the record of a distinct era in his writing, than that it should make a strong impression of development. In the context of the deepening Depression, a poem like 'New England Verses' seemed almost wilfully at odds with the times, as Filreis suggests; and if he is correct to assert that none of the poems added was composed later than 1924, it is an additional sign that Stevens wanted to define a personal epoch, rather than bring his readership up to date.[9]

It may also be the case that he still felt himself to have made no very significant progress – a view which would have been corroborated by the scantiness of his output since then. There were, nevertheless, some who felt differently; in February 1931 Conrad Aiken had replied to Blackmur's enquiry about Stevens by comparing 'The Comedian...' favourably with *The Waste Land*, and asserting that he thought Stevens 'as sure of a permanent place of importance as Eliot, if not surer'.[10] The appearance of a second edition of *Harmonium*, however, did not provoke in Stevens any obvious renewal of his poetic mission: shortly before it came out he told Kirstein that it would take a coup d'état to get him writing poetry – although he looked forward to reading Blackmur's article on his work (*L* 261); in August the following year (1932) he told Monroe that whatever else he did, he did not 'write poetry nowadays' (*L* 262), although he then enclosed a 'scrap', in partial expiation for having sent 'The Woman Who Blamed Life on a Spaniard' (*OP2* 66) to *Contempo*. What he sent Monroe was probably 'Good Man, Bad Woman' (*OP2* 65; see *L* 262n.), and both poems appeared that same year; it seems likely that they had been written a good deal earlier – possibly around the same time as 'Red Loves Kit' (1924; *OP2* 63). Whether disingenuously or otherwise, he gave Monroe the impression of having had to scrape around to find such scraps for the benefit of editors; none of these poems was admitted into his collections – presumably because he felt them to be too personal.

By this time, while he was raiding his poetic larder, reviews of the revised *Harmonium* had appeared. The first, by Percy Hutchison in the *New York Times Book Review* for 9 August 1931, saw Stevens as the exponent of 'pure poetry' that was 'brilliant as the moon' and 'equally dead'; he concluded that 'the very remarkable work of Wallace Stevens cannot endure'. On 27 September in the *New York Herald Tribune Books*, in a review entitled 'Highly Polished Poetry', Horace Gregory criticised Stevens for having remained 'static': by implication, in a world which had radically moved on, Stevens was to be found in the same place. Both reviewers, then, saw *Harmonium* (1931) in the perspective that had largely governed reactions to the 1923 edition. In the September *Nation*, however, Eda Lou Walton, taking a tack similar to Aiken's in his letter to Blackmur, compared Stevens to Eliot, and decided that whereas the latter had retreated into 'scholarship' and 'religion', Stevens was more honestly engaged in trying to reconcile his sensuous poetry with the current circumstances. Entitled 'Beyond the Wasteland' (*sic*), her review was the first manifestation of a trend observable in criticism of Stevens over the following decades, of praising him because he was not Eliot. She disputed the justness of Munson's label 'dandy' – and in doing so showed an awareness of adversarial views of the poetry, that was also shown in Morton D. Zabel's review in *Poetry* that December. Zabel (who would briefly succeed Monroe as editor) was, similarly to Walton, concerned to show that an authenticating attitude, defined as Stevens's 'sincerity' and 'private fortitude', gave a substantiating seriousness to his poetry, in spite of its gaudy appearances; where others had seen an extravagant miscellany (possibly including Stevens himself, who would later define his *Harmonium* period as one when he had believed in 'pure poetry', *L* 288), Zabel insisted the volume was informed by 'a set of pure principles which made his work a unity'.

These reviewers were orienting their responses with regard to what they took to be the prevalent attitude to Stevens's work: its pointless stylishness, ever more objectionable in the Depression. This, too, was a starting point for Blackmur's highly influential essay 'Examples of Wallace Stevens', published in the *Hound and Horn* (Winter 1932), and subsequently collected in three of Blackmur's own books (in 1935, 1954, and 1957), as well as appearing thereafter in several anthologies of Stevens criticism. It was a piece of work with which he had taken considerable pains, as he wrote to Stevens. Its first paragraph defined two groups of readers: those who disliked Stevens for being 'finicky' and those who liked him for being 'ornamental', and set out to instruct their prejudices. This it did by close attention to the verbal detail, insisting that the exoticisms of Stevens's vocabulary were always justified by their function within the poem. Whether a hostile reader would have been persuaded by the revelation of 'little surds of feeling' inhabiting Stevens's 'mood of Euphues' is, I suppose, debatable; but Blackmur (reversing Wilson) favourably contrasted Stevens with Cummings, and later compared him with Pound and Eliot, in a manner that presumed his equal importance with those primary figures of high Modernism. Following Stevens's own comments in a letter to him, he stressed the '*intentional* ambiguity' of the poetry, which had the effect of rendering the poems inexhaustible, and differentiated between the kind of difficulty Stevens presented, and that of Pound or Eliot: '[his] difficulties to the normal reader present themselves in the shape of seemingly impenetrable words or phrases which no wedge of knowledge brought from outside the body of [his] poetry can help much to split'. As well as deploying a terminology and approach which would become fundamental to the practice of what was then emerging, and would later be institutionalised, as the 'new criticism', this was the first essay to offer close readings of several previously unnoticed poems; thus, a doubly canonical process was in train, that involved both methodology and material. Blackmur showed how Stevens was worthy of consideration alongside Pound and Eliot by virtue of his credentials as a 'difficult' poet, but one whose difficulties were intellectually recuperable; and at the same time implicitly validated his own critical procedures by their ability to show it.

Williams had a point, when he accused Eliot of having by *The Waste Land* given the poem back to the academics: difficult modernist writing justified the priestly interpositioning of the literary critic ('to the specialist the task of explaining them', as Pound would say of his *Selected Cantos* in 1966). Blackmur's essay marked a point of confluence between Stevens's poetry and the rise of this clerisy; and *Hound and Horn* itself, modelled on a *Criterion* which by this stage was altering the proportions between creative and critical writing to the latter's advantage, was a sign of the times. Defining Stevens as a 'rhetorical' poet, and setting his work in an essentially intellectual rather than socio-political context, Blackmur inaugurated an influential twofold development, of treating the poems as self-contained utterances, which triumphed over time and chance (that is, achieved canonicity) by their innate structure of ideas. This would be the beginning of a process which would see Stevens instituted as essentially 'philosophical', writing a 'poetry of thought':[11] a process which would in its way have the effect of moving his work from the edge and toward the centre of what was regarded as literary value. But Blackmur's influence would be apparent in the medium and longer terms, rather than instantaneously, however gratified Stevens was by his high praise; although by March of the following year (1933) Stevens told Zabel that 'for some reason' he had had quite a few requests for poems (possibly stimulated by the article), he was not writing enough or liking what he wrote enough to satisfy them all (*L* 265). He implied that he was painfully shaking off the rust that had accumulated during years of disuse; but it now seems possible that he had already composed – or was on the point of doing so – two of the stronger poems of his subsequent volume, 'The Idea of Order at Key West' and 'Evening without Angels'; and that the spur to his creativity had not been Blackmur, but a shadowy multinominate individual who had approached him under the name of Ronald Lane Latimer.[12]

'Ronald Lane Latimer' was one of several aliases used by James G. Leippert, who while still an undergraduate at Columbia University had involved himself in the publication of poetry. Himself the writer of undistinguished verse, his real distinction lay in his passion for and presciently discriminating taste in the contemporary poets, from whom he was remarkably successful in soliciting contributions for his proposed little magazine – which ran through as many alternative titles as its editor had aliases, before settling on *Alcestis*. The magazine lasted for four issues (featuring some high-calibre contributors), but its name survived in the Alcestis Press Leippert went on to run (with Willard Maas), and which published books by Stevens, Williams, Tate, John Peale Bishop, and Robert Penn Warren. Clearly, there was a significant component of (possibly pathological) play-acting in his character, which spilled over into a life sufficiently complex to include simultaneous engagement to a young woman of good family and gay relationships in Greenwich Village, as well as the need to juggle his identities. During this period, Stevens seemed to be retreating ever further from avant-gardism: in a letter to Monroe he sneered at the New York sophisticates observed at the Hartford première of the opera *Four Saints in Three Acts* by Gertrude Stein and Virgil Thomson (February 1934; *L* 267), and bemoaned the deterioration of Key West into a colony for writers and artists (February and March 1935; *L* 274, 278). Yet despite warnings from suspicious friends like Bynner or, later, Williams, he persisted in an epistolary relationship with the shadowy 'Latimer' which obliged him at times to send letters via a gay bar or a grocery store; and with unruffled equanimity he entrusted the doubly-obscure young man for over a year with the evidences of his poetic revival, denied to more illustrious editors.[13]

The flexibility and accommodatingness of Stevens's relations with 'Latimer' may have been part of the older man's desire to help his junior make a start (Stevens was also prepared to offer more practical help); the very fact of Leippert's being so much younger would have eased matters between them, and however absolute Stevens could on occasions be with his inferiors, it is also clear from colleagues' reminiscences that he had no difficulty in delegating responsibilities. The legacy of this involvement lay not only in the poems 'Latimer' appeared able to encourage him to produce, where no others had succeeded, and in the two books of verse they published together; it also consisted in the remarkable series of letters written by Stevens to his young publisher, replying with what appears to be wholly relaxed candour to numerous enquiries about his poetry – some of which, as Filreis has shown, were actually posed by Leippert's left-wing collaborator, Maas. 'Latimer' had originally approached Stevens in February 1933; and it was the following month Stevens had written to Zabel of his dislike for his own new poems ('writing again after a discontinuance seems to take one back to the beginning rather than to the point of departure', *L* 265). In October the next year, he was to be found holding off Zabel yet again, although making a commitment to provide something. This contrasted with his letter to 'Latimer' the following month, responding to the suggestion that he should think of a new collection with an enthusiasm for poetry absent from his correspondence for a dozen years: he could not imagine anything, he told 'Latimer', that he would like more (*L* 271). There were two problems Stevens foresaw: the scantiness of material (he contrasted his own meagre productivity with that of Williams), and the necessary consent of Knopf – although he correctly doubted, in the case of Knopf, that a serious objection would be made in the prevailing commercial climate.

After publishing three poems a year in 1932 and 1933, 1934 saw his decisive resurrection, with 16 new poems published in four different magazines and one anthology (*Modern Things*, ed. Parker Tyler). In the case of two of these, *Alcestis* and *Direction*, Stevens contributed to the first issue of a new venture; and *Direction*, set up by Kerker Quinn at Bradley University, achieved in its opening number an array of talent as impressive as Leippert would muster: Aiken, Aldington, Frost, Pound, Stevens and Williams were represented. In Stevens's case, however, the eight poems he published in *Alcestis* (October 1934: the month he was putting off Zabel), principally 'The Idea of Order at Key West' (*CP* 128) and 'Evening without Angels' (*CP* 136), but also 'Lions in Sweden', were unquestionably his most important poems of that year. The others were slighter pieces, although 'Gallant Chateau' achieved a grim concision (plausibly read as offering a comment on the state of its author's marriage, as might also be the case with 'Secret Man' in Tyler's anthology, or 'The Widow', sent privately by Stevens to 'Latimer', see *OP2* 67, *L* 274). Both the ideas of order and the un-angelled evening – whilst being offered as answers to questions of the spirit, and appearing to affirm the essentially Coleridgean imagination as the only available 'religious' principle – have their perplexing aspects. In the first, the triumphantly absolutist 'she' who makes her only world by singing it, is nonetheless relativised within a universe that includes the antecedently created ocean as well as the poem's speaker and – it would surprisingly appear – the Ramon Fernandez so passionately interrogated at its close. Two men observe the remote ecstasy of a woman (reminiscent of Susanna and the Elders?) applauding a solipsism their presence disproves: whose 'idea' and what 'order' are established here? 'Evening without Angels' also seems to be a poem in which high-church recidivism overcomes a fundamentalist reductive tendency.

Early December 1934 saw Stevens fulfil his undertaking to Zabel by sending *Poetry* 'Like Decorations in a Nigger Cemetery' (published February 1935), and continue his discussions about a new book with 'Latimer'. The poem, dedicated to his friend Judge Powell, consisted of 50 poetic observations mostly composed, as Stevens told Zabel, as he walked to and from the office. It would be a mistake to suppose that the title had the same objectionable force 60 years ago that it has today; but its use indicates that, no matter what Blackmur asserted about Stevens's precision in matters lexical (and he was surely right about the poet's exploitation of the stranger recesses of language), certain resonances of certain words were inaudible to him. It is unlikely that Stevens gave the matter very much strategic thought, but he would surely have been aware that, after so long a silence, his use of (the first) ten pages of *Poetry* would be construed as an important statement. Insofar as he was concerned to make a specific impression, he may have wished to mark an obvious difference between this new long poem and 'The Comedian...'; where that was a sustained narrative in a rococo style, these improvisatory pieces were – as the title indicates – concerned with a much humbler and more spontaneous ornamentation. The invocation of Whitman in number I (*CP* 150) seems like Stevens's affirmation of an all-American bardic ancestry – not much noted by reviewers of *Harmonium*. I doubt, however, that he set very much store by this poem; again, his diffidence in its regard, excusing it because he found it difficult to find the time to write poetry (*L* 272), contrasts with the letter written four days later to 'Latimer', whom he told of rooting about in the chill of the attic (by this time he was in his new house), trying to find enough to justify a new collection. There was a comedy of errors about whether Stevens had been asked to introduce a selection of Ernest Dowson's or Austin Dobson's poetry 'Latimer' envisaged publishing; but this idea was swept aside in any case, as he warmed to the task of writing enough new poems to make a volume (*L* 272–3).

Having assembled what he had found in his attic (not much) and what he had recently been composing, it seemed to Stevens that the overall effect lacked colour; which defect – since, as he put it, the tone of the whole book was important – he proposed to alleviate by composing some poems which would 'give a little gaiety and brightness'. By the time he next wrote to 'Latimer' (a month later, on 8 January 1935), he was able to report some success in his campaign to 'pump up floods of color' (*L* 273), as he had written a poem describing 'a deathbed farewell under the new regime' (!).[14] He went on to talk about the composition of poems, in a way which emphasises the important role 'Latimer' was playing in his poetic reawakening:

> One of the essential conditions to the writing of poetry is impetus. That is a reason for thinking that to be a poet at all one ought to be a poet constantly. It was a great loss to poetry when people began to think that the professional poet was an outlaw or an exile. Writing poetry is a conscious activity. While poems may very well occur, they had very much better be caused.
>
> (*L* 274)

Having now a reason to keep to writing, Stevens jovially anticipated turning his imagination into a veritable fire of creativity; and early the next March he sent his publisher four poems (to add to 'The American Sublime' already in his hands) for publication in the third number of *Alcestis*. Days later he followed this up with another new poem, 'Sailing after Lunch', which he already had in mind as the first poem in his projected book, whose title he proposed should be *Ideas of Order*. Nothing underlines the nature of his relations with 'Latimer' more than his willingess, in this letter, to offer (without having been asked) an explanation of the latest poem:

> The thing is an abridgment of at least a temporary theory of poetry. When people speak of the romantic, they do so in what the French commonly call a *pejorative* sense. But poetry is essentially romantic, only the romantic of poetry must be something constantly new and, therefore, just the opposite of what is spoken of as the romantic. Without this new romantic, one gets nowhere; with it, the most casual things take on transcendence, and the poet rushes brightly, and so on. What one is always doing is keeping the romantic pure: eliminating from it what people speak of as the romantic.
>
> (*L* 277)

Stevens emerged from his post-*Harmonium* silence to embark on a sustained consideration of the poet's role, specifically (his own case) and generally; and the issue seemed to be – adopting terms from these two letters – how to reconcile poetry as a 'conscious activity' with the 'transcendence' it should achieve. If 'The Idea of Order...' was composed comparatively early in this resumption of poetry writing, then it is an interesting (if fulsome) note toward his theory of poetry: the solitary singer contemplated, who is referentially beyond the poem as she is 'beyond the genius of the sea' (we don't know what she sings about), may exemplify an obsolete romantic intoning and declaimed clairvoyance (see *CP* 387), inappropriate to the reasonable world of the speaker and Ramon Fernandez. Her world is her, theirs the town they return to – or so it might be thought; yet they return to a place apparently transfigured, after her example: she has at least located the voice that is great within her (see *CP* 138), and answered the challenge posed 'To the Roaring Wind'. Pondering another's creativity was an activity undertaken directly as well as indirectly by Stevens at this period, in the preface he provided for Williams's *Collected Poems 1921–1931* (1934) and his review for *Life and Letters Today* (December 1935) of Marianne Moore's *Selected Poems* (1935); in both he addressed the issue of the transformation of the 'romantic' in the contemporary setting. In his preface, Stevens asserted that Williams was a romantic poet with a touch of sentimentalism; his chief virtue lay in the reaction against these impulses, his passion for the 'anti-poetic': 'as a phase of a man's spirit, as a source of salvation, now, in the midst of a baffled generation, as one looks out of the window at Rutherford or Passaic, or as one walks the streets of New York, the anti-poetic acquires an extraordinary potency' (*OP*2 213–14). Stevens defined the contemporary romantic poet as a dweller in an ivory tower who valued it for the view it afforded of the public dump and advertising hoardings.

This was another of his suavely adversarial readings of Williams's work, in part designed to recuperate an apparently radical poetics within a more inherently quietist literary tradition. In a letter of March 1935 to T.C. Wilson of the *Westminster Magazine*, responding to an invitation to review Moore's book, Stevens made it clear that he thought her a much more significant poet than Williams, by virtue of her reconstructive as well as destructive powers; Williams, he opined, represented an 'exhausted phase' of the romantic, whereas Moore showed more clearly the search for a new romantic (*L* 279); hence the title of his review, 'A Poet that Matters' (*OP*2 217 ff.). Like Blackmur's approach to his own poetry, Stevens started by paying close attention to aspects of Moore's language and construction; then he broadened his argument, to assert that whereas in the pejorative sense the romantic connoted obsolescence, in her case, 'it means, now-a-days, an uncommon intelligence. It means in a time like our own of violent feelings, equally violent feelings and the most skilful expression of the genuine' (*OP*2 220). Enlisting yet another ally in what would look to a contemporary like an alliance of right-wingers, Stevens found pleasant things to say of Eliot in this regard (although to call Eliot a 'brilliant instance of the romantic' would be, he well knew, as infuriating to Eliot as were his similar compliments to Williams). Stevens paid Moore's work the tribute of seriousness withheld from Williams's: 'In any project for poetry (and one wishes that the world of tailors, plasterers, barkeepers could bring itself to accept poets in a matter-of-fact way) the first effort should be devoted to establishing that poets are men and women, not writers' (*OP2* 221).

Writing about the two poets with whom he was most friendly, Stevens in each case read their work in the context of the altered times to which they responded. In Williams's case, he seems to have needed to protect himself from any perception that that particular response was the most valid available, and did his best (in what seems, rhetorically, a typical spoiling tactic) to diminish Williams's challenge to his own aesthetic, by presenting the work as an already obsolescent form of the modern (emphasising that the poet was over 50, and likening him to a 'grand old plaster-cast'; in a letter to 'Latimer' of October 1935, Stevens called him 'old Dr Williams', *L* 286). He misread 'The Attic which is Desire' (1930), apparently conceiving the 'unused tent' to be an item in it rather than what it resembles, and proposing a diversionary Freudian interpretation; the only other poem from the 1930s which he noted was 'The Cod Head' (1932), whose itemisation (of what earlier in his own life Stevens had dismissed as 'silly jumble', see *L* 45) he affected to regard as 'pure sentimentalization'. Clearly, he greatly preferred the signs 'C.J. Poole, Steeple-Jack' and 'Danger' noted in Moore's poem 'The Steeple-Jack', as striking a human note absent from the electrified 'SODA' sign in 'The Attic which is Desire'; and the valuable difference between the radical Williams and the much less abrasive Moore lay in the lines Stevens quoted from her poem: 'it is a privilege to see so/ much confusion' – where the fact of seeing has led to a morally formative response. The kinds of randomness routinely fitted in by Williams to his poems were as routinely excluded by Stevens from his; unlike the poetry of either Williams or Moore, which usually convinces the reader of its reference to things witnessed, the sense of there having been a physical perception as the basis of his poems is irrelevant. We do not necessarily believe Stevens ever saw a woman singing by the sea at Key West (still less whilst walking there with Ramon Fernandez), and an appropriate summary of their response to her display might be, it is a privilege to see so much order.[15]

Yet if he felt that Williams's 'confusion' paid too little tribute to inherencies of order, he did not wish the poems he himself was writing between 1933 and 1935 merely to present the opposite condition. Even his references to the 'baffled generation' and its 'violent feelings' – like his awareness of a possible relation between his poetry and the lives of tailors, plasterers, and barkeepers (quixotic as such a hope might be) – suggested an ideological difference from the poet of *Harmonium*. That Stevens wished this to be noticed by any readers of his second volume was signalled by the plurality of its title, rejecting the concordial aspirations of 'harmonium': *Ideas of Order* rebukes and relativises the over-confident singularity of 'The Idea of Order...' as well, making poetry out of the quarrel with himself just as other poems seem to offer dismissive commentary on *Harmonium*. 'Sad Strains of a Gay Waltz' (1935; *CP* 121) is explicit in its rejection of the solipsistic tendencies of Hoon (from 'Tea at the Palaz of Hoon'), whose abstention from humanity has left him vulnerable; what is needed, the poem suggests in a direct repudiation of *Harmonium*'s totalitarianism of the spirit, is an 'harmonious skeptic' who will order the 'epic of disbelief' into an appropriately 'skeptical music'.[16] The waltz may have become obsolete, but some form of music must be necessary: this is the main thrust of *Ideas of Order* which, if not a thesis as Stevens insisted to 'Latimer' (*L* 279), was nevertheless thematically more coherent than his first book. Whereas the First World War had been the starting point for some of his poems initially excluded from *Harmonium*, which were only admitted once that connection had been obscured, the links between several of the poems in *Ideas of Order* and the early 1930s were manifest (as in 'Mozart, 1935').

Stevens was responding both negatively and positively to the social and socialist pressures of the times. By mid-decade the Depression was past its worst, and the First New Deal of President F.D. Roosevelt (elected 1932) had inaugurated a vast series of public works that began to restore a sense of national purpose and make inroads into the huge numbers of unemployed (although unemployment remained high until the Second World War). At the time, considerable controversy surrounded the New Deal proposals, some of it emanating from conservative business groups like the insurance companies.[17] The evident failure of old-style capitalism led (as in Britain) to a belief that Stalin's effectively stage-managed Soviet system, with its trumpeted five-year plan (from 1929), illustrated the better path forward. The Left/Right political debate swung decisively leftward in most liberal-intellectual circles (seen for example in Edmund Wilson's admiration for Lenin, from which his post-war friend Vladimir Nabokov was unable to disinfect him), further polarised by the rise of fascism and its consequences, in Europe: Hitler acceded to the

German Chancellorship (1933), remilitarised and occupied the Rhineland (1936); Mussolini's Italy invaded Ethiopia in 1935, the Spanish Civil War began in 1936, ending three years later in victory for Franco, and, in Asia, Japan invaded China in 1937. The emotional map of the decade might be described as one in which the despair caused by the Great Depression had hardly given way to hopes that societies could be rebuilt, before it was replaced by the awareness that the world was lurching toward another war, in which the forces of evil might very possibly prevail; an awareness complicated by the breakdown for many of the simple moral binarism of Left (=good) / Right (=evil), induced by the dismaying revelations of the Moscow 'show trials', and then by Stalin's pact with Hitler (1939). It was all this that led W.H. Auden, in 'September 1939', to talk of the expiring 'clever hopes' of a 'low, dishonest decade'.

In April 1935 Stevens delivered the proofs of his new book into the hands of Lew Ney, its printer, who alarmed the poet by threatening to come and see him at the Hartford when holidaying, in shorts, with his wife (*L* 283). By mid-August the book had been published: a limited edition totalling 165 numbered copies, all signed by the author; 20 were presentation copies printed on handmade paper, 135 copies for sale at $7.50, and 10 copies for review. If *Harmonium* (1923) sold like the Ford Edsel, this seemed aimed at the Rolls-Royce sector of the market; whatever the poems themselves had renounced in verbal or thematic splendour had been incorporated in their physical presentation. Stevens was delighted with the book's appearance, commenting on its contents only that it would be impossible to try reading them again (*L* 283). As he had explained in his earlier letter, the main principle of arrangement had been contrastive (*L* 279), which is perhaps most clearly seen in the transition from 'The Idea of Order...' to 'The American Sublime'; overall the book seems more obviously aware of, and concerned with, a possible reader than its predecessor – even if the degree to which it sets out to woo that reader is debatable. The opening poem, 'Sailing after Lunch' (*CP* 120), with its presentation of a poet speaking *in propria persona* and finding his plight to be that of an 'inappropriate' man in an 'unpropitious' place, seems like a plea for understanding from the much-maligned author of *Harmonium*, keen to establish that he was a man rather than a writer; but whatever sympathy might have been felt by any tailor, plasterer, or barkeeper for his plight could well have been modified, by doubting just how 'matter-of-fact' was the predicament of one who in 1935 seemed as sure of his lunch, as of the opportunity to go sailing afterwards.

The reviews of this new volume were not unfriendly; few failed to notice the difference from *Harmonium*, and several observed its address to current contexts (Howard Baker in the *Southern Review* for Autumn 1935 noted that it laboured 'a little inconclusively with the social and economic problems of these disturbed years'); Marianne Moore in the *Criterion* sternly averted her gaze from any such impurities. F.O. Matthiessen in the *Yale Review* thought the book deserved a Pulitzer prize. Babette Deutsch in the *New York Herald Tribune Books* fretted, not entirely without cause, at the expensive and therefore restrictive fact of its being a limited edition, whilst accepting that the poems seemed more serious than those in his first collection. In the *New Republic* Theodore Roethke, who would later in his own verse show some debt to Stevens, regretted that, despite the differences from *Harmonium*, Stevens had not sought to project himself 'more vigorously upon the present-day world'. There was something of an irony in the fact that the book of poems by which Stevens turned his attention toward the contemporary world, with its obvious economic problems, should be an expensive limited edition, physically expressive of poetry's semi-religious apartness: it symbolised the paradox inherent in his conception of poetry's relation to the everyday (as a 'tune beyond us, yet ourselves', *CP* 165). It was a point of honour with Stevens to make no money out of the Alcestis edition, but that in itself could not detach the book as intellectual object from involvement in the market-place. As we have seen, several poets were also involved with the Alcestis Press and similar ventures, so that Stevens's association with it was not at all anomalous; but if he had hoped that the limited circulation would make the whole event less publicly exposed than had been his experience with *Harmonium*, he was disappointed, and the book's appearance propelled him deeper into the public engagement of his art.

It is not clear why else he should have been so stung by Stanley Burnshaw's notice in *New Masses* (October 1935); at this stage, the magazine was straightforwardly Marxist, and Stevens presumably came to its review (probably the first that he read) with equivalent expectations: commenting to 'Latimer' on 9 October 1935, he described it as 'interesting' for having placed him in a new setting;

'I hope I am headed left, but there are lefts and lefts', he went on, 'and certainly I am not headed for the ghastly left of MASSES. ... MASSES is just one more wailing place and the whole left now-a-days is a mob of wailers. I do very much believe in leftism in every direction, even in wailing. These people go about it in such a way that nobody listens to them except themselves; and that is at least one reason why they get nowhere. They have the most magnificent cause in the world' (*L* 286–7). This doesn't read quite like the reaction of an author to an 'interesting' review; just as the politics affirmed here are not usually associated with Stevens – who in paying 'leftism' the tribute of being a 'most magnificent cause' was turning leftward his own tribute to the imagination as the 'magnificent cause of being' in 'Another Weeping Woman' (*CP* 25). Burnshaw had cited these lines from *Harmonium*, and had dismissed the poetry of that book as 'the kind of verse that people concerned with the murderous world collapse can hardly swallow today'; but he had gone on to assert that Stevens had indeed moved on, and had found that 'his harmonious cosmos is suddenly seething with confusion', to which *Ideas of Order* represented the honourable if necessarily inconclusive response of a 'troubled, searching mind'. Burnshaw summed up by identifying Stevens (and Haniel Long, also reviewed) thus: 'Acutely conscious members of a class menaced by the clashes between capital and labor, these writers are in the throes of struggle for philosophical adjustment. And their words have intense value and meaning to the sectors within the class whose confusions they articulate. Their books have deep importance for us as well.'

It was possibly finding himself thus conscripted to the rhetorical polarities of the class struggle (wherein he could either be, in Burnshaw's terms, potential ally or potential enemy) that so irritated Stevens, even if, as Filreis argues, he must have known of the growing political radicalism at the Alcestis Press. He was aware of the ideological imperatives embedded in the current poetical debate, in England as well as in the USA: he owned the Hogarth Press edition of Cecil Day-Lewis's *The Magnetic Mountain* (1933), which he had considered to the extent of writing comments from the *Hound and Horn* (April 1933) on the flyleaf. Day-Lewis's book, owing a heavy debt to Auden and prefaced by a couplet from Rex Warner welcoming the 'movement of masses' as 'beginning of good', and with its programmatic narrative of a journey toward class enlightenment involving a rejection of the 'enemy', may well have represented for Stevens a sort of poetry he had little desire to write, but needed to answer. At the point when – with *Ideas of Order* – he had shown awareness of his potential audience, soliciting its concern for the problems aired in 'Sailing after Lunch', he was criticised for having failed to make sufficient headway and judged by the binaristic mode it had been part of his book's purpose to evade. Moreover, by the time of Burnshaw's review he had already taken a step further, in 'The Old Woman and the Statue', which had appeared in the inaugural number of the *Southern Review* (Summer 1935); this poem he described in 1936 as concerning 'the effect of the depression on the interest in art. I wanted a confronting of the world as it had been imagined in art and as it was then in fact' (*OP2* 225–6). The poem was as wordily bad as anything in *The Magnetic Mountain*; and the immediate consequence of reading the *New Masses* review was that, by way of riposte, Stevens set about composing its successor, a long poem which he had completed by the end of that month, called 'Mr Burnshaw and the Statue', published the following year in Kreymborg's *The New Caravan* (1936). This was the second in what was taking shape in his mind as a series of poems about statues, prompted initially by an apparent interest on the part of Dent's in London (prodded by Conrad Aiken; see *L* 279, 296), and encouraged by the Alcestis Press's desire to publish a further book by him. He told 'Latimer' that this new poem represented his attempt to consider Communism from the perspective of poetry (*L* 289).

Looking over his latest volume, in the interesting letters he wrote to 'Latimer' in the latter part of 1935, Stevens saw that an important theme concerned the 'status of the poet in a disturbed society' (*L* 292), although in his following letter he chose 'How to Live. What to Do' (1935; *CP* 125) as his favourite poem (*L* 293): which seems to celebrate its protagonists' emancipation from the 'muck' of received ideas, both religious and political. But it was such ideas he was to wrestle with in the long, dull poems he was then engaged in writing, whose ideologies of order have an effect contrary to the 'freshening of life' he desired of the poet (*L* 293). These poems would be issued as *Owl's Clover* by the Alcestis Press on 5 November 1936; but while he was composing them, Stevens was revealing to 'Latimer', in response to his questions, just how serious was his vision of the place of poetry in the modern world: 'the real trouble with poetry is that poets have no conception of the importance of the thing. Life without poetry is, in effect, life without a sanction' (*L* 299; 10 December 1935). A similar ambition would later characterise Stevens's discussions with Henry Church, about the possible foundation of a Chair of Poetry at Harvard; just as something which might be called a 'sense of community' discriminates the poetry of this period from that of *Harmonium*, so his forthright projections of the poet's role differentiate the post-*Harmonium* Stevens from the diffident avant-gardist at Arensberg's salon. His emergence as a more confident, publicly oriented poet is to be observed, also, in his attitude to publication. In November 1935 he had written to 'Latimer' of his desire that Knopf would decline to publish a trade edition of *Ideas of Order* (*L* 296); this would leave Stevens free to proceed as he wished, and he expressed his indifference to large sales. But at the same time, he acknowledged the beneficial effects of enlarged circulation; thus, when in March 1936 Knopf expressed his willingness to take the book on, Stevens was assenting to a version of poethood subtly different from that he had pursued with the Alcestis Press and with the relatively obscure magazines in which his 1930s verse had predominantly appeared.

He provided three new poems for Knopf: 'Farewell to Florida' and 'Ghosts as Cocoons' at the beginning, and 'A Postcard from the Volcano' inserted after 'Like Decorations...'. Instead of the indecisiveness of 'Sailing after Lunch', the new opening poem (*CP* 117) struck an assertively rhetorical tone, replacing the 'old boat' by a 'high ship', and presenting the poet-speaker not as misplaced romantic but as Ulyssean homecomer (*The Magnetic Mountain* had also alluded to the *Odyssey*); the Florida escaped from is the land both of the lotus-eaters and of Circean enchantment. 'Farewell to Florida' is sure of its direction: a renunciation of feminine southern comfort, for a masculine north imaged as cold, turbulent and metropolitan; the purposive northwardness of this liberating voyage also contrasts with Crispin's inconclusive mock-epic. The terms of the poem's north/south opposition (with the north representing post-Depression realism) was historically unfair, since Stevens knew better than most how badly Florida had been hit; but perhaps the most noteworthy feature of the poem is its evident function as a manifesto of his own changed poetic direction, addressed to a readership presumed to need dissuading from its preconception of him as the aesthetic hedonist of *Harmonium* – even though, in his jacket statement for Knopf's edition, he misleadingly defined the book as 'pure poetry'

(*OP*2 222–3). 'Delightful Evening' was retained as the final poem; its deliberate diminuendo reinforced the volume's sense of itself as embracing a world of fortuity and ordinariness, rather than reaching after verbal altitudinosities. Knopf's edition came out in October 1936 (1000 copies at $2), then came the Alcestis *Owl's Clover* (85 copies available, at $10 apiece). Stevens's further emergence into the public arena, and his increasing stature as a poet, were signalled by his invitation to give a paper at Harvard: 'The Irrational Element in Poetry' was read on 8 December, bringing to a close an impressive year, in which he had also been awarded the *Nation*'s poetry prize for his poem about the Spanish Civil War, 'The Men that are Falling'.

In his blurb for *Ideas of Order*, Stevens closed by asserting that the more 'realistic' life was, the more it required the 'stimulus of the imagination'; this was essentially the animating perception of the five long poems in *Owl's Clover* (*OP*2 75–101), which was his attempt to prove that a set of social and economic circumstances apparently intractable to aesthetic treatment were in fact both in need of and amenable to it. On 6 December 1936 Ruth Lechlitner (in the *New York Herald Tribune Books*) and Eda Lou Walton (in the *New York Times Book Review*), both of a radical persuasion, reviewed *Owl's Clover*; both noted the difference it represented from his earlier work, although Lechlitner was more alert to the fact that, stressing the individual rather than the collective imagination, it laid him open to 'attack from the left' (on which possibility Stevens commented humorously in a letter the next day to 'Latimer', *L* 313). Neither felt the book to be wholly successful, but each honoured the effort made to accommodate the contemporary scene. Marianne Moore's comments in *Poetry* the following February were eloquent in their refusal to attend with any closeness to the book notionally under review, quoting instead from several *Harmonium* poems in possibly implied rebuke, and ending with a statement (or rallying-cry) more optative than definitive: 'America has in [him] at least one artist whom professionalism will never demolish'. But perhaps the most effective review was Ben Belitt's in the *Nation* (12 December 1936); responding with a note of thanks, Stevens accepted the justice of Belitt's definition of his particular difficulty that, 'moved to formal discourse in the quest for order and certitude, his art has not up to the present permitted him to pursue such discourse or his temperament to accept it' (quoted *L* 314n.). This was indeed astute;

for although Stevens had toyed with the title 'Aphorisms on Society' (*L* 311), the main weakness of *Owl's Clover* lay precisely in its distended discursiveness and failure to achieve aphoristic precision. It could be argued that throughout his career he would overestimate his aptitude for the long poem, and that ('Comedian...' aside) he comes closest to success in those poems which are in essence assemblages of constituent parts: an *e pluribus unum*.

Stevens wrote to Belitt that he had no better idea than his critic what would happen next; but despite the perhaps over-generous praise received for the blank verse of *Owl's Clover*, it was becoming clear to him that he needed to condense his style and sharpen his approach – and it is possible that at the time of his letter he had already started composing the poems which would become 'The Man with the Blue Guitar' (1937): on 17 March 1937 he wrote to 'Latimer' that during the preceding winter he had composed nearly 40 short pieces, about 25 of which he felt were up to standard (*L* 316). Two were printed in the British magazine *Twentieth Century Verse* the next month, and 13 as 'The Man with the Blue Guitar' in *Poetry* (May 1937); but not until Knopf published *The Man with the Blue Guitar and Other Poems* in October 1937 did the poem of 33 sections appear. The 'other poems' consisted principally of a version of 'Owl's Clover' severely pruned to 607 lines, as if in token of the author's already growing dissatisfaction with this poem. This also marked the diminution and then termination of his relations with 'Latimer', whose financial difficulties forced him to abandon his Alcestis Press. Initially there had been the possibility of his being interested in 'Blue Guitar', but as it became clearer to Stevens that Knopf (who would more than once in Stevens's case find himself irritated by dealings involving other publishers[18]) wished to have it, that receded; to be replaced by a scheme for 'Latimer' to issue a limited edition amounting to the 'Collected Poems' up to that date. This would have involved a considerable financial risk to the publisher, and so Stevens (who seems to have figured as the one stable point in Leippert's progressively disintegrating world), instructed by Knopf's disapproval, had to abandon the project. In his last letters to 'Latimer' Stevens was advising him to go to Ceylon – a country of which his knowledge was confined to his recently opened correspondence with L.C. van Geyzel, descended from Dutch colonists, who had sent him some representative items. It was perhaps appropriate that Stevens should encourage a person who was in many ways a figment of his imagination, to emigrate to a land which was a wholly mental construct.

For all his operatic dissimulations, 'Latimer' had been an essential part of Stevens's return to writing, and should be given due credit for the remarkable burst of creativity in which, twelve years after his belated first volume, Stevens issued three new books of verse in successive years. In addition to stimulating the poetry, by his interrogations 'Latimer' encouraged Stevens to develop a rationale for his art, which led toward the critical prose; most importantly of all perhaps, he enabled Stevens for the first time to enter into a sustained dialogue about his writing: and by asking in a non-adversarial way the kind of question which a radical antagonist might have put, he helped Stevens to formulate his own position with regard to the social and political context, and, indeed, to conceive of his writing as a dialogic engagement. Thus, from the apparent indifference to the reader that *Harmonium* exemplified, *Ideas of Order*, *Owl's Clover*, and *The Man with the Blue Guitar* show an ascending graph of awareness of a contingent world and how it might look to a contemporary; '...Blue Guitar' goes furthest in its imagination of a dialogue between opposing viewpoints, which are not (as in *Owl's Clover*) lost in the solvent of Stevens's rhetoric, but inhabit the very voice of the poem and inhibit its incipient sublimities. 'He talks out his ideas', marvelled Eda Lou Walton in her review (*NYTBR* 24 October 1937), and marked the poem as a 'distinct advance'; Ruth Lechlitner was similarly appreciative, and in the *New Republic* that November Williams, whilst reserving his highest praise for 'The Men that are Falling', strongly approved the rhetorical economy forced on Stevens by the four-beat line of his new poem. Following Pound's antipathy to the pentameter line, he declared that 'five beats have a strange effect on a modern poet; they make him think that he wants to think', and justifiably took the turgidities of *Owl's Clover* as his evidence.

Williams may still have been smarting from Stevens's application to his own work of the label 'anti-poetic'; but two of his scepticisms seem appropriate: he doubted the rumours that Stevens had turned definitely to the left, and he asserted that 'though he seems at times not to wish to acknowledge it, he is primarily a lyric poet'. In the overall perspective of Stevens's life and career, it seems strange that a leftward inclination had ever been suspected (although, as Filreis painstakingly suggests, being was not always the finale of seeming, in this regard); and in the context of '...Blue Guitar', the degree to which the antagonistic interlocutors are actually answered by the poem, as distinct from being incorporated into the strategies of its rhetoric, is debatable. They are like the huddled masses of 'Sad Strains...', who cry without knowing for what and require an order beyond their speech – thus necessitating and validating the poet-orator who will do so for them.[19] The guitar may well be a more democratic instrument than the harmonium, and much better for the blues; but its player makes fewer concessions than might be supposed to his audience, who compliantly require exactly what he wants to provide for them: a rhapsodic statement of things as they are. Because Stevens had been supposed to be so far on the right wing of aesthetic absolutism, he did not need to move very far toward the centre, to make a disproportionate impression of having shifted his ground. Entranced by its deceptive clarities, readers did not always notice the overpowering energy of longing behind that 'imagined pine' and 'imagined jay' with which '...Blue Guitar' closes. Even the last poem in the book, 'The Men that are Falling', however unclear its affiliations in respect of the emergent civil war in Spain, is clear about the duty this devolves upon the poet to come up with the appropriate modes of revealing desire.[20]

And this, finally, may be what happened to Stevens in the 1930s, and what that highly politicised era accomplished for him: he entered the decade virtually silent, and associated with a 'creed outworn'; but by manifesting an unanticipated ability to respond to the times, he managed to evade the fate of being tarred with the brush of the old guard, even if he had not moved as decisively leftward as some supposed. The polarising debates of these years defined his artistic mission for him, as nothing in the previous decade had: he saw his role as poet to be that of resisting the conscriptive forces brought to bear, by functioning as spokesman for the people who, he believed, needed more than the definitive ideologies on offer. The purpose of his poetry became precisely that of opposing itself to political or economic determinisms, by asserting a 'world elsewhere' of imaginative transfiguration: the 1930s gave him the opportunity to assert his notions of poetry as a 'slight' transcendence *within* rather than – as with *Harmonium* – in detachment from, a social context. The animating sense of his life, that poetry and economics were at odds, became a message of the relevant irrelevance of art that centralised it rather than marginalised it (nobody, after all, bothered to tell Crispin what sort of poems they wanted him to write). Out of this period, for better or worse, came Stevens's increasing concentration on notions of the poet as a kind of necessary hero and secular priest; and we would be justified in applying to the 1930s in general the comment Stevens made about his involvement with *New Masses*: 'merely finding myself in that *milieu* was an extraordinarily stimulating thing' (*L* 296).

6
1937–47: Helping People Live their Lives

In his jacket statement for *The Man with the Blue Guitar and Other Poems* (1937) Stevens defined 'Owl's Clover' as concerning itself with the 'opposition between things as they are and things imagined', and 'Blue Guitar' with the 'incessant conjunctions' between these two categories (*OP2* 233). As early as 1923, 'Academic Discourse at Havana' (as subsequently titled) had opposed 'politic man' to the 'imagination'; and one way of thinking about Stevens's poetry of the 1930s is to see it as an interrogation of that opposition, which finished by subsuming politics as a (somewhat mechanistic) phase of the imagination. The decade was one in which Stevens was preoccupied with making the appropriate adjustments to times of change in both his careers: his paper on 'Insurance and Social Change' (*OP2* 233ff.) was published in the same year as *The Man with the Blue Guitar*. Just as in his poems he was trying to preserve poetry from subordination to extraliterary concerns, so in this piece he suggested the need of the insurance market to remain flexibly responsive to the changing times, in order to ward off any danger of government appropriation (i.e. nationalisation); and both poetry and insurance could be described as pragmatic responses to a world conceived idealistically ('The objective of all of us is to live in a world in which nothing unpleasant can happen. ... Insurance is the most easily understood geometry for calculating how to bring the thing about' *OP2* 234). In 'Surety and Fidelity Claims' (1938), the description he gave of the job emphasised its distance from the reality with which it dealt: 'you never see a dollar. You sign a lot of drafts. You see surprisingly few people. You do the greater part of your work either in your own office or in lawyers' offices. You don't even see the country; you see law offices and hotel rooms' (*OP2* 237). The end product of this concern with paper realities is a man 'who comes almost to believe that he and his papers constitute a single creature, consisting principally of hands and eyes' (*OP2* 239). Having brought this odd monster to birth, however, Stevens dismissed it as representing the truth; which, he insisted, was that the real 'human interest' of the situation lay in the humanity of the surety claims man himself.

His assertion of the human element in what might otherwise seem an abstract process is similar to his emphasis in 1937 on the 'presence of the determining personality' of the artist as an essential factor. As 'Surety and Fidelity Claims' shows the variety of objective situations that may confront the subjectivity of the claims man – to which the adequacy of his response will depend on the person he is as much as on a book of rules – so one of the tests of the poet would be a quality of adaptability; as Stevens put it in a letter to 'Latimer', 'the only possible order of life is one in which all order is incessantly changing' (*L* 292–3). This Protean requirement was not well met by the discursive, formally monotonous sprawl of *Owl's Clover* (in either version); but his account of 'Blue Guitar' as given on the dust-jacket pointed both the difference from its predecessor and the way forward: considering the important spiritual function of poetry, Stevens told the reader he had been 'making notes on the subject in the form of short poems'. This conjunction of the momentous with the haphazard was accompanied by a democratisation of attitude; gone was the hectoring assertiveness of the earlier poem, to be replaced by a conception of the poet as 'any man of imagination' (*OP*2 233). Gone, too – or at least diminished – was the defensiveness underlying his alternative title for *Harmonium*: it now seemed that 'preliminary minutiae' were the nearest one could hope to come to any 'grand poem'. Such a conception was truer to the circumstances of his composing, as well as enabling the retention of an air of provisionality that countered any tendency toward monolithic solidification: in June 1938 he told 'Latimer' that what he had already done was merely 'preliminary'; for him, thinking about poetry was 'an affair of weekends and holidays, a matter of walking to and from the office. ... I very much like the idea of something ahead; I don't care to make [an] exhaustive effort to reach it, to see what it is. It is like the long time that I am going to live somewhere where I don't live now' (*L* 333).

He made these remarks in the context of the decision to abandon any plans for the Alcestis Press to issue his 'collected' poems; for Stevens, a book of poetry continued to be a 'damned serious affair': his delayed first volume and his later procrastination over the *Collected Poems* alike indicated a fear of the literary equivalent of premature burial. His stated aversion to re-reading his own books seems part of a disinclination to regard the past as fixed; and titles such as *Ideas of Order* or *Parts of a World* (1942) stress the plurality of contents rather than the singularity of the volume. By virtue of being non-profit-making ventures, the limited editions issued by the Alcestis Press may be seen as a way of acquiring what Pierre Bourdieu has defined as 'symbolic capital'; while simultaneously their pleasingness as artefacts bore physical witness to values other than the purely commercial, and contributed to the spiritual effect. They were a kind of secular prayer-book, part of the world and yet beyond it, their specialness a function of the resistance to overt commodification signified by their relative unavailability in the market-place. The trade editions issued by Knopf for however modest profit were different in kind, and made an implicitly different statement about both poetry and poet (Stevens would experience some difficulty over what in 1945 he defined as Knopf's 'acute sense of property' in respect of his poetry).[1] A reader coming across poems in a current little magazine would suppose the material to be entirely new; but poems gathered in a volume would for the most part be *not* new: their collocation was a statement of interrelationships within the *oeuvre*, and a definition of the poet's progress (or lack of it). If the poem published in a little magazine was living tissue, then the context of the collected volume was a step toward embalming: the implicit difference is between reading something for the first time, and re-reading it. Unlike his two most successful contemporaries, Frost and Eliot, Stevens did not issue preliminary *Collected Poems*; instead he preferred to present his various collections as successive versions of work in progress, hoping thereby to temper any institutionalisation of his work.

Having thawed out at 40, as Williams put it, and having thawed out again at 50 or so, Stevens had no desire to freeze over at 60 – even while humorously acknowledging that a poet should be 30 not 60 (*L* 343). The matter was very much on his mind in the late 1930s; his comments on the adverse consequences of Eliot's 'prodigious reputation' (referred to in Chapter 1) were published in 1938; and, confirming his own status, that year eleven of his poems (including 'Sunday Morning' and '...Key West') were published in the *Oxford Anthology of American Poetry* (eds, Benét and Pearson), together with a 'Note on Poetry' (*OP*2 240) that almost defiantly eschewed any theoretical account of his poems, and instead related their existence to his 'need' to have written them. Yet it was the theoretical content of his writing that was coming to the fore – perhaps best seen in the replacement of 'Latimer' by Hi Simons as his principal correspondent: the first was publisher and *agent provocateur*, the second was essentially a worshipper at the shrine, who was compiling a bibliography and would produce some critical essays on the poetry before his sudden death in 1945. The kind of enquiry Simons made was more an invitation to Stevens to reflect on what he had written, than a stimulation to write more; and so far as he provoked the poet, it was to regret at having run the risk of killing his poems by leaden explanation. 'There is a kind of secrecy between a poet and his poem', Stevens asserted, 'which, once violated, affects the integrity of the poet' (*L* 361): an interesting revival of notions of secrecy and violation that must have been implicit in Elsie's earlier dismay at the plundering of 'her' poems. In the longer run Henry Church would be a more significant correspondent than Simons, but even he encouraged the poet's theoretical bent: it was through their association that Stevens came to deliver the papers 'The Noble Rider...' and 'The Figure of the Youth...'. But writing to Church in June 1939, he tried to disentangle himself from the perspective in which he had most recently been viewed: 'What counts, I suppose, is one's relation to contemporary ideas. ... I am, in the long run, interested in pure poetry. No doubt from the Marxian point of view this sort of thing is incredible, but pure poetry is older and tougher than Marx and will remain so. My own way out toward the future involves a confidence in the spiritual role of the poet' (*L* 340).

The 1940s would be a decade during which Stevens spent much energy in thoughts upon that subject. It would also be the period in which public ratification of his status gathered momentum, from the special number of the *Harvard Advocate* devoted to his work in 1940, to his induction into the National Institute of Arts and Letters in 1946, and receipt of his first honorary degree in 1947. During these years he published *Parts of a World* (Knopf; 1942), *Notes toward a Supreme Fiction* (1942) and *Esthétique du Mal* (1945) in limited editions from the Cummington Press, and *Transport to Summer* (Knopf; 1947). He delivered the following papers in the following places: 'The Noble Rider and the Sound of Words' (Princeton, May 1941); 'The Figure of the Youth as Virile Poet' (Mount Holyoke College, August 1943); 'Three Academic Pieces' (Harvard, February 1947); 'Effects of Analogy' (Yale, March 1948: repeated at Mount Holyoke); and 'Imagination as Value'

(Columbia, September 1948). I should say that the story of the 1940s was of Stevens's not always successful efforts to resist the effects of such incorporation; as he gained in public stature, the danger of turning into a statue, an Ozymandian item of High Culture, increased. If *Harmonium* was criticised for not taking itself seriously enough, then the essential struggle of these years lay in remembering the playfulness embedded in – and indeed constituent of – his high seriousness: it lay in protecting the integrity of minutiae against encroachments of a grand design, by preserving the balance between poetic occasion and quasi-philosophical superstructure. To adjust Auden's words about Yeats, the public life of the poet needed to be kept from his poems: too great a concern with the 'role of the poet' ran counter to the production of 'pure poetry'.

Public realities in the closing 1930s and the first half of the 1940s were, of course, virtually impossible to ignore, as events in Europe and then Asia developed their implacable momentum. In 1936–7 revelations about the repressive nature of Stalin's regime, indicated by the infamous 'show trials' in Moscow, caused splits and perturbation amongst Soviet sympathisers, whose position was calamitously undermined by his non-aggression pact with Hitler in August 1939. The Munich agreement in the autumn of 1938 between Chamberlain and Hitler had secured a phoney peace followed, after September 1939, by nearly nine months of the so-called 'Phoney War', which abruptly terminated with the unforeseen German invasion of France through the Low Countries in May 1940; by the end of June the British Expeditionary Force had been expelled (via Dunkirk), France had fallen and Paris was under German occupation (and Stalin seized the opportunity to invade Poland and Finland). There then ensued the Battle of Britain, in which Germany attempted but failed to inflict a similar lightning defeat by means of air-power; which strategy was superseded that autumn by the more attritional process of night-time bombing raids on London and other British cities. For Americans, the spectacle was one which excited their horror and sympathies (mostly on the British/French side), whilst at the same time stimulating an intense desire not to become involved. The foreign policy of the Roosevelt administration during these years consisted in trying to circumvent consitutional obstacles, so as to send as much of the desperately needed supplies to Britain as possible, without incurring the wrath of a Congress determined not to embroil the nation in another European war. As early as October 1937, Roosevelt had warned a Chicago audience against trusting to 'isolation and neutrality', but that same year a Gallup poll suggested that 94 per cent of Americans wished to do just that; Congress, however, had shifted ground sufficiently to approve the 'Lend-Lease' bill in March 1941. There then occurred the two decisive events of the war: in June 1941 Hitler's armies invaded Russia, and – not to be outdone in folly – the Japanese mounted a devastating air attack on the US Naval base at Pearl Harbor that December, bringing the USA into the war and accomplishing at a stroke everything that British foreign policy had been aiming for since it began.

Although as with the First World War Stevens's knowledge of events came at second hand, those affected were closer to him. Foremost amongst these was Henry Church, whose inherited fortune had enabled him to live the life of patron of the arts at Ville d'Avray near Paris, but who had been unable to return because of the war. Church was founder and co-editor of the French little magazine *Mesures*, to which Stevens had subscribed through Anatole Vidal, his Paris bookseller; Church first contacted Stevens in the spring of 1939, seeking permission to publish French translations of some *Harmonium* poems in a special American number that summer. As events forced him to stay in America and he looked for ways of salvaging what he could of activities he valued, as well as for ways of helping those left behind, Church's acquaintanceship with Stevens grew and deepened; and through him the poet was brought much closer than might otherwise have been the case to the realities of life under Nazi occupation. When he gave his paper at Mount Holyoke in August 1943, he sat next to Jean Wahl, a Jewish philosopher and friend of Church, who had been interned in the infamous transit camp at Drancy and probably owed his release (and therefore his life, as most of the internees were *en route* to Auschwitz) to Church's ability to ransom him. Jean Paulhan, co-editor of *Mesures*, was (correctly) suspected of involvement with the French Resistance, and was subjected to Gestapo interrogation (which he withstood).[2] The active engagement of these intellectuals in a deadly struggle gave Stevens models for heroic conduct and its connection with the life of the mind, as well as affirming what he saw as his spiritual affinity with France (however unrepresentative they may have been of the behaviour of the majority, under German occupation). Examples such as theirs were nutritive to Stevens, during the years in which he focused on the role of the poet, as much as on the function of poetry.

As with his fellow countrymen, however, for many of whom 1939 was more remarkable for the film of *The Wizard of Oz* than the outbreak of war in Europe, it took Stevens time to move from an essentially isolationist position to one supporting American intervention. The war came at an inappropriate moment for him, psychologically: the family had taken a comparatively rare holiday together, at a resort on the Maine coast; out of this came the poem 'Variations on a Summer Day' (1940), a poem, he told Simons, from which he had deliberately excluded thoughts of the relation between poetry and a world at war, in order to concentrate on 'agreeable things' (*L* 346). Another agreeable thing occurring at this time, if somewhat ironically, was the World's Fair in New York (1939–40). Stevens paid many visits to this, in the company of his family and business associates, and clearly delighted in the spectacle and the various exhibitions. Erected on the site of a former ash dump, the fair's very situation symbolised the rejection of a wasted past and the affirmation of a technologically optimistic vision of the future, to which it was dedicated (several of the exhibits made play with notions of time-travel). At the Medicine exhibit there was the educational Transparent Man, who may have contributed to Stevens's 'man of glass' in 'Asides on the Oboe' (1940); there were numerous state-of-the-art displays of virtual realities; but Stevens's personal favourite, according to Wilson Taylor, was the French Pavilion, at which his visits would always terminate with a drink and a meal.[3] This was the peak of his commodification of France: here was more than the literature and the occasional *objet d'art* he had hitherto acquired (and would continue to acquire); here were art exhibitions and an attempt to import a whole Gallic ambiance for New York's consumption. It seems appropriate that Stevens's interest in purchasing an electrically-lit stained-glass forest scene that was a feature of the pavilion foundered (according to Taylor) when what had been perceived as a uniform surface was discovered from the back to consist of inserted pieces of glass of very irregular thicknesses, that required equally diverse strengths of light-bulb arranged behind, to achieve even illumination. This unexpected diversity of what had been perceived as homogeneous could stand as an image for Stevens's view of France; yet even he, visiting the pavilion after May 1940 (the fair closed that autumn), must have known that this futurist extravaganza was in reality a souvenir of the past. In 1939–40 he had spent much time theatre-going with Holly; and the World's Fair offered, technologically, a series of *coups de théâtre*; but by 1940 he had seen that these were easily upstaged by current events, and that (as in 'Of Modern Poetry') the 'theatre of war' would predominate (the phrase, interestingly, occurs in *The Magnetic Mountain*).

In the winter of early 1940 Stevens, unusually, took his wife and daughter with him on his visit to Florida, on what turned out to be the last visit he paid to Key West, and the last family holiday they spent together. The previous summer they had visited Pennsylvania, apparently due to Elsie Stevens's desire to look into her ancestry; but her interest in genealogy was one which her husband pursued enthusiastically with regard to his own bloodline. In both their cases there was a superficial – and somewhat snobbish – reason: to establish eligibility for membership of exclusive societies based on the nationality of traceable forebears. But although Stevens's consuming interest in genealogy during the war years can be viewed as another instance of self-indulgent escapism, it is better seen as one form of his reaction to the general spectacle of death, and a desire that death should not amount to simple waste. His elder brother had died at the end of 1937, having spent the last few years of his life asking for (and receiving) handouts from his two other brothers; John, Stevens's younger brother, died in July 1940, and his sister Elizabeth in February 1943. It is perhaps ironic, if entirely human, that Stevens's interest in his family history should awaken just as the other members of his generation were dying out; but surely a 60-year-old man's sense of the communality of death was a point at which he could feel a legitimate connection to the collective deaths of war. These were years in which, for Stevens as for many, the questions of 'how to live, what to do' were intimately linked to those of how to die, what to do. His awareness of the war and its likely consequences altered in response to the news: if at the very end of 1939 he could evoke the predicament of a soldier waiting for the call of duty on the Maginot Line, and thinking how poetry might best serve such a man (*L* 346), by the end of August 1940 his imagery drew on the current London Blitz, declaring that he felt 'pretty much as a man must feel in a shelter waiting for bombing to start. ... the climate is changing, and it seems pretty clearly to be becoming less and less a climate of literature' (*L* 365).

In the *Partisan Review*'s questionnaire about 'The Situation in American Writing' (Summer 1939), he had replied to a question concerning American entry into any world war, and the responsibility of writers in that situation, as a 'very theoretical question respecting an extremely practical state of affairs. ... The role of the writer in war remains the fundamental role of the writer intensified and concentrated' (*OP2* 310). In some ways, however, his own practical response to the darkening international situation was highly theoretical: 'Man and Bottle' and 'Of Modern Poetry' were published as 'Two Theoretic Poems' in May 1940, and even after Pearl Harbor 'Examination of the Hero in a Time of War' (April 1942) was not a poem to impress a reader with any sense of immediacy. I think it can be argued that the pressures of war were harmful to Stevens's writing, to the degree that they encouraged a violation of the privacy between him and his poems, evidenced in an increasingly obtrusive theoretical superstructure. The reasons for this awkwardness are suggested by his answer to an earlier question, when he declared that 'writing poetry is one thing; publishing it is another. Often I wish that I did not publish it, because the act of publishing it involves a seriousness different from the seriousness of writing it' (*OP2* 310). The saving levity of 'Blue Guitar' was absent from the programmatic inflations of 'The Woman That Had More Babies Than That' and 'Life on a Battleship', published in *Partisan Review* (Spring 1939); poems which saw him revert to *Owl's Clover* mode (and which, like it, were omitted from *Collected Poems*, although included in *Parts of a World*). Combining with his own desire to make a contribution to the theory of poetry (see *L* 585) and his appetite for the long poem, the war may have altered for the worse Stevens's conception of his relations with his readership. Partly as a result of his correspondence with Simons, he was responding to the implication that explicability (i.e. the presence of a basis in theory) was a bridge between himself and his audience – to ignore which in wartime was tantamount to irresponsibility. He saw that war altered his relations with both reality and the imagination; so he felt inhibited from taking the liberties that are evident in the earliest poem in *Parts of a World*. In 'A Rabbit as King of the Ghosts' (October 1937), the actual rabbit digging up bulbs in his

garden (see *L* 321) was transfigured into an anti-hero of Emersonian solipsism, in a poem which both celebrates and mocks such
powers of transcendence (*CP* 209). 'Examination of the Hero...', by
contrast, last-published and printed last in the volume, is quite dull
poetry, in which the desire to articulate a train of thought has
overwhelmed the poetic occasion. It is true that no other poet could
write quite like this, but questionable whether any would wish to.

The qualites by which Stevens deserves a place at the forefront
of modern poetry – which were felicitously described by Randall
Jarrell as the poems in which he was 'all windhover and no Jesuit'
– were not best represented in *Parts of a World*, even though shortly
after publication he declared it to be his best book. Knopf issued it
on 8 September 1942, in an edition of 1000 copies at \$2; all but a
few of its 64 poems had been published in various little magazines
between late 1937 and early 1942 ('Extracts from Addresses to the
Academy of Fine Ideas' was published in Oscar Williams's
anthology *New Poems: 1940*). The principles of arrangement were
different from those previously followed: whereas in the cases of
Harmonium and – to a lesser degree – *Ideas of Order* Stevens had
broken up sequences first published in magazines and disrupted
the chronology of composition, here for the most part he preserved
chronology, and invariably kept the arrangements of magazine
publication. He departed from chronology to the extent that the
twelve poems commencing the volume were not the earliest,
having been first published as 'Canonica' in the *Southern Review*
(Autumn 1938); but he retained their original order. Expressing a
vivid discontent with single systems or permanent points of rest,
they well reflected the book's title (derived from the later
'Landscape with Boat'); and 'Dry Loaf', restlessly evoking artistic,
natural, and military compulsions, gained force from its
reappearance in the context of actual war.[4] Stevens heightened the
relation between his book and the global conflict by ending it with
a prose statement on 'Poetry and War' (*OP2* 241–2), in which (if I
understand him, and I am not sure that I do) he implied that
poetry and war have a similarity, insofar as each involves a
confrontation with things as they are for which the imagination
proposes alternative arrangements: achieved by the individual
poem or by force of arms, in each case. In other words, war may be
the failure of politics, but it is in some ways a radically practical
extension of poetics: the soldier and the poet are both
interventionists. In this view, Stevens is clearly seen to be very far

from any imagist or objectivist position; as he wrote to Simons in February 1942:

> When a poet makes his imagination the imagination of other people, he does so by making them see the world through his eyes. Most modern activity is the undoing of that very job. The world has been painted; most modern activity is getting rid of the paint to get at the world itself. Powerful integrations of the imagination are difficult to get away from. ... This power is one of the poet's chief powers.
>
> (*L* 402)

This line of thinking informs the opening metaphor of *Notes toward a Supreme Fiction*, the series of poems he would begin composing the following month (see *L* 443); but the immediate context of their discussion was the lecture Stevens had delivered at Princeton in May 1941. Although he had been most unwilling to do this, it was a sign of his increasing self-confidence (and of his desire to oblige Church, who had financed the series) that he at last consented. 'The Noble Rider and the Sound of Words' was published in *The Language of Poetry* (ed. Allen Tate) in 1942, along with the papers given by Philip Wheelwright, Cleanth Brooks, and I.A. Richards; it would be nine years before it could be considered in the context of Stevens's other lectures, when Knopf brought out *The Necessary Angel* (1951). Taking as its starting point the image from Plato's *Phaedrus* of the human soul as charioteer with mismatched horses (which seems to have contributed, years before, to the closing image of 'Le Monocle...'), the paper set out to examine the history of the idea of nobility, as suggested by a chronological sequence of arbitrarily chosen equestrian images. The procedures and methodology are pure Stevens: choosing a topic which could hardly be adequately rendered other than in a scholarly treatise, and confidently appropriating for analysis a three-dimensional object (Verrocchio's statue of Colleoni in Venice) which he can only have known at second hand. From Colleoni (whose name commemorated his fabled tri-testicularity: a source of nobility Stevens overlooked) to Clark Mills's statue of Andrew Jackson, to a reproduction of a painting of a carousel called 'Wooden Horses', Stevens plotted an increasing inaccessibility of concepts of nobility resulting from the essentially democratic pressure away from the elevated toward the demotic, from the connotative use of language to the denotative, partly as a result of the levelling effect exerted by the era of mass communication. In a sense this reprised the argument of 'Blue Guitar'; and Stevens saw the process as loss of the capacity to respond to an important spiritual register, without which we are less than ourselves. He saw it as the poet's function to restore this capacity, and illustrated its benefits by citing lines from Wordsworth's sonnet 'Composed upon Westminster Bridge', to show how a particular integration of the imagination could transfigure a scene without misrepresenting it.[5] It is doubtful that Stevens's audience at Princeton would have had a paraphrasable notion of his argument – any more than most readers do – but they could not have been left in any doubt about the importance he attached to his theme:

> What makes the poet the potent figure that he is, or was, or ought to be, is that he creates the world to which we turn incessantly and without knowing it and that he gives to life the supreme fictions without which we are unable to conceive of it.
>
> (*NA* 31)

Between the delivery of 'Noble Rider...' and the composition of *Notes toward a Supreme Fiction* in March/April 1942, the USA had entered the war; so the pressure of reality had increased. In December 1941 he had been approached by the Cummington Press in Massachusetts about the possibility of their publishing a limited edition of his poems; that month and at the beginning of 1942 he was busy finalising *Parts of a World* to send to Knopf, but by the beginning of June he had his typescript ready for Katharine Frazier at the Press; and *Notes* appeared on 13 October in an edition of 273 (3 presentation copies, 80 signed, at $4.50, and 190 unsigned at $3.00); he had declined the Press's offer of payment.[6] Stevens arranged for copies of both *Parts of a World* and *Notes* to be specially bound by Gerhard Gerlach and was, as he made clear, willing to pay up to $150 for this – insisting that the effect he desired was dignified rather than foppish (*L* 418). An effect of dignity rather than foppishness was in essence what he wished to achieve by his poetry; and he may have succeeded too well in this, for he grumbled to three of his correspondents that there had been no indication in reviews of *Parts of a World* that the reviewer had actually enjoyed the book (*L* 430, 433, 436). He commented that reviews were significant only insofar as they contributed to a poet's being 'accepted' by his readership; but in fact the reviews did indicate a degree of acceptance. The poet Weldon Kees, for example, writing in the *New Republic* (September 1942) judged that Stevens's 'distinguished place in American poetry' had never been securer, but at the same time suggested that his audience was likely to be smaller than that of any other 'poet of his importance'. Horace Gregory (*Accent*) thought the book his 'most important since *Harmonium*', but found himself disliking the longer poems. Louise Bogan (*New Yorker*) thought him 'more and more philosophic, closed in, and obscure', and Mary Colum (*NYTBR*) diagnosed too great a dominance of what she called the 'speculative instinct'. Hi Simons – who would later take issue with the evaluations of Gregory and Colum – contributed a review to *Poetry* which stressed the poet's relativism, and his growing search for a humanist solution. Predictably, Louis Untermeyer thought there was still a good deal of foppishness to be found in Stevens (*Saturday Review*).

Kees's comments were quite fair, insofar as the initial print-run of 1000 was not one which suggested that Knopf expected heavy sales for *Parts of a World*; three years after first publication he issued a second printing of 500, but the total remained modest, compared with the figures for an equally non-populist poet such as Eliot: whose *Collected Poems 1909–1935* (1936) had been published in the USA with a run of 4700, and whose *Four Quartets* was published in 1943 in an edition of 3500 (Eliot's American print-runs were smaller than in Britain – where Stevens, of course, was not published until later). The year 1943 saw a second edition of *Notes* (330 copies at $2), as well as the publication of two reviews. Blackmur in *Partisan Review* emphasised that the poem was a 'set of notes' rather than the proposition of a system, and Dudley Fitts in the *Saturday Review* saw it as a confirmed development beyond the earlier poetry 'from decoration *sui causa* towards philosophical statement'. Others, however, were less pleased with Stevens's progression beyond *Harmonium*: in his influential essay first published in his book *The Anatomy of Nonsense* (1943) and several times reprinted, Yvor Winters summed it up as 'The Hedonist's Progress'; although Winters could find bad poems by Stevens from the *Harmonium* period, he asserted that he couldn't think of any good ones after 1923. He ignored *Notes* along with the bulk of Stevens's work from the previous decade; and this may be taken to mark the beginning of a trend toward a preference for *Harmonium*, running counter to the actual effort Stevens had made in the 1930s to dissociate himself from that era of his creativity. This trend was strengthened by the poems by which he was increasingly represented in anthologies, which were weighted toward his first volume (by 1952, when he came to compile his *Selected Poems* for the British market, Stevens himself would choose a preponderance of *Harmonium* material).

Whereas Eliot, between the first edition of *The Sacred Wood* (1920) and the second (1928), could relegate the status of poetry to that of a 'superior amusement', and in *East Coker* (March 1940) could assert that 'the poetry does not matter', for Stevens the case was entirely otherwise. He could never, as did Eliot in that quartet's second part, comment on the poem as 'a way of putting it – not very satisfactory'; for in his universe ways of putting it were virtually all there are. When the Eliot of 1928 had passed on to 'the relation of poetry to the spiritual and social life of its time and other times', he found poetry diminished in significance; whereas Stevens's consideration of that relation from the mid-1930s onward made him consider poetry ever more central.[7] It is not a question of deciding one or other poet is right; although it may well be such an attitude in Eliot that made Stevens define him to Church as a 'negative rather than a positive force' (October 1940; *L* 378): it is, rather, a question of appreciating just how important poetry was for Stevens. At the end of March 1943 he was again discussing with Church the idea of a Chair of Poetry at Harvard, and the names of both Frost and Eliot (again) came up; Stevens then declared that 'the belief in poetry is a magnificent fury, or it is nothing' (*L* 446): one could draw the (*possibly* unintended) inference that neither of these better-selling and more celebrated poets exemplified that fury. It happened that by then both men had already written their best work; Stevens's possession of – or by – such a belief enabled him to keep on writing good poems until he was virtually on his death-bed. It is almost certainly not an exaggeration to assert that poetry was the most important element in his life, exceeding any human relationship he had: for what, except for it, did he feel love?

Notes toward a Supreme Fiction was the work in which he addressed the many issues bound up with his ideas about poetry and its relation to the actual world; in it he tried to render an account of how he felt poetry mattered enormously to a world at war, and why he felt that its mattering enormously depended on its not making too many concessions to the claims of such a world. The letter he wrote to Simons just before starting to compose *Notes* enlarged on the issue of poetry as 'escapism' (touched on in 'Noble Rider...'), and glossed it as 'benign illusion' (*L* 402); discussing the poem in a letter to Church (December 1942), he saw how this would lead on to the question of 'illusion as value' (*L* 431); *Notes* is a subjectivist's *credo* in an objectivist world, but rendered in a manner that does justice to the inevitable provisionality of such enunciations, since the last thing Stevens desires is to propound a system. To return to Eliot's comment quoted above, Stevens would not *say* the poetry does not matter, because in his best work the extent to which it does not matter is already implicit in his way of putting it; the extent to which it does matter is both explicit and implicit. *Notes* is some of Stevens's best work; along with – in an entirely different mode – 'The Comedian', it seems to me his most successful long poem. Thematically and structurally there are similarities to 'Blue Guitar', which he also considered to be 'notes'; but the ambition was greater, and his use of the tercet rather than the distich gave greater scope and flexibility, whilst imposing a similar restraint. Stevens knows why it is noble for his rabbit to conceive itself the centre of its universe; but he knows, also, what is both ludicrous and dangerous in its doing so. As he had written 25 years before *Notes*, he knew noble accents and inescapable rhythms; but he also knew that the blackbird was involved in what he knew.

But if the blackbird was an epistemological and rhetorical necessity, so was the angel: the poet's function is to be sufficiently attentive to both, and *Notes* is the poem in which Stevens set forth his dominant preoccupations. As much of his poetry of the 1930s had been a response to the social and political pressures of those years, so *Notes* was produced by the pressure of war, and in some ways can be read as his *apologia* – or at least an explanation of why his continuing to be the sort of poet he was, represented the best service he could offer to the common cause. The spring of 1942 was a dark time for the allies, with the tide yet to turn visibly in their favour; to write about supreme fictions in the prevalent military and political context might well have seemed like playing checkers on the Maginot Line, ignoring the fact that it had been overrun by the enemy. Sending a copy to Robert Frost two days after publication, Stevens wrote that it would be 'nice ... to sit in the garden and imagine that we were living in a world in which everything was as it ought to be' (*L* 423); that same day, Eliot's *Little Gidding* was first published in the *New English Weekly*, and this poem's clear addressing of the national predicament offers an apparent contrast to the serene abstraction evident in Stevens.[8] Or so it might be thought; but just as it happened to be the case that *Notes* was written while Eliot was *not* writing *Little Gidding* (he completed an unsatisfactory first draft in summer 1941, but did not radically revise and finalise until a year later), so the things with which it deals are not found in Eliot's poem – whose religious synthesis it repudiates, whose historical perspective it does not reflect, and whose communitarianism it neglects, in favour of a focus that is essentially individualist, even if of general relevance. It seems clear that *Little Gidding* was conceived by Eliot as his poetic *chef d'oeuvre*; but although *Notes* can be and has been read as Stevens's equivalent, the ambition was always modified by its embedded provisionality. Although Stevens may well have felt the need to declare himself, in the context of world war, it is possible that he could only have done so by means of a specialised limited edition.

In 'The Noble Rider...' Stevens had rejected notions that a poet should acknowledge any 'sociological or political obligation', and asserted that 'his role, in short, is to help people to live their lives' (*NA* 27, 29): the implication was that this true role is best fulfilled by eschewing specious ones, such as social relevance. This may have been in order to distance himself from his 1930s incarnation; yet even that decade had offered some odd confirmations of the escapist tendency: in 1931 the song 'Life is just a bowl of cherries' enjoyed great popularity in America, when large numbers of those listening to it were experiencing life as anything but that; and the 1935 Astaire/Rogers musical film *Top Hat*, set amid globe-trotting American high society in a fantasy London and Venice, envisioned a world utterly removed from the circumstances of its audiences, without impairing its popularity then or its staying power now.[9] At the time *Notes* was first published, Stevens was in his own family confronted by what he took to be a misplaced sense of sociological or political obligation, on the part of his daughter Holly, who had decided to withdraw from Vassar because it felt pointless to be there in wartime; and his attempts to dissuade her are relevant. He argued that *because* of the 'huge struggle for survival that is now going on' it was essential not to have a knee-jerk reaction to the contemporary, but to maintain a contemplative distance in order to establish true priorities. 'Take my word for it', he surprisingly wrote, 'that making your living is a waste of time. None of the great things in life have anything to do with making your living' (*L* 426).

This might sound like the rejection of one of the founding tenets of his own philosophy (as instilled by his own father). There may have been an unvoiced gender context (daughters of well-off fathers don't need to get a job *versus* the modern woman has to make her contribution too), as well as the evidently voiced desire 18-year-old Holly had, to be free of parental constraints. But Stevens's denunciation of making one's living is striking. It might mean that he had now found it to be so, since the things for which he had made his money (including giving his daughter a privileged education, better than his own) had turned to ashes in his mouth; but it seems more serious, a declaration that the aspects of life which really matter have nothing to do with money. He had declared to Elsie before their marriage that he did not 'desire money, and yet my thoughts must be constantly on that subject' (*L* 100) – and one wonders what it must have meant to him that the profile of the woman he loved (or ought to love) was actually used on US coinage. The whole logic of his having worked to live, was in order to finance his spiritual independence in the poem – an independence glimpsed, for example, in his declaration to Hi Simons (September 1944): 'I write poetry because it is part of my piety: because, for me, it is the good of life, and I don't intend to lift a finger to advance my interest, because I don't want to think of poetry that way' (*L* 473). When Stevens wrote to a contact on the college faculty, to see if she could arrange for Holly to be befriended by 'some girl of intelligence and tact' who would try and talk her round (*L* 424), nothing illustrates his at-least-partial sense of the spiritual unwholesomeness of the proposal more than his offering to *pay* any such tactful intelligencer.

Stevens did not, however, wish his daughter to remain at Vassar from any reverence for the academic life; he had come back from Princeton having had, as he put it to Simons, a glimpse of a life he was glad not to share ('how they keep alive is more than I can imagine', *L* 392); and at the end of *Notes* the Sorbonne is half-humorously dismissed as unlikely to come up with right answers in any near future. Other than – presumably – in law, Stevens was never at his ease with systematic thinking, as his essays demonstrate; and academies looked best to him when they achieved a shimmering inexactitude, as in a moment of awakening when:

> We more than awaken, sit on the edge of sleep,
> As on an elevation, and behold
> The academies like structures in a mist.
>
> (*CP* 386)

This dissolution of the architecture of knowledge into a suggestive imprecision is an apt image for what *Notes* sets out to accomplish. It searches for a first idea unclouded by divine origination; but of course to imagine oneself at the beginning is to be where no human was, at the muddy centre before we even breathed; and any myth of beginning is, logically, preceded by ever-receding anteriorities. To instruct the ephebe that the sun should be unnamed, and then immediately to qualify it as 'gold flourisher' (*CP* 381), is to demonstrate the ineluctable modality of the lexical (as Joyce might have put it), and to affirm that there is no accessible bliss of unenunciated pre-consciousness, in which we can retreat from our fallen knowingness. Henri Focillon, whose *The Life of Forms in Art* (tr. 1942) Stevens would enthusiastically cite in 'The Figure of the Youth...', asserted that 'between man and nature, form intervenes'; and according to his mood, Stevens viewed language – the most obviously intervening form – as both power and prison, reconciling us to and separating us from the world of which we are too distantly a part. A poem is a 'more than rational distortion' (*CP* 406) which 'refreshes life so that we share,/ For a moment, the first idea' (*CP* 382), enabling us to experience the 'freshness of transformation' as both the 'freshness of a world' and as the 'freshness of ourselves' (*CP* 397–8). It is, however, momentary. Stevens wrote to Simons at the beginning of 1940 that 'there are many "immediate" things in the world that we enjoy; a perfectly realized poem ought to be one of these things' (*L* 349); in the environment of the poem – and poems were mental places to Stevens – we enter an act of mediation that achieves a simulacrum of immediacy: 'A largeness lived and not conceived, a space/ That is an instant nature, brilliantly' (*CP* 301). Our doing so is simultaneously an act of affirmation and admission of destitution: 'Of Bright & Blue Birds & the Gala Sun' (1940; *CP* 248) is a concisely brilliant illustration and example of this; its niño is the ephebe's playful antecedent.

Stevens thought well enough of his coda to *Notes* equating poet and soldier as different types of warrior, to wish it to be featured on the cover of the Cummington Press edition. It forms, I think, a regrettable addition to the main poem; but its composition and the prominence he wanted it to have show his desire to orient himself with regard to the war. In 'The Virile Youth...', delivered at Jean Wahl's invitation at Mount Holyoke in August 1943, Stevens differentiated poetry from philosophy as an 'unofficial view of being' (*NA* 40); and it might be thought that the conscriptive necessity of war represented the official view in an extreme form. Writing to Simons in January 1940, however, Stevens had abruptly turned from a discussion of his own politics (dismissing this as a fruitless topic) to declare that he was much more interested in getting rid of the Archbishop of Canterbury (*L* 351); the official view of being he wished to supplant was essentially the religious one: this accounts for the axiomatic atheism of *Notes* and other poems. But if the poet was to replace the priest, it was not by usurping his functions with regard to any afterlife: Stevens availed himself of a high romantic vocabulary of the imagination, as well as of imagery that seems religious in its tenor; but explicitly asserted the need to avoid 'the hieratic' (*NA* 58) produced by a 'false conception of the imagination as some incalculable *vates*' (*NA* 61); the poet, he had already noted in his 'Adagia', mediates between people and the world they live in, 'not between people and some other world' (*OP2* 189). His prickly response to preconceptions of the poet derived from the Romantics or French Symbolists (e.g. *L* 413–15) stemmed from his sense and experience of poetry as a rational pursuit rationally engaged in. Poetry was continuous with ordinary unexalted life – even if one of its desirable functions, in expressing its unofficial view, was to identify the irrational element in ordinary being, and to affirm the benefits of intermittent exaltation. Truth may depend on a walk around a lake, but there may also be times of inherent excellence; poems, too, are parts of the world.

If, as Filreis reports, Stevens intensified his gallery-visiting in 1942 and 1943, this was not necessarily because he sought refuge in art from a world at war; he could as easily have been wanting to ascertain what, in art, could suffice at such times.[10] His poem 'Dutch Graves in Bucks County' (*CP* 290), first published in *Sewanee Review* (Winter 1943), clearly originated in the genealogical researches he had commissioned, but was not for all that an exercise in antiquarian retrospection; instead, it brings the dead forefathers and the world at war into conjunctive disjunction: each five-line stanza depicting the expansive violences of the present is followed by a two-line refrain evoking the dead ancestors in their constricting graves; yet if their world has so little in common with the present, the present will, in time, have everything in common with their world. Although the poem's title might suggest a state of deracination (similar, say, to that in the title 'Anglais Mort à Florence'), in the historical context it could also be read as a statement of America's umbilical connectedness to Europe: if Dutchmen are buried in Pennsylvania ensuing blood-ties, such as Stevens was investigating in his own regard, made it appropriate for Americans – metaphorically if not actually descended from those pioneers – to return: some of them to graves in Europe, whose poignant displacedness, in the poem's terms, enacts a central American experience. At about the time the poem was published, Stevens visited the Van Gogh exhibition in New York at the Wildenstein Gallery, set up to encourage American support for the occupied Netherlands: looking at pictures could be connected with the war-effort, and just as in the Depression the WPA programme had enlisted creative artists in some of its regenerative projects, so during the war there was a role for art.

At Mount Holyoke that August Stevens's audience had been composed principally of expatriated French intellectuals (see *L* 457; also there were Marianne Moore and John Peale Bishop); organised by Wahl and entitled '*Les Entretiens de Pontigny*' (signifying its continuation of a series made impossible in France by the German occupation), the conference was a gesture of Franco–American solidarity to which Stevens responded, as Filreis shows, by citing as many French writers as possible in 'The Figure of the Youth...'. In his Princeton lecture, Stevens had stated that his interest in the role of the poet was 'paramount', but he immediately continued by making clear that such a role was not incompatible with addressing an élite, 'for all poets address themselves to someone and it is of the essence of that instinct ... that it should be to an elite, not to a drab but to a woman with the hair of a pythoness, not to a chamber of commerce but to a gallery of one's own' (*NA* 29). Now that America was involved in the war, the question of the poet's role had moved on a phase, with isolation no longer on offer. His later paper has a more communitarian feel, to the extent that is defined by Klaus Mann's comment on André Gide which Stevens quoted, that the main crisis of the times lay in the 'reconciliation of the inalienable rights of the individual to personal development [with] the necessity for the diminution of the misery of the masses' (*NA* 64); but it was fairly clear that the poet's true sense of his individual rights remained his best way of helping the masses. Nevertheless, Stevens's increased sense of the contingency of war (fuel rationing affected him personally, and provoked the poem 'No Possum, No Sop, No Taters') contributed to the superiority of 'Esthétique du Mal', written in June and July 1944 and therefore coincident with the Normandy landings, to 'Extracts from Addresses to the Academy of Fine Ideas' (1940), with its rather placid contemplation of evil and death.[11]

In March 1944 Stevens noted to a correspondent that the poems he had written recently were 'intended to express an agreement with reality' (*L* 463); whether this would have been apparent to a reader encountering 'Repetitions of a Young Captain' published that spring in the *Quarterly Review of Literature* is open to question, but for Stevens 'reality' was a pliable concept (although not sufficiently pliable to accommodate Holly's marriage, that August, to a man who serviced the adding-machines in the office where she worked: when she broke the news to her father, the pseudo-classical interior of the Hartford's head office echoed to his bellows of rage).[12] By the end of the year, however, with allied victory in Europe seeming ever more assured, Stevens was beginning to look ahead to life beyond war: negotiations were under way for a selected edition of his work to be published in England by the Fortune Press; the Hartford had emerged as the largest company of its kind in the USA; and he was seeking to re-establish his Parisian contacts, as well as opening up a new correspondence with a young Cuban poet, José Rodríguez Feo. When, therefore, the anthologist Oscar Williams asked him for a prose commentary on war and poetry Stevens turned him down flat, arguing that although the war was 'something that must be carried on and finished', the future of labour relations in the USA, in the light of the 'proletarian politics' of the New Deal, was of much greater moment; the same day (4 December 1944; just before the surprise German counter-offensive in the Ardennes) he wrote to Allen Tate that 'the big thing politically in the world is not the war, but the rattle and bang on the left and in the labor movement' (*L* 479, 479n.).

In this, he was voicing a concern that came to be widespread, about the social consequences of millions of demobilised

servicemen returning home to seek employment in an economy
that was bound to contract in peacetime (although in the event its
resilience was such that the transition was made much less
painfully, and there was no return of the slump; there was
considerable industrial turmoil in 1946, and a brief rise in
unemployment, but nothing to confirm the worst premonitions).
Thus a poem like 'The House was Quiet and the World was Calm'
(1945; *CP* 358) could be read either as an evocation of a world
restored to peace, or as an invocation to keep at bay the gathering
forces of unrest, excluded by a paranoid reader determined to find
'no other meaning' than that offered by the book he reads. Writing
to Henry Church (who was paying his first visit to post-war
France) in August 1946, Stevens – having acknowledged the
importance of Europe to America – spoke darkly of the 'growing
sense here of the increasing strength of the powers at work to
promote interests other than our own' (*L* 531). The same year saw
the publication of 'A Woman Sings a Song for a Soldier Come
Home' (*CP* 360), which seems to me his best poem about
soldiering: its diminishing stanzas tactfully enact the difficult
process of reintegration for the returning combatant, who must
leave his disparity of experience at the 'edge' of the village, before
he can find his old place at its centre. He must make a voluntary
renunciation of things he cannot bring himself to talk about; there
is no officious suggestion that what he needs is a curative dose of
the right poetry. This too, however, might be read as a poem
nervously imposing its quietist template over a threatening
situation: the twelve million ex-servicemen to be reabsorbed were
perceived as a source of potential unrest, much in need of being
calmed down – as, indeed, might be the women singing at their
homecoming, likely to be required to give up wartime jobs they
had grown used to having.

If such a poem seems to address its public context with an
understated comprehendingness, then 'Description without Place',
which Stevens had been invited to read to the Phi Beta Kappa
chapter at Harvard in June 1945, as part of the university's
commencement ceremonies, strikes many as overstatedly
uncomprehending of all external contexts. Filreis has shown how
Stevens departed from convention both in the poem's length –
which greatly exceeded custom and expectation – and in the
degree of its thematic dissociation from the immediately preceding
Oration delivered by a former undersecretary of state, which

predictably dealt with the embryonic post-war world order; but he has made a case for there actually being a deeper continuity between the two contrasting addresses the audience heard that day.[13] It is difficult, however, not to see the poem as another of the many occasions on which Stevens showed an impaired sense of audience – despite having at the outset asserted to Church that the idea that we live in description rather than place was appropriate both to audience and occasion (*L* 494). His refusal to play the role of public poet – as many of his contemporaries were content to do at similar occasions throughout the nation – signals both his move away from notions of the poet's duty in wartime, and his disinclination to become an elder statesman. When earlier that spring Knopf had proposed bringing out a Collected Poems, Stevens had backed off, giving as his reason the comparative failure of *Parts of a World*, which led him to wish to make his mark with another volume before considering such a move (*L* 501). The desire to continue developing was also seen in his telling Knopf that by the time *Notes* was published commercially, it was likely to be 'at least double its present length' (*L* 502). A month after his Harvard address he was commenting to Church that old people like themselves didn't appreciate 'how completely young people are in the grip of established reputations' (*L* 510); in a similar spirit, two years later, he would complain to Church's widow that the prospectuses of some little magazines he had perused showed that 'the trend is against experiment, which is unfortunate. Experiment means growth' (*L* 566).

The letters Stevens wrote in 1945 and 1946 suggest an alternating engagement with the emergent global politics, and a desire to retreat from it to the sanctuary of his garden, with a bottle of 'really decent wine' (*L* 512). In April 1946 he replied to a question posed by *Yale Literary Magazine* about the problems faced by the contemporary American writer, by observing that currently all roles yielded to that of the politician, and that whereas the poet absorbed the public life, the politician was absorbed by it. The poet, declared Stevens, 'must remain individual. As individual he must remain free. The politician expects everyone to be absorbed as he himself is absorbed. This expectation is part of the sabotage of the individual. The second phase of the poet's problem, then, is to maintain his freedom, the only condition in which he can hope to produce significant poetry' (*L* 526). Such sentiments marked an obvious move away from the consensualist attitude of wartime, and underlying them is an American individualism reasserting itself against the collectivism of the Soviet state, newly perceived as potential enemy. Along with Stalin, another saboteur of the individual was Freud: if one saw the personality defined by externally determinist forces, the other saw it undermined by its own internal compulsions; both are rejected by the 1946 poem 'Mountains Covered with Cats' (*CP* 367). 'Credences of Summer', written that summer, celebrated an American plenitude that is its own adequacy; later, Stevens described this poem as a turning away from the imaginative emphasis of *Notes* (*L* 636); but it may be that the very fervency of its desire for 'things certain sustaining us in certainty' (*CP* 375) was an index of the unacknowledged but still threatening order taking shape beyond the Oley hayfields it evoked. It is this that may be registered in 'Burghers of Petty Death', published along with 'A Woman Sings a Song...' and 'Mountains Covered with Cats' (and nine other poems) in the *Quarterly Review of Literature* (Fall 1946). In some ways a miniature 'Dutch Graves...' in its contemplation of ancestral burial (almost certainly – hence the word 'burghers', appropriate to the Dutch), the poem sets these minor variations against the major and implacable theme of 'total death' and 'devastation', 'covering all surfaces,/ Filling the mind' (*CP* 362). This apocalyptic vision supervening on a country churchyard seems to me likely to owe a good deal to the dread inspired by the advent of nuclear warfare; the first bombs had, of course, been dropped on Hiroshima and Nagasaki in 1945; but in July 1946 the first peacetime testing of atomic bombs took place near and on the Bikini atoll and, in the same year that had seen Winston Churchill put the phrase 'iron curtain' into common parlance (in a speech given in the USA), the image of the mushroom cloud refurnished the collective nightmare (Robert Frost's quatrain 'US 1946 King's X', about the consequences of the bomb for America, was first published in December 1946).

By winter 1946 Stevens was returning the corrected proofs of his next volume to his editor at Knopf's, and when at the end of February 1947 he received his advance copies, the congratulations he had extended on the cleanness of the page-proofs became virtual whoops of joy as he contemplated the finished product (*L* 537, 547). Perhaps Knopf had responded to Stevens's evident interest in the work of little presses (the Cummington Press had waived any 'rights' over *Notes* and 'Esthétique...') by showing how good a commercial outfit could be; he certainly seems to have felt that his author was becoming more marketable: shown in the initial run of 1750 (Stevens's highest to date), as well as in his decision to issue 1000 copies of a 'completely reset' third edition of *Harmonium* three months later. Whatever commercial factors operated in this, it may also have been intended to start Stevens thinking again about a collected edition; and in addition it had the effect of ensuring that his latest book could be read side by side with his earliest (Louis Martz compared *Transport to Summer* somewhat unfavourably with *Harmonium* in his review). As published that March, the volume's 57 poems were arranged for the most part in their sequence of first publication, with the glaring exception of *Notes*, which despite being the earliest-written poem in the volume was placed last – thereby giving a rather misleading sense of Stevens's development. It may well have been the case that Knopf was unwilling to open a book of poems he was publishing with a long poem already published elsewhere, albeit in a limited edition. The title of the volume seems intended to give extra prominence to 'Credences of Summer', as the long poem in the volume that better represented its point of arrival than did *Notes*, which was in fact its point of departure; but consequent upon the revelations about Nazi mass-extermination programmes and the ensuing judicial process for war-crimes at Nuremburg, the word 'transport' had acquired some especially terrible resonances; it is not clear whether Stevens was alert to these, nor clear if he wanted the ending of one of the poems in 'The Pure Good of Theory' (1945) inflected with particular horror: 'He was a Jew from Europe or might have been' (*CP* 331).

Writing in *Yale Poetry Review* (Vol. 2, Autumn 1946), Louis Martz had observed that the recent publication of substantial essays by Hi Simons and Wylie Sypher, albeit that he disagreed with both, usefully indicated that Stevens's *oeuvre* had achieved 'the range and complexity and richness which demand a summing-up' (p. 13).[14] This was before the appearance of *Transport to Summer*; by the time that came out there was an even greater body of work to attend to. Reviews were quite good, with only Louise Bogan in the *New Yorker* dismissing the poetry as an impossible 'luxury product'; opinion-forming critics such as F.O. Matthiessen (*NYTBR*), Martz (*Yale Review*), and Blackmur in *Poetry* all found aspects of high excellence. At the same time, however, each expressed some reservations: Matthiessen preferred the shorter poems, Martz thought that too many were laboured and 'muddy', and Blackmur went so far as to apply the term 'prolix', judging the greater part of the contents to be poetry not 'truly alive'. Of as great significance as these views may be the fact that several of the rising generation of poets responded admiringly to their clearly-respected senior: Richard Eberhart, Delmore Schwartz, and Robert Lowell all found much to praise – even though Schwartz devoted more review space to Auden's *Age of Anxiety*, and Lowell started by acknowledging Stevens's international standing to be less than that of either Pound or Eliot, and his popularity less than that of Frost. None of this was news to Stevens, who had in 1942 told a correspondent – without any rancour – that Edgar Lee Masters was better known than he was (*L* 413); Lowell himself won the Pulitzer Prize (for *Lord Weary's Castle*, 1946) in the month his review of Stevens appeared in the *Nation*, and was perceived to be the brightest of the rising stars – so stellar, indeed, as to merit a photo-feature in *Life* magazine. Only just emerging from the fire-breathing Catholic phase which had produced the exorbitant rhetoric of 'Quaker Graveyard in Nantucket' (1946), Lowell was perplexed by Stevens's attitude, which he took to be incommensurate with his stature: why should such a poet toss off unfinished improvisations, he wondered, and offered: 'there seems to be something ... that protects itself by asserting that it is not making too great an effort'.

The 30-year-old Lowell may well have confirmed for Stevens his earlier jest about the right age for a poet; and in many ways Lowell's good looks, Brahmin background, and self-assured assumption of the poet's mantle, together with the enthusiasm of his reception, fitted him to be the kind of cultural/spiritual hero that Stevens had so often written about. Lowell's comments on Stevens, however, throw up two issues: of the poet's role and responsibilities, and of poetic technique. On the first of these issues Lowell partly echoes Pound's earlier suspicion that Stevens failed to take the poetic vocation seriously; and as an issue it was thrown into sharpest focus by Pound's own case, who having in 1946 been found unfit to stand trial for his 'treasonable' broadcasts from Mussolini's Italy, had been confined to a ward for the criminally insane in St Elizabeth's Hospital, Washington, DC. Pound might well look like a culture-hero gone badly wrong, ironically fulfilling (as Lowell would do) the prejudice Stevens wished to dislodge, that poets were at bottom extraordinary madmen. Stevens had been approached at the time of Pound's initial return to America, to contribute to a symposium on the case; but he replied, more as a lawyer than a poet, that the circumstances were not sufficiently clear to be sure that Pound wasn't guilty as charged, and that the fact of his being a genius was not sufficient excuse, since it did not exempt him from 'the common disciplines' (*L* 516–17). There was, in other words, no cultural-political 'outsidership' that entitled any artist to claim secular benefit of clergy. Stevens described himself and Eliot as dead opposites, but this is even truer of himself and Pound at this period: Pound had been ritually excluded from society for his presumptuous (or treasonable) meddling in wartime affairs of state; Stevens was becoming culturally centralised, precisely because of his perceived reluctance to allow social or political concerns to intrude upon the realm of the aesthetic. Events would soon demonstrate this polarity.

The year of publication of Stevens's new book, 1947, was also the year in which the phrase 'Cold War' came into being, the year in which the House UnAmerican Activities Committee began investigating Hollywood, the year in which the CIA was set up. Pound, the alleged traitor, could stand as a potent symbol of such manifestations: awareness of the 'enemy within' (seen also in President Truman's instructing the FBI that year to locate potential security risks; hindsight suggests they should have started with the Bureau's Director, J. Edgar Hoover). Obviously, such a fear had been part of the 'hot' war, and produced random policies of internment, on both sides of the Atlantic; but with demobilisation, large numbers of servicemen wished to turn back to the America evoked by Stevens in June 1945 as a 'vast countryside' (*L* 507). Stevens, however, had been prescient enough to suggest to his British correspondent that that 'was all over for the present, and for the next generation or two': it can be seen now that a sense of national vulnerability, instilled into Americans keener to do nothing else than beat their swords back into ploughshares, was a politically useful means of preventing a recurrence of isolationism. The twin planks of foreign policy in the post-war period, containment of the Soviet threat and reconstruction of gutted Europe, required an enormous outlay of American capital; and as with any electorate, it was easier to persuade people to part with taxes if self-interest could be activated by showing that the war in fact continued in a different guise. As 'Credences of Summer' suggests, Stevens was as keen as any to return to pastoral satisfactions (and his letters suggest him to be no great lover of the

IRS); so the bad-tempered outburst in his poem 'Memorandum' (winter 1947), which evoked the Ephrata of his boyhood summers, shows how dismayingly he sensed that ideal to have been compromised by Stalinist intrusions:

> Say this to Pravda, tell the damned rag
> That the peaches are slowly ripening.
> Say that the American moon comes up
> Cleansed clean of lousy Byzantium.
>
>   (*OP2* 116)

Implicit in this uncharacteristically direct utterance, however, was the inference that 'truth' is better established in America than Russia, in the rural rather than the urban, and in disinterested poetry rather than politically motivated journalism. It was precisely this overtly political address that would be missing from his poetry, as a mark of his difference from the state bards of Stalin; and as the exponent of an American aesthetics of depoliticisation, it could be argued that Stevens entered precisely that realm of clandestine political activity (for the *kulturkampf* was part of the new war as of the old) that was most characteristic of the post-war decade.

Thus, Lowell's sense of there being a quality of protective disengagement in Stevens's sense of his role, was justifiable; somewhat less so, was his complaint about the improvisatory nature of the verse: for this failed to see the extent to which Stevens (who excised but seldom revised) valued spontaneity and playfulness. In June 1945 he had written a long letter to Rodríguez Feo, in which he quoted a 'precious sentence' by Henry James (encountered in Matthiessen's study of the novelist), to illustrate the fact that in the world of 'actuality' one was always 'living a little out of it':

> To live *in* the world of creation – to get into it and stay in it – to frequent it and haunt it – to *think* intensely and fruitfully – to woo combinations and inspirations into being by a depth and continuity of attention and meditation – this is the only thing.
>
>   (*L* 506)

James's declaration of faith has something in common with the exclusively concentred reader depicted in 'The House was Quiet...';

and, like James, Stevens was always aware of the forms of orderliness to be brought by 'the sublime economy of art' in its application to the 'inclusion and confusion' that is life (the terms come from James's Preface to *The Spoils of Poynton*). There are certain moods, too, in which Stevens would assent to James's dismay over 'the fatal futility of Fact' when not the object of human observation and evaluation; but he also was aware of those times when the actual was a 'deft beneficence' (*CP* 155) – although of course it can only be judged to be so by an essentially subjective response. Thus in a further letter to Cuba that October, he emphasised James's 'world of creation' as only one of the areas of the world of thought (*L* 513), as if to draw back from what might have seemed the Old Adam of aesthetic absolutism. In May 1945 he had written to his Ceylon correspondent Leonard van Geyzel about his interest in establishing the place of poetry in thought, 'and certainly I don't mean strict thought, but the special thinking of poetry' (*L* 501). This arose, he said, from 'the desire to contain the world wholly within one's perception of it. As it happens, in my own case and probably in yours, within perceptions that include perceptions that are pleasant' (ibid.).

The special kind of thinking which Stevens felt poetry to exemplify was thought perceived as feeling, constructed emotionally as well as logically. If a sequence of thought were exhaustible in logic, it would also lose its emotional force, since reason cannot give adequate response to desire (see the end of 'Dezembrum', *CP* 218).[15] Stevens's wish not to reach conclusion, his pleasure at not having written a book full of complacently grandfatherly wisdom (like, say, Frost), but of having nonetheless achieved a 'momentary end/ To the complication' (*CP* 303), are of a piece with the essential evasiveness of his poetry; which was able to interrogate itself as part of its own process – as seen in the uneasy repetitions of this poem's last line, and its title, 'The Lack of Repose' (1943). By this I mean partly his need, like James, to live a little out of actuality since (as in 'Credences of Summer', VII) it is difficult to sing in the presence of the object of one's song; but also I mean the characteristic deferral of closure in his poems. The poem should resist the intelligence because to yield to it would be to suffer its own extinction: the reader may suppose that there is a 'meaning' behind the words on the page which they themselves obstruct, so that his desire is to transcend them and thereby gain access to some paradise of noumenal immediacy, yet Stevens insists that the words of the poem *are* the poem, and any attempts to rise above them – as if they were merely the foyer to some grander structure – end when we see that there is no 'beyond', and that *there* is really *here* (my allusions are to 'Crude Foyer', *CP* 305). There are evocations in his poetry of what might be called a semantic eschatology, when the temporary changes of poetic perception fall away; but these are invariably evoked conditionally, as in 'Description without Place':

> There might be, too, a change immenser than
> A poet's metaphors in which being would
>
> Come true, a point in the fire of music where
> Dazzle yields to a clarity and we observe,
>
> And observing is completing and we are content,
> In a world that shrinks to an immediate whole,
>
> That we do not need to understand, complete
> Without secret arrangements of it in the mind.
>   (*CP* 341)

Yet this is really what he described elsewhere as a tentative idea for the purpose of poetry, expressing a desire but not defining a position: because for Stevens, too great a clarity involves the cessation of thinking. Just as he celebrated the permissive 'vagueness' of Henry Church's will (*L* 477–9), so he endorsed the nutritive evasiveness of a poetry that responded to the unfixedness of being; as he wrote in his letter to van Geyzel, people usually think of poems as 'integrations of ideas: that is to say, of what they mean. However, a poem must have a peculiarity, as if it was the momentarily complete idiom of that which prompts it, even if that which prompts it is the vaguest emotion' (*L* 500). This momentary but momentous adjustment of words to impulse was, for Stevens, of the essence of poetry, best representing the mental texture of living; and although the resistance offered by poem to intelligence could produce frustration, its resolution into clarity unnervingly prefigured death:

> We must endure our thoughts all night, until
> The bright obvious stands motionless in cold.
>   (*CP* 351)

7

1947–55: Private Man as Public Figure

The eight years Stevens lived after the publication of *Transport to Summer* were years of comparative public prominence — although the comparison is with his earlier career, rather than with those of celebrated contemporaries such as Eliot or Frost. Notwithstanding his personal disinclination, he gave lectures and public readings of his verse; and he received honorary degrees from Wesleyan University (1947), Bard College (1951), Harvard (1951), Mount Holyoke (1952), and Yale (1955). In 1950 he received the Bollingen Prize in Poetry for the previous year, and in 1951 he was awarded both the Gold Medal of the Poetry Society of America and the National Book Award in Poetry for 1950; in 1955 he was again awarded the National Book Award in Poetry, and the Pulitzer Prize, for his *Collected Poems* the previous year. It was his custom to request that any honororia he was offered for readings should be used to help younger poets; and this reflected his status as a senior in the craft, for whom the exercise of modest patronage was appropriate; he was also called upon to serve on awarding committees. With the sudden deaths of Hi Simons in 1945 and Henry Church in 1947, he had lost the two contacts closest to himself in age and in interests; and although he continued his friendship with Church's widow, Barbara, his correspondents were, characteristically, younger men (for the most part) who were making their way as writers and scholars. At the same period, the birth of his grandson in April 1947, followed by Holly's separation (1949) and divorce (1951), effected a reconciliation and growing attachment between the poet and his daughter: she lived near enough for him to call in on his way back from the office, and she visited Westerly Terrace at weekends. She would on occasions accompany him on visits to Barbara Church's social gatherings in New York, and this inaugurated an involvement with his literary life that would become the dominant feature of the rest of her own life, as the keeper of her father's flame: editing his letters and journals, contributing odd little memoirs here and there, and responding to scholarly enquiries.

Moving toward and into his seventies, it was hardly suprising
that habits of sedentariness increased their power over Stevens: as
usual, summer holidays were not considered and, as he told Barbara
Church in 1948, he and Elsie shrank from everything; one of the chief
pleasures in taking a trip to New York was that of returning home at
the end of it (*L* 626) where, as he informed her, 'nothing could be
more exciting than to sit in the quiet of one's room watching the
fireflies. ... Of course it isn't the fireflies that make it exciting, it is the
sense of peace: the feeling that one is back again where one was as a
child' (*L* 639). Letters – from Barbara Church on her travels in
Europe, van Geyzel in Ceylon, Rodríguez Feo in Cuba, Thomas
McGreevy in Ireland, and from Paule Vidal in Paris – relieved him of
the necessity of exploring a world which he persuaded himself they
made available: he received a book about the Jesuit church at
Lucerne, and later dropped a reference to it in a lecture, as if he had
walked around in the building (*NA* 137). 'I like natives', he told
Barbara Church: 'people in civilized countries whose only
civilization is that of their own land. Not that I have ever met any: it
is merely an idea' (*L* 613). Living in a world merely of ideas and
preferring the predictable routines of home or office, Stevens almost
invited mockery; but ideas were, in actuality, extremely powerful at
this period, and were shaping the lives of many more people than
those actively engaged with them. The most obvious idea, which is
reflected in Stevens's correspondence of this period, was the threat
of communism. Abroad, this evidenced itself in the installation of
puppet regimes in Hungary and Czechoslovakia, in the Soviet
blockade of Berlin and the consequent airlift to preserve the allied
presence (1948–9), and in the Korean War (1950–3); at home, it was
seen in the increasing fears of internal subversion, most obviously
given voice in the McCarthy investigations (1950–4) and in the spy
trials, and led to President Eisenhower's outlawing of the
Communist Party in America (1954). The peculiarly qualified terms
of Stevens's interest in the wider world may also be thought to be
representatively American: in that at the same time that the USA
despatched its military personnel to increasingly diverse foreign
bases, it ensured that they would be protected, in those alien
geographies, by the cocoon of a homogenising American way of life
imported along with them. Beyond their compounds, ideational
'natives' peopled ambiguous wildernesses.

But whatever the appearances of calm and orderliness, Stevens
was not the helpless victim of his rocking-chair. An uncollected

poem that he wrote in 1947, 'First Warmth' (subsequently revised to 'As You Leave the Room'; *OP2* 117 for both), wondered whether his questionings about reality had not condemned him to the life of a skeleton; and although both first version and revision offer a degree of reassurance, the question was severe. The last word of 'Credences of Summer' had been 'happiness'; but 'The Auroras of Autumn', the long poem which Stevens wrote the following year (1947), both in title and in content can be seen to move beyond 'Credences...' to a much less consolatory version of American beginnings and endings, and an existence much more menaced and conditional. Defining the 'fat girl' of *Notes* for Church in October 1942, Stevens had described her as standing for the earth, amplifying this by saying that a politician would probably have used the term 'globe' (*L* 426). 'Earth' is much more suggestive of place and locale, conflating as it does with the very ground we stand on; whereas 'globe' is a perception available only to one looking from outside; and the difference between 'Credences...' and 'The Auroras...' could well be summed up thus: the first is a poem of earth, whereas the second enforces a planetary perspective in which the northern lights are a phenomenon less tractable to the imagination than was the ripening sun of 'Credences...'. The difference should not be taken to be a permanent change from lightness to darkness in Stevens: the uncollected poem 'Outside of Wedlock', which was probably written in late 1941 or early 1942 (*OP2* 112), paints as bleak a picture of the futility of living as any; and after 'The Auroras...' Stevens went on to compose 'An Ordinary Evening in New Haven', which was a much more domesticated vision. What it does suggest, however, is the way in which Stevens tended to progress by reacting against himself.

At the beginning of 1948 he told Barbara Church that he had been invited to give another one of 'those lectures which I do so badly' (*L* 574). It is difficult to dissent from the justice of his self-assessment; read now these papers, with their Emersonian disregard for the syntax of thinking, do little to advance his cause as a theorist of literature; no one who is not already animated by an interest in Stevens is likely to seek or find enlightenment in the pages of his critical prose – and this is very different from the case of Eliot, whose best literary criticism, notwithstanding its propagandist function with regard to his own ideas, also throws light on its notional subject. Stevens had read 'Three Academic Pieces' at Harvard in 1947, and went on to give 'Effects of Analogy' at Yale (and at Mount Holyoke) and 'Imagination as Value' at Columbia in 1948, and 'The Relations between Poetry and Painting' at the Museum of Modern Art in 1951. 'Three Academic Pieces' consisted of one prose section and two poems ('Someone Puts a Pineapple Together' and 'Of Ideal Time and Choice'); and although in 'As You Leave the Room' he cited the pineapple poem as one proving he hadn't lived a skeleton's life, few would endorse his judgement.[1] All of the essays are concerned with the relation between poet, reality, and poem, and on the psychological level seem to represent Stevens's efforts to produce a rationale for why it was a necessity of his being to refract life through the prism of the poem. 'Effects of Analogy' ends with a declaration both resonant and qualified: 'Thus poetry becomes and is a transcendent analogue composed of the particulars of reality, created by the poet's sense of the world, that is to say, his attitude, as he intervenes and interposes the appearances of that sense' (*NA* 130).

In 1949 he also read an eleven-canto version of 'Ordinary Evening...' at the sesquicentennial celebration of the Connecticut Academy of Arts and Sciences, at New Haven; Louis Martz claimed that (highly unusually) Stevens had tried the poem out, first, on his wife; who had covered her eyes and opined, 'They're not going to understand this!' No matter what tribute the poem's title paid to its occasion, one suspects that Elsie Stevens must have been right; and her comment would equally apply to most of the public addresses her husband gave, both prose and poetry. He was ill-adapted to the role of public speaker, as well he knew, and his experience giving the Bergen lecture at Yale – when he had felt himself to be the object of ridicule for having asked that the lectern be adjusted to accommodate his height (*L* 583), and a member of the audience had asked him to speak up – encapsulated the horrors such events could hold for him. He resisted until quite late requests that he should make a recording of some of his poems; and I take it that all this points to the continuing difficulty Stevens had in reconciling the notion of poetry as a public art with its very private function in his own emotional and spiritual economy: physically confronting an audience, he was brought face to face with precisely what his poetry shied away from; as he put it to

McGreevy in June 1948, 'I know exactly why I write poetry and it is not for an audience. I write it because for me it is one of the sanctions of life' (*L* 600). This being so, to address a hallful of people was a kind of profanation, a further violation of the secrecy between poet and poem – as well as being, in the light of Stevens's acute self-consciousness and vulnerability on such occasions, an awkward reversal of the power relations implicit for him in the act of composition. What a difference there must have been, between composing poems on his way to work and then giving them to his secretary, and reciting these poems to an audience which might ask him to speak up, or in some way corner him about his work. And just as Kreymborg recalled Stevens accosting him with the manuscript of 'Peter Quince...', itself rendered as self-effacing as possible by the minute handwriting, and swearing him to secrecy about it, so, much later, secrecy was still the watchword: telling Bernard Heringman in May 1949 that he was at work on 'Ordinary Evening...', Stevens stressed that the information was confidential and not to be talked about (*L* 636).

The maintenance of secrecy was, as it happened, a national priority at this time; and ironically, it was the perception of Stevens as a writer who observed the aesthetic purity of his calling by abstaining from overt political activity, that was influential in making of him a writer who fulfilled a public function through the exemplification of privacy in art. The occasion of this was the controversy created by the decision of the awarding committee of the 1948 (and first) Bollingen Prize, to give it to Ezra Pound for *The Pisan Cantos* published in the USA that year. At that stage the prize was administered by the Library of Congress, whose fellows (including Eliot, Auden, Aiken, Tate, Louise Bogan, and Robert Lowell) were the jury. The decision was so sensitive that it was insisted that a second, postal ballot be held; but when this confirmed the verdict, there was a predictable furore that an arraigned if unconvicted traitor should be so honoured. The award committee was essentially underwriting the principle that poetry was distinct from politics, and that aesthetic judgement was independent of concerns relating to the world of current events; but this was a profoundly political position, designed also to draw attention (since the *Pisan Cantos* dealt in part with the brutal circumstances of Pound's literal encagement at the US army detention camp near Pisa) to Pound's ongoing incarceration: with the implication that this might be more appropriate to Stalin's

Russia than Truman's America. Opponents of the award were scarcely more logical in their position, believing as they did that Pound's disgrace should colour value judgements about his poetry, whilst implicitly preferring a poet to be the exponent of politically unengaged high art. The fall-out of the affair was that the prize was detached from its adjacency to government, and thereafter administered by Yale University Library. It was felt that some of the damage done to the Bollingen's prestige by the Pound controversy needed to be repaired; and Stevens's receipt (in 1950) of the 1949 prize restored stability at the same time that – by not giving the prize to the populist Frost – the awarders affected a degree of independence from public opinion, thereby demonstrating the separateness of poetry from things of the moment.[2]

Writing to Delmore Schwartz at the *Partisan Review* in spring 1948 Stevens had declared that the 'basic meaning of the effort of any man to record his experience as poet is to produce poetry, not politics. The poet must stand or fall by poetry. In the conflict between the poet and the politician the chief honour the poet can hope for is that of remaining himself. Life and reality, on the one hand, and politics, on the other, notwithstanding the activity of politics, are not interchangeable terms. They are not the same thing, whatever the Russians may pretend' (*L* 591). The post-war cultural climate, in which the separation of politics from art was perceived to be a symptom of American or Western libertarianism, as distinct from the political conscriptiveness of Soviet aesthetics, is clearly expressed here. Later the same year, in a letter to Barbara Church, Stevens sounded a note that would again feature in cold war perceptions, that communists took advantage of American liberal institutions to undermine them – this would become an argument for an abridgement of civil liberties in the McCarthyite assault on claiming the Fifth Amendment, and would eventuate in the ban on communism. 'The total freedom that now endangers us has never existed before, notwithstanding Voltaire', he wrote; 'We might need a police state before long to protect ourselves against Communism' (*L* 620). Something of this sense of embattlement seems to inform his figures of speech later in the same letter, when he proposed poetry as a 'combat with' rather than a 'transmutation of' reality; and these inflections of conflict and danger – with the need for protection, such as perhaps the poem alone could give, against systematic ideology (the unfair weapon of enemies both within and without) – were deeply embedded in the era's cultural and political constructions, and formed the larger climate within which Stevens was assembling his next book of verse.

This was first spoken of in May 1949, in the same letter to Heringman that told of 'Ordinary Evening...'; the next month Stevens wrote to Knopf, proposing that he issue one more book, to be called *The Auroras of Autumn*, and whose manuscript the poet undertook to complete by the end of the year (*L* 638). We can infer how keen Knopf was to bring out a Collected Poems, from the persuasive effort Stevens put into this letter, which stressed how much he had been thinking about his new book and how committed he was to it; in essence, he told Knopf that if he brought out *The Auroras of Autumn*, then Stevens would agree to a collection. Within a week Knopf had assented to the proposal, and Stevens was writing to Barbara Church about the different circumstances in which this book would be composed: as opposed to the casual construction of his previous volumes, this one required him to 'plan ahead for a long period of thinking and writing' (*L* 639). That July he told McGreevy that he needed to compose some short poems to fulfil promises he had made to editors, and commented that short poems were more difficult to write because a long poem acquired its own impetus, whereas each short poem required a fresh start, and he could only write a very few each month (*L* 640).[3] In fact, as he told Barbara Church in mid-September, he had composed ten short 'things' during August, and was now at the point of beginning what he planned to be the last long poem for *Auroras*. Since, however, the group of poems referred to must have been 'Things of August', and since the only other long poems had already been written (he reported having finished what must have been 'Ordinary Evening...' that June, *L* 639), it seems as if this last long poem never materialised – or that it was displaced by the short 'Angel Surrounded by Paysans', the last poem in *Auroras*, which was written within the first two weeks of October, inspired by a still life by Tal Coat Stevens had just received from Paule Vidal. He kept to his word and sent Knopf the manuscripts (his own plural) in December; but evidently he had not accomplished what he wished, for in February 1950 he told Heringman that he felt the book to have been damaged by not having had enough time (*L* 666; see also *L* 669); by the time of its publication, however, he judged it 'perfect' (*L* 686).

In September 1949 he had told Barbara Church of his 'sense of anxiety about the future, which everything seems to exploit'

(*L* 648); the recent establishment of a communist state on mainland China (followed the next year by the Sino–Soviet treaty) had augmented the sense of threat. The apocalyptic intimations of his new volume's title poem, together with the barely-suppressed violences of poems such as 'Page from a Tale' (1948) and 'Puella Parvula' (1949), give a somewhat vertiginous feeling to the book; but perhaps the truer tone is struck by the shorter poems, which better exemplify what Stevens drew attention to in his rather impersonal inscription in Holly's copy ('From Her Father'), that poetry was 'a response to the daily necessity of getting the world right'.[4] This presumably described the sudden rightness of the poet, rather than the systematic rightness of the politician: the momentary visitation of a necessary angel. Knopf brought out *The Auroras of Autumn* in September 1950, in an edition of 3000; and while the sharply increased print-run may have been due to his perceptions of the book's quality, it is more likely to have been due to the calculation that Stevens's receipt of the Bollingen Prize earlier that year (to which attention was drawn on the dust-jacket) would improve his marketability. If so, this was a fair assumption: two years later, a second edition of 1000 copies was required; which had doubtless been given added impetus by the book's having won (in 1951) the 1950 National Book Award. The reviews were respectful rather than ecstatic; Bogan commented on the human emptiness, and more than one reviewer found mastery rather than versatility: Randall Jarrell in *Partisan Review* saw that Stevens was one of the century's important poets, but found the volume 'monotonous' and 'overwhelmingly characteristic', lacking in immediacy. William Van O'Connor, author of the first book-length study of Stevens (*The Shaping Spirit*, 1950), made an important point when he suggested that Stevens's 'aesthetic', formerly so unpopular in America, was now becoming more respectable: for precisely those qualities for which *Harmonium* had been condemned on its first appearance, were attributes highly desirable in an era committed to the separation of art from politics. In particular, Stevens's apparently hermetic lyrics were highly suited to the well-wrought urn-estness of New Critical procedures, rapidly ascendant in the academy; and the same climate which advanced the ideological content-lessness of Abstract Expressionism, saw the institutionalisation of Stevens as a representative American poet, whose jar in Tennessee need never threaten to break out beyond the classrooom (these years found him increasingly approached by university students working on his poetry).

By the same token, Stevens's increased visibility made the issuing of his critical writing seem desirable. He had previously been disinclined to divorce these papers from the contexts of their occasions, and his editor at Knopf's had also been unenthusiastic; but Knopf, provoked – as Stevens supposed – by his recent publicity, asked about the papers, and brought out *The Necessary Angel* in an edition of 3000 in November 1951. This, too, was part of the institutionalisation of Stevens; for, as the example of Eliot showed, unless a poet also established his credentials as a critic, he would not be admitted to the first rank. The other significant step in the consolidation of his reputation lay in the compilation of a Selected Poems: which involved a volume which was projected but never issued, a volume which was issued but should not have been (and was withdrawn), and, last of all, the *Selected Poems* issued by Faber in 1952, which marked Stevens's first volume for the British market, where hitherto he had been represented only in anthologies. The rather complicated sequence of events also had its consequences for the definition of Stevens's canon. His reluctance to sanction a collected poems was such that, despite his undertaking to Knopf at the time of proposing *Auroras*, the publisher seems to have countenanced the notion that a selected volume be released for the American market; and in May 1950 Stevens submitted a list of 86 items for consideration. As ever fearful of any sense of an ending, he insisted that this did not represent a 'final choice', but we safely suppose that he chose poems he liked: he selected 31 poems from *Harmonium*, 14 from *Ideas of Order*, the title poem and 'Men that are Falling' from *Blue Guitar*, 17 from *Parts of a World*, 14 from *Transport to Summer*, and eight from the not-yet-published *Auroras*. For once the editors at Knopf, who had been making it plain for some while that if they were to act on readers' reports they probably wouldn't publish Stevens, were able to act on their instincts, and rejected the selection as too miscellaneous.[5]

From Stevens's letter to Barbara Church of 13 June 1950, it appears that Knopf had intended to force the issue somewhat by letting older volumes go out of print, in order to necessitate a collected volume; but he was persuaded by the strength of his author's disinclination to opt instead for a reissuing of the old work: *Harmonium* (August 1950; 1500), *Transport to Summer* (January 1951; 1500), *Parts of a World* (June 1951; 1500), *The Man with the Blue*

Guitar, including Ideas of Order (February 1952; 2000), and *The Auroras of Autumn* (November 1952).[6] At this stage 'Owl's Clover' remained part of *Blue Guitar*, but the 1937 volume preceded the 1935 *Ideas of Order* in the new combined volume; which may have had a bearing on Stevens's choice for the Faber *Selected Poems*. Toward the end of 1951 negotiations were successfully concluded with the British firm (with Peter du Sautoy rather than Eliot taking the lead), for the issuing of a selection of Stevens's poems, not to exceed 160 pages; Stevens's initial preference had been for someone else to make the choice – Marianne Moore was suggested – but in the event he did the job himself, although Moore left her mark in suggesting that he include the uncollected 'Final Soliloquy of the Interior Paramour'. This pleased Stevens as providing a good ending poem (*L* 733–4), but the choices he himself made are interesting, and were based, as he told Herbert Weinstock at Knopf's, on a different theory from his previous selection: representative rather than what he wished to preserve (*L* 732n).[7] This selection was very much more weighted toward his first volume: 34 of its 58 poems were from *Harmonium*, with only four from his second book, two from *Blue Guitar*, five from *Parts of a World*, eight from *Transport to Summer* and four from *Auroras*. He did not, as with the earlier project, use excerpts from longer poems, printing *Notes* in full (although retaining the eleven-canto version of 'Ordinary Evening...'); he placed the selection from *Blue Guitar* before the poems from *Ideas of Order*. The book appeared in February 1953, in a run of 2000 (of which 820 sold in the first year, but which thereafter sold sluggishly until brought out as a paperback in 1965); and to everyone's surprise there simultaneously appeared a *Selected Poems* edited by Dennis Williamson, and issued by the Fortune Press under the terms of a contract whose option had expired in 1946; arms were duly twisted and the offending volume was withdrawn.[8] To his delight, Stevens managed to acquire a copy which had been sent out for review in Ireland.

When he corrected the proofs of the Faber selection, Stevens confided to Barbara Church that the book had struck him as insubstantial and extremely irrelevant to the actual world (10 September 1952; *L* 760); but this may have been partly due to the fact that Knopf had written at the end of August to urge a collected volume, and Stevens had replied (2 September 1952) trying to make the case for an American selected poems, to coincide with his 75th birthday in 1954. Meanwhile he was able to turn his attention to helping Renato Poggioli, Professor of Comparative Literature at Harvard, prepare an annotated translation of some poems into Italian (*Mattino Domenicale ed altre Poesie*, Turin, 1954), offering explanatory glosses similar to those he had in the past provided for 'Latimer' and Simons. This could only be a diversion from the inevitable, however; and when Knopf wondered whether the poet might produce a new volume for his birthday, Stevens realised that he had to face facts and consent to a collection, which he did in a letter on 22 April 1954 – although his aversion to the prospect was such that five days later he was still wondering whether there might be a case for preferring an enlarged selection; but really he knew the game was up (*L* 829, 830–1). As he explained to Barbara Church early in May, he had held off from a collection for years because 'in a way, it puts an end to things' (*L* 832); but the reality of termination was beginning to make itself felt to him, as his letters spoke increasingly of the encroachments of fatigue. Early in 1950 he had fallen on ice and broken his ankle; and although his enforced immobility (which according to his company chauffeur Stevens fiercely resented) offered the rare opportunity for him to need Elsie, and for her to respond to that need, the longer legacy seems to have been an increased sense of physical limitation, with all its implications. But this in turn would inform his remarkable late poems.

He told Barbara Church that he had chosen to omit a 'few rather stuffy things' from his *Collected Poems*. What in fact he left out, as specified in his letter to Knopf of 27 April, was 'Owl's Clover', 'Life on a Battleship' and 'The Woman That Had More Babies Than That'; these are, in all conscience, bad enough poems to justify their omission: but the loss of 'Owl's Clover' in particular meant that the volume issued by Knopf that October gave a rather misleading picture of Stevens's development. He was himself sufficiently aligned with the current critical estimate of his work to have declared, at the end of 1953, that certain things in *Harmonium* pleased him more than any of his subsequent poems (*L* 807); and it cannot have been wholly accidental that the poems he omitted were precisely those least likely to be valued in the cultural climate of the early 1950s, with the anathematisation of political verse and the elevation of formalist and aesthetic criteria. It may have been his perception of the rising stock of his once-despised first volume that led Stevens to propose 'The Whole of Harmonium' as a title for his Collected Poems, as well as his desire to indicate the

rounded completeness of his *oeuvre* (with 'Owl's Clover' dismissed
as a kind of divagation); but Knopf and his advisers were unhappy
with the idea, and the machine-made title of *The Collected Poems of
Wallace Stevens* was what was issued, in an edition of 2500 copies –
which was quite quickly followed by a second and then a third
impression (February 1955, 2100; May 1955, 4000). As well as the
already published books, the collected volume included a final
section, eventually entitled 'The Rock', in which were printed 25
poems previously uncollected – but accidentally omitting one of his
finest late poems, 'The Course of a Particular' (1951, *OP*2 123; see *L*
881). The British *Collected Poems* was issued by Faber a year later, in
a printing of 2000 (subsequent impressions: 1959, 1966, 1971).

Stevens had predicted to Barbara Church that this would be his
last book (*L* 832), although he anticipated that he would carry on
writing poems. But the congruence between the completeness of his
book and the completeness of his life (as it would turn out) made
manifest the always-implicit metaphor of the book as a life. The
increasing public recognition he attracted was also a mark of the
degree to which his career was being assimilated as a model;
although populist writers such as Frost and – as Stevens himself
noted – Sandburg might reach a broader audience, their very
popularity detracted from their being viewed as exponents of
cultural high seriousness; whereas his difficult poems entitled him
to be considered in the same intellectual league as Eliot. He was
thus welcomed by the academy (which was itself affected by
McCarthyite encroachments) at the same time that, as a happy
capitalist and aider of those who would live in the spirit, he could be
offered as a most appropriate cultural embodiment of the American
way. Just as *The Tempest* was read as Shakespeare's culminatingly
serene dispensation of wisdom, so the poems contained in 'The
Rock' – in which there was more than one allusion to *The Tempest* –
offered confirmation of the view that (to switch plays) ripeness was
all. The most emphatic canonical response was Randall Jarrell's
judgement that the poems were 'magnanimous, compassionate, but
calmly exact'; yet for all its triadic stateliness, his view was not
misleading: in consenting to the collection Stevens had internalised
the reality of his own dying, and the poems about being old and
looking back on a life which was simultaneously persistence and
absence seem to be written from the centre of his own condition.

Although his genealogical researches had come to an end in the
late 1940s (with his failure to qualify for the Holland Society),

Stevens had been thinking of his roots; in 1947 he wrote to Barbara Church that during his early New York years he had occasionally gone back to Reading as 'a way of getting back to an earth which always filled me with whatever I really needed' (*L* 563); and to McGreevy in September 1951 he wrote of going home from Harvard, and of feeling as if he was 'going back to mother earth' (*L* 728). The poems in 'The Rock' are poems of thresholds, of desiring the 'beyond', and poems of return or searching for origins: the systole and diastole of Stevens's poetry. The two movements are most effectively combined in 'The Poem that took the Place of a Mountain' (1952; *CP* 512), where the visionary ascent ends with the climber looking back down upon the sea he has left behind, as his 'unique and solitary home' (the poem owes something to Stevens's hikes along the Palisades a half-century before; but its conflation of the imagined with the actual makes any simply categorical interpretation hazardous). The poems are of earth rather than about the globe – to use my earlier distinction – but if 'The Irish Cliffs of Moher' (1952) imagines a father at the beginning, and 'Madame la Fleurie' (1951) a mother at the end, neither parent is a consolatory force; one of the strongest poems, 'The River of Rivers in Connecticut' (1953), tries to establish a mythology appropriate to the region, in a language that acknowledges its own inevitably falsifying figurations.

The bracingly instructive confrontation between the formative mind and a world not answerable to the meanings it imposes is the matter of some of the most memorable poems of this last period: 'The Course of a Particular', 'The Plain Sense of Things' (1952), 'A Clear Day and No Memories' (1955), 'July Mountain' (1955), and 'Of Mere Being' (1955), for additional examples (all but the second in *OP*2). The facing-up to a challenging vacancy is, as with 'The River of Rivers...', a particularly American phase, implicitly repudiating grandiose old-world structures of belief: this also underlay 'St Armorer's Church from the Outside' (1952), a poem in which the unfettered spontaneities of a nonconformist 'chapel of breath' were contrasted with the bare ruined choirs of the defunct old church. A reconciliation to minor rather than major structures of the imagination was perhaps the distinctive feature of these poems, whose author had repeated to Barbara Church the French saying that long poems were written by those who couldn't write short ones: thus, his poem about the domestic rituals of Penelope ('The World as Meditation', 1952) was more successful than his evocation of her ocean-going husband in 'The Sail of Ulysses' (*OP2* 126; 1954) – his last attempt at a long poem. Certainly, the small occasions were what most effectively animated him: the letters and postcards he received, constituting the life he lived vicariously through his correspondence (he survived on postcards from Europe, he told Barbara Church in 1953; *L* 797). 'One picks up a kind of freedom of the universe, or at least of the world, from the movements of other people', he had written to McGreevy two years earlier (*L* 727); and thus he dwelt in Hartford, constructing the world from postcards and news reports, while his wife gardened manically outside.

Although he had decided on fewer public addresses and readings, after his increasing dissatisfaction with the ones he had given (his paper 'A Collect of Philosophy', delivered at the University of Chicago in 1951, had been rejected by the journal he then offered it to), Stevens did consent to compose a poem for the Phi Beta Kappa exercises at Columbia University at the end of May 1954, as well as agreeing to do some recording and broadcasting for the Voice of America programme. By contrast with the aberrance from its occasion of 'Description without Place', Stevens went to great lengths to conform to the apparent stipulation that he 'do something on the theme or slogan which they are exploiting: freedom of knowledge and free use of knowledge' (*L* 816). Although he insinuated that this seemed unsuitable to a 'normal, mature audience', he complied as best he could in 'The Sail of Ulysses', which in a rather formulaic way rings changes on notions of being and knowing, and which he disliked so much after the event that he refused to let anyone have copies, and which he radically shortened and retitled for its appearance in the *Times Literary Supplement* that September.[9] Filreis is surely right to see the poem as virtually unreadable when divorced from its social and political contexts, whatever its thematic continuities with the sort of thing Stevens tended to say; but it remains unclear whether he was asserting American speculative freedom in a straightforwardly McCarthyite way ('this is what makes us better than thought-policed Communists'), or as an implicit critique of the threat to such freedom posed by the Wisconsin senator's inquisitorial proceedings. Stevens's piece for the Voice of America, 'Connecticut Composed' (*OP2* 302–4) written in the spring of 1955, seems a straightforward affirmation of Yankee perdurability, evoking the state as 'mother' (albeit aspic-nippled) whose sons honoured her because 'it is a question of coming home to the American self in the sort of place in which it was formed. Going back to Connecticut is a return to an origin.' The final sentence locates Yankee virtues 'all over the world'; but rather than diluting the specificity of his tribute to Connecticut, this conforms perfectly to the propagandist undertow of the Voice of America: how easily the non-American could become American, and how much better for it, were it to do so. The wilderness remained ripe for conversion.

The unprecedented second National Book Award for his *Collected Poems* in 1955 showed the extent to which Stevens had gained 'acceptance' and was, perhaps, being read in the pew, by an audience keen for a certain type of American Poet: wise, disinterested, and unobtrusively patriotic. The importance to certain readers of the kind of man he was perceived to be is further illustrated by the mystery and dispute surrounding his final days. At the beginning of 1955 Elsie suffered a stroke; in April that year Stevens was admitted to hospital, where an exploratory operation revealed incurably-advanced cancer of the stomach, of which he was not told. He recuperated from the operation in a convalescent home, returning to his office for a few hours each day in the summer, but by mid-July was readmitted to the convalescent home and, six days later, to St Francis Hospital, where he died in the morning of 2 August. Although his letters of late June and early July speak of recovery, it is hardly to be doubted that by the time of his readmission to the convalescent home (outside which he is pictured in the photograph facing p. 887 in *Letters*) he knew his condition to be terminal. Having made contact during his first spell in hospital, during his final stay Stevens reportedly had considerable contact with the Chaplain, Father Hanley, with the result that he was received into the Roman Catholic faith, and died in the bosom of the Church. Father Hanley is reported as recalling, 'All the time in the back of my mind was, how can I get this man in the Church?' (Brazeau, p. 294); and Holly Stevens, who vigorously disputed the conversion story, claimed that Stevens had complained to her of being bothered by the priest. The event was kept secret because of fears that Elsie might make a scene, and because the Archbishop judged it best; but it was confirmed in writing by Father Hanley in 1977 and again in 1981 – although no other documentary evidence in support of his assertion exists.[10]

It is not for us to judge the decisions of a dying man, until we are ourselves confronting death; and it seems improbable that an ordained priest would bear false witness in so significant a matter. If poetry helps people live their lives, perhaps religion helps us to die our deaths; despite irregularities, the story of Stevens's conversion seems more likely to be true, than not. His lifelong preoccupation with Christianity and its potential substitutes, his emotional inhabitation of so many of its forms, together with the apparent absoluteness of his rejection of its tenets, quite plausibly set the stage for an essentially Pauline conversion. What is of interest, is the opposition to the event felt by some readers – chief amongst them, his own daughter. This has to do with the importance of Stevens as exponent of humane scepticism, and as exemplar of the bleak courage required of the mind facing annihilation without the consolations of an afterlife; incontestably, the chief thrust of his writing up to the very end conformed to those perceptions. To conceive of Stevens as a stalwart atheist (although he denied the label to Sister Bernetta Quinn) was part of the image of the life derived from the art, serving further to discriminate him from churchwarden Eliot. Possibly Holly Stevens's objections were rooted in the degree to which her own life consisted in a retrospective act of acquaintanceship with her father, through the medium of his writings; for our parts, we shall never know whether he embraced Catholicism in the spirit of fact or the spirit of fiction: perhaps it was an ultimate elegance that transformed a sensed ending into a threshold.

Stevens died at the height of his reputation; there was not a publicly visible period in his own lifetime when he had seemed written out, or obsolete. Yet the time at which he died was a time when poetry in America was about to change, and the kinds of decorum he believed in would be overturned. Elvis Presley was about to start rocking and rolling, Allen Ginsberg was about to start performing *Howl*, *Lolita* was about to demonstrate some of the wilder functions of formalist fiction. The patron saint of the most immediately audible and visible younger generation poets would be Williams, rather than Stevens – although there would be lines of descent to writers such as James Merrill and John Ashbery. Nevertheless, as poetry became increasingly entwined with college English, Stevens's corpus was particularly well placed to survive. Its amenability to New Critical treatment was obvious, and then, when Structuralism and its theoretical successors came to the fore, the degree to which his poems had already internalised theoretically sophisticated models of interpretation and linguistic self-awareness was ripe for discovery. Although his widow (who died in 1963) had been quite assiduous with her scissors, there yet remained enough material, as the academy moved beyond the Eliotian credo of the separation between life and writing, to build a picture of the man behind the poems and, more recently, his writing has been the site for New Historicist excavations of the interactions between text and context. Stevens has turned out to be a poet for all seasons.

In his acknowledgement of the 1954 National Book Award for his *Collected Poems*, Stevens projected a realm of desire beyond the actual book, asserting that his 'true' poems were not the ones he had written, but the ones he would like to have written, the 'uncollected poems' he had not had the strength to realise. He went on:

> Humble as my actual contribution to poetry may be and however modest my experience of poetry has been, I have learned through that contribution and by the aid of that experience of the greatness that lay beyond, the power over the mind that lies in the mind itself, the incalculable expanse of the imagination as it reflects itself in us and about us. This is the precious scope which every poet seeks to achieve as best he can.

> (*OP2* 289)

The swelling rhetoric perhaps overbears the doubts we might legitimately have about his presumption to speak here for 'every poet'; as with the definition of poetry (in his introduction to *The Necessary Angel*) as 'the imagination manifesting itself in its domination of words', we learn about the power and the glory, but the nature of the kingdom is obscure. The mind's power over itself was not necessarily sought or realised in the art nor what Lowell called the 'generic life' of younger poets such as Dylan Thomas, Theodore Roethke, Elizabeth Bishop, Delmore Schwartz, Randall Jarrell, John Berryman or Lowell himself – although a poet like Richard Wilbur might exemplify it. The poetry of Stevens, Eliot, and Moore suggests the poem to be a closed rather than an open system, whose object was less the exposure than the retentive definition of 'self'.

Stevens, who shared none of Eliot's asceticism, was not ashamed to be a bourgeois poet, affirming that a life of material comfort was preferable to a life of deprivation. Money was a kind of poetry, insofar as each potentially ensured a degree of freedom from life as basic subsistence; but the kinds of value and recognition attaching to each meant that, beyond this similarity, divergence increased. In his acceptance speech, Stevens declared that the value of such prize-givings was that they recalled the poet to the fact that he lived in the world of Darwin rather than the world of Plato; and for him, it is clear that these public occasions were events which focused the dumbfoundering abyss between his personal sense of the centrality of poetry, and the public view of it as an optional and even negligible activity – a disparity which reactivated his old struggle with his father. As a bourgeois, he had much in common with his fellow-citizens; but as a poet, he knew that he addressed himself to an élite, consisting of those who had the time and ability to devote the degree of concentrated attention necessary to appreciate his poems. Increasingly, this has comprised the professional or semi-professional readership constituted by teachers and students of literature – a circumstance which, it seems to me, throws up some particular problems in the case of Stevens, with his exceptional alertness to the difference between what one does for a life, and what one does for a living. Having learnt at his father's knee, so to speak, about the status of pure acts of the mind in a world of work, the surrogate religion which he made of poetry was one, in which the notion of the poem as an activity deliberately disengaged from any functional effect became a cornerstone of his 'piety'. The refusal to make money by it, or to use his poetry as a means of advancement (*L* 473), was part of what preserved its holiness. He was acutely aware of the differences as well as the connections between the man in the office and the poet in the park or at home, between his vocation and his avocation – great as was his reliance on each condition.

Stevens may be much more challenging, in his very playfulness, than is frequently supposed. Those who read him for professional reasons, and write books about his work (including this one), risk a betrayal of that spirit of disengagement which may constitute what is most fundamental to his poems; substituting for it 13 ways of looking at a blackboard which, however varied, overestimate the poetry as epistemological model, and underestimate it as a linguistic playground full of jocular procreativity. Abstruseness notwithstanding, his poems exist most truly, because most strange, beyond the classroom, insistently unfamiliar in what he called the wild country of the soul (*CP* 240). Keats despised poetry which has 'a palpable design on us'; and Stevens's semantic inconclusivity enacts that undesigningness. The poem becomes a virtual reality, born of a lonely impulse of delight whose value is, precisely, to have no status in a world of causes and effects (whether logical or mechanical); instead, it resembles the sublime uselessness of music, nominated by Walter Pater as representing the highest condition of art.

As the poet acknowledged when older, this is a dangerous name to invoke; yet the early Stevens can be seen as a quarrelsome disciple of Pater, seeking protection from the latter's aesthetic extremism by counterbalancing it with Matthew Arnold's arguments for the spiritual centrality of poetry, which in turn he leavened with a Jamesian Pragmatism. A later influence was the French aphoristic essayist Alain, whose *Les Dieux* (1934) he is likely to have acquired soon after publication, and which offers striking parallels with Stevens's own ways of thinking and writing about the genealogy of gods. More or less throughout his career he can be seen to be in debate with Emerson, whom he not infrequently derides, but with whom his spiritual affinity is strong. Yet none of these sources or connections accounts for what is valuable in Stevens or likely to ensure his survival, since citing them conduces to a discussion of his theory rather than his practice. One of the 'Adagia' defines living as 'the struggle between thesis and instinct' (*OP2* 187): the formative confrontation between Platonic ideas of order, and a Darwinian incommunicable mass which may be as much deformed as charmed by an Orphean lyre. The poem is the site of this primordial struggle, and its success depends on the struggle's outcome being undecided: as Stevens wrote to Blackmur in November 1931, 'If I am right in identifying a certain ambiguity as essential to poetry, then I am wrong in explaining, because if I destroy the ambiguity I destroy the poem'.[11] In the same letter, Stevens voiced his unconcern that a poem might mean one thing to one reader and something different to another; and certainly the amenability of his poetry to different critical schools has been a function of its longevity; yet equally important may be the nature of his unconcern, which is not to be confused with lack of seriousness (back to Pound's strictures). One of the ways in which we know Stevens to have been a true poet, rather than one of the many *soi-disants* poets cluttering the scene then and now, is that he kept on writing poems as sort of necessity; and one of the ways in which he knew himself to be a true poet, was that he wrote them for their own sake, not to advance his career or make his name: 'One does not write for any reader except one', ran another stern adage (*OP*2 191).

Ben Jonson's famous tribute to Shakespeare declared his friend to be 'not of an age, but for all time': staking Shakespeare's claim to classic status, as if pre-emptively aware of the efforts that would be made by contemporary criticism, to drive out bardolatry and to establish how far the playwright was in fact the man 'of an age'. In the smaller sphere of Stevens studies a similar historicism is observable; but just as audiences and readers of *King Lear* (in whichever version) may obstinately persist in believing the play to have something continuously valid to disclose about, say, growing old, so Stevens's poetry, if it survives as more than a cultural-historical *exemplum*, will do so by remaining readable in contexts very different from those in which it happened to be generated – readable, indeed, in ignorance of those contexts. Of course each reader brings his or her own peculiar plot to the act of interpretation; but the poem remains, however variably constructed, as primary instigation. Stevens adhered to quite a few beliefs which are currently unfashionable: he believed that there was such a thing as literature, and such a quality as aesthetic value; that discerning readers consituted a minority (certainly) and an élite (probably); and that to some degree – as Henry James asserted – art 'makes' life.

It does so, as one of the highest manifestations of the rage for order or formative impulse that is characteristic of conscious apprehensions of reality; although this same impulse, when expressed as art, may also imply resentment at what James called the 'fatal futility of Fact'. Stevens's thinking about poetry was deeply structured, it seems to me, by such an oppositionalism, inherent in the poem's relation to the world beyond itself; an oppositionalism which also rehearses the incompatibility between the visionary and the mercenary which he appeared to enact in his own life. His view of the poet's function was that it should release the reader's own poetic potential, and expressed in this way can be seen to have a similarity to Emerson's version of the 'poet', given in *Nature* (1836), as a receptivity to the 'integrity of impression', which 'distinguishes the stick of timber of the wood-cutter, from the tree of the poet'; the farmer looks at the countryside and observes the fields by which he hopes to profit; the poet 'whose eye can integrate all the parts' appreciates the 'landscape', which cannot be bought and sold. 'Enjoy the land, but own it not', was Thoreau's injunction; for Emerson as for Thoreau, the moral/aesthetic 'value' is achieved by an act of withdrawal, and is located within the (implicitly solitary) perceiving mind.

Considered as a literary life, Stevens offers a particularly intense version of that commitment to creative transformation of the simply given order, that surely is the fundamental art-impulse: in his case moving toward an evasive postulation of the imagined world as the ultimate good (see 'Final Soliloquy of the Interior Paramour', 1951). His is the peculiarly authoritative record of the primacy of subjective states, of life lived in the mind – the more authoritative for the persistence of his creativity as well as his incontestable engagement with the unimagined world. To make such an emphasis may risk reidentifying him with the stereotype that Filreis, for example, has tried to supplant: as the liver of 'an eerily unimportant American life'.[12] But it seems to me that Stevens's profoundest perception was that all our lives are eerily unimportant, no matter who we are; but that in the matter of who we *think* we are – in the active rather than the presumptive sense – we touch the central of our being. This changes; in it is no protection from pain or death; but it is where the transcendence of desiring interacts with the pragmatics of being.

In the first version of his elegy for Yeats, Auden asserted that time worships language: meaning that it is by a writer's mastery of the craft of words that the work stands or falls, and not because of what it is 'about'. Stevens possessed the gift of language, without which writing poetry is simply a form of personal therapy, opinion mongering, or attention seeking. Although many of his poems were characterised by linguistic opulence and extravagant effects, his range comprised the quieter register as well, as shown in 'The Planet on the Table' (1953); in which he summarised his career, and judged that what was important was not that his poems survived, but that they bore witness to earth's 'affluence' in the 'poverty of their words' (*CP* 533). Sometimes it was a case of rich earth, poor poem, and sometimes the reverse; but what we see in Stevens is a consistent sense, observable not only in what he wrote but in how he lived, of the poem as marginally central, importantly unimportant. This was thrown into sharper relief by his Americannness, in which his tributes to the penurious affluence of, say, Connecticut, show an inevitably thwarted (because unreciprocated) love for the rocks and stones and trees he was so loyal as never to have left. It is the Americanness which, in 'A Clear Day and No Memories' (1955), reveals itself as a sense of (confected) pastlessness at once vertiginous and stimulating:

> Today the air is clear of everything.
> It has no knowledge except of nothingness
> And it flows over us without meanings,
> As if none of us had ever been here before
> And are not now: in this shallow spectacle,
> This invisible activity, this sense.
>
> (*OP*2 139)

But as the poem acknowledges, the mind is not part of this weather; and the man who spent considerable sums of money researching his own ancestry, who felt Europe (especially France) to be his spiritual outpost, who responded to the residual barbarous euphony of the old Indian place-names, was one for whom the mind was substantially its own place: never resting, never satisfied, looking for what was where it used to be; intensely aware of death, but happiest in the moments of slight transcendence imparted by the poems – moments when, all sublimely and perhaps a little fatuously, we choose to play.

Notes

1. THE MÉTIER OF NOTHINGNESS

1. My title alludes to a phrase in 'Seventy Years Later' (*CP* 525–6), the whole of which late poem is suggestively relevant to this chapter. Sources of quotations from Stevens's published writings will be given in the running text, using the abbreviations already described.
2. Samuel French Morse, quoted by Peter Brazeau in his *Parts of a World: Wallace Stevens Remembered* (New York: Random House, 1983), p. 152. Subsequent references to this book will be incorporated in the running text as (Brazeau, p. –).
3. *We Dream of Honour: John Berryman's Letters to his Mother*, ed. Richard J. Kelly (New York & London: W.W. Norton, 1988), p. 207; 'So Long? Stevens' can be found in the collection *His Toy, His Dream, His Rest* (London: Faber & Faber, 1969), p. 148.
4. Thomas C. Grey, *The Wallace Stevens Case: Law and the Practice of Poetry* (Cambridge, Mass. & London: Harvard University Press, 1991), p. 12.
5. Pound's remarks about Stevens date from 1933, and are quoted by Alan Filreis in *Modernism from Right to Left: Wallace Stevens, the Thirties & Literary Radicalism* (Cambridge & New York: Cambridge University Press, 1994), p. 147.
6. John Timberman Newcomb, *Wallace Stevens and Literary Canons* (Jackson & London: University Press of Mississippi, 1992), pp. 3–4.
7. Henry James, *Hawthorne*, ed. Tony Tanner (London: Macmillan, 1967), pp. 55, 56.
8. D.H. Lawrence, *Studies in Classic American Literature* (Harmondsworth: Penguin, 1971), p. 70. In citing Sacvan Bercovitch, I am thinking principally of *The Rites of Assent: Transformations in the Symbolic Construction of America* (New York & London: Routledge, 1993).
9. Stevens acquired a copy of *Emma* in 1902, having already read *Sense and Sensibility* at Harvard (see Bibliography for articles detailing the books in Stevens's personal library). The quotation I use is found on p. 241 of the Penguin edition of *Emma*.
10. Stevens had also read his Emerson, whose assertion near the end of *Nature* that 'the ruin, or blank, that we see when we look at nature is in our own eye' was precursive of 'The Snow Man', and was itself precoursed by James Thomson's sentiment in 'Winter' (from *The Seasons* (1744), ll. 704–6): 'All nature feels the renovating force / Of Winter – only to the thoughtless eye / In ruin seen'.
11. This comes from Moses Coit Tyler's *History of American Literature 1607-1765* (1878), quoted by Kermit Vanderbilt in *American Literature and the Academy* (Philadelphia: University of Pennsylvania Press, 1986), p. 100. I was pleased to find a similar interpretation of the 'bucks' of 'Earthy Anecdote' as Indians, in Joan Richardson's biography of Stevens (see Bibliography), Vol. I, p. 531 n. 1.
12. A letter from his father to Stevens at Harvard implies a discussion between them about the Venus de Milo (*L* 15).

2. STARTING WITH NOTHING

1. The 1936 fistfight between Hemingway and Stevens is recounted by the former in his published *Letters*; the incidents of the tray of drinks and the honorary degree are in Brazeau (pp. 74, 58–9); the story of the British philosopher comes from Frank Kermode.
2. Brazeau, p. 28; for Elsie Stevens's insulting behaviour, see Brazeau, p. 246.
3. Roethke's poem is 'A Rouse for Stevens' (1955). An article by Steve Kemper in the Connecticut paper *Northeast* (24 March 1996), entitled 'Looking for Wallace Stevens', makes clear how unpopular Stevens was with his Hartford colleagues, and how slight the traces he has left in the city where he wrote most of his poetry.
4. John Updike, *Hugging the Shore: Essays and Criticism* (Harmondsworth: Penguin, 1985), p. 612. An attempt to discuss the importance of Stevens's roots is made by Thomas F. Lombardi in *Wallace Stevens and the Pennsylvania Keystone* (Selinsgrove: Susquehanna University Press & London: Associated University Presses, 1996).
5. Garrett's letters to his son and their relationship at this time are well described by Milton J. Bates in *Wallace Stevens: A Mythology of Self* (Berkeley & London: University of California Press, 1985). References to this book will hereafter be incorporated in the running text as 'Bates, p. –'.
6. George Santayana, *Interpretations of Poetry and Religion* (New York: Harper, 1957), p. 20.
7. *The Poetry of Robert Frost*, ed. E. Connery Latham (London: Jonathan Cape, 1971), p. 156.
8. Quoted by Ann Douglas in *The Feminization of American Culture* (New York: Alfred Knopf, 1978), p. 235. My debt to her researches is clear. (Her later study of the diversities of American Modernism, *Terrible Honesty: Mongrel Manhattan in the 1920s* (1995), can also be recommended.)
9. Douglas, p. 82. See also the figures given by Harold Beaver in his description of 'The Literary Market-Place' in *New Pelican Guide to English Literature*, ed. Ford, Vol. 9 *American Literature* (London & New York: Penguin, 1988), pp. 59–60.
10. Douglas, p. 8.
11. Frank Lentricchia, *Modernist Quartet* (Cambridge & New York: Cambridge University Press, 1994), p. 2. This is a useful study of the contexts of American Modernism as exemplified in Frost, Eliot, Stevens, and Pound.
12. Lentricchia, p. 59.
13. A well-known fictional description of the slaughter of these birds occurs in Chapter 22 of J.F. Cooper's *The Pioneers* (1823). 'The last immense nesting took place in Michigan in 1878. During the next thirty years the remaining flocks dwindled until they were gone. The last passenger pigeon in the world expired at the Cincinnati Zoo at 1.00 p.m. Central Standard Time, September 1, 1914' – thus runs the

note in the Audubon Society's 'Baby Elephant Folio' edition of *Audubon's Birds of America* (New York: reprint of 1981 edn). It is not impossible, therefore, that Stevens might have seen these birds in the wild, though only as 'casual flocks'.

14. See his comments in 'The Irrational Element in Poetry' (*OP2* 225). The April after his Canadian trip, he noted in his journal that 'Spring comes this way, trait by trait, like a stage sunrise, *bien calculé*' (*SP* 131).

15. This alludes to one of the 'Adagia' (*OP2* 188). His observation of the mountains resurfaced in 'Arcades of Philadelphia the Past' (1939): 'The mountains are scratched and used, clear fakes' (*CP* 226).

16. Bynner's comments on Stevens are quoted by Joan Richardson (see Bibliography) in Vol. I, p. 553 n. 52.

17. The jar in question, Roy Harvey Pearce pointed out (*WSJ* 1977, pp. 64–5), may have been a 'Dominion Wide Mouth Special' fruit storage jar.

3. STRICT ARRANGEMENTS OF EMPTINESS

1. Their niece recalls the poet's widow insisting on being addressed as 'Mrs Wallace Stevens' rather than as 'Aunt Elsie' (Brazeau, p. 252).

2. See the unpublished letter quoted by Joan Richardson, Vol. I, p. 342.

3. See the unpublished letter quoted in Richardson, I, p. 260.

4. Richardson, I, p. 296.

5. Richardson, I, p. 260.

6. Definitions of Elsie as his second self can be found in letters quoted in Richardson, I, pp. 254, 288, 291.

7. The importance of this kind of private publication of poetry (as by Emily Dickinson) has been underlined by Jerome McGann in *Black Riders: The Visible Language of Modernism* (New Jersey: Princeton University Press, 1993).

8. Unpublished letter (WAS 1842) quoted in Richardson, I, p. 344.

9. Richardson, I, p. 339.

10. Williams's sonnet can be found in *The Collected Poems 1909–1939*, eds Litz & MacGowan (Manchester: Carcanet Press, 1987), p. 21. Eliot's early work and its sources can be studied in *Inventions of the March Hare: Poems 1909–1917*, ed. Ricks (London: Faber & Faber, 1996).

11. Joan Richardson explores the possible influence of the *Vagabondia* poems on Stevens; I, p. 276ff.

12. Newcomb, *Wallace Stevens and Literary Canons*, p. 26.

13. Here and elsewhere in this study I have used information given in *American Literary Magazines: The Twentieth Century*, ed. Edward E. Chielens (Westport, CT & London: Greenwood Press, 1992).

14. For further explorations of these areas see Glen Macleod's two books: *Wallace Stevens and Company: the Harmonium Years 1913–1923* (Ann Arbor: UMI Research Press, 1983) and *Wallace Stevens and Modern Art: From the Armory Show to Abstract Expressionism* (New Haven & London: Yale University Press, 1993).

15. Robert Hughes, *The Shock of the New* (London: Thames & Hudson, 1991) p. 15.
16. A comparator here would be Renoir's 'Le Coup de Vent', in the Fitzwilliam Museum, Cambridge: where a landscape ruffled by wind is presented in the state of blurring that the eye might actually perceive.
17. Williams made these comments in his 'Author's Introduction' to *The Wedge* (1944).
18. In the earliest version of 'Nude...' (1911), it is clear that the staircase is spiral: a pleasingly predictive allusion to our century's unlocking of the doubly-helical structure of DNA.
19. Unpublished letter (WAS 1789) quoted in Richardson, I, p. 262.
20. These remarks of Cézanne's are quoted in *The Shock of the New*, pp. 124, 18.
21. *Wallace Stevens and Company*, p. ix.
22. Bynner's linkage to the literary old guard about to be displaced by the new writing was, Newcomb suggests, a significant factor in the early eclipse of his reputation.
23. Unpublished letter of 13 September 1909 (WAS 1902), quoted in Richardson, I, p. 365.

4. 1914–23: ACCENTS OF DEVIATION

1. Macleod, *Wallace Stevens and Company*, p. 65
2. Chielens, *American Literary Magazines*, p. 231.
3. See Chielens, p. 231ff.
4. Alfred Kreymborg, *Troubadour* (New York: Boni & Liveright, 1925), p. 221.
5. See Hans Richter, *Dada: Art and Anti-Art* (London: Thames & Hudson 1965), for comments about Stieglitz, and Arensberg.
6. Information in this paragraph derives from Roger Conover's foreword to his 1997 edition of *Mina Loy: The Lost Lunar Baedeker* (where he asserts that the five-in-a-bed spent a chaste night); Neil Baldwin's study of *Man Ray* (p. 73); and William Ewing's *The Body: Photoworks of the Human Form* (p. 27). A reminiscence by John Crockett suggests that behavioural excess was a feature of Holly Stevens's life, if not of her father's; see 'Of Holly and Wallace Stevens in a Hartford Light', *WSJ*, Vol. 21 No. 1 (Spring, 1997), pp. 3–35.
7. See Newcomb, *Wallace Stevens and Literary Canons*, pp. 35–7.
8. These figures are derived from J.M. Edelstein's *Wallace Stevens: a Descriptive Bibliography* (Pittsburgh: University of Pittsburgh Press, 1973).
9. Significant reviews are most easily accessible in Charles Doyle's *Wallace Stevens: The Critical Heritage* (see Bibliography).
10. Braithwaite's choice was limited by Stevens's having published no poetry in 1920, and in 1921 only two slight pieces in a mimeographed issue of *Contact* before 'Cortège...'; the clearly superior 'Man Whose

Pharynx Was Bad' in the *New Republic*, mid-September, probably appeared too late for inclusion.

11. Quoted in Bates, p. 93
12. See Richardson, I, p. 509.
13. Macleod, p. 19.
14. See *The Poetry of Robert Frost*, p. 277; the poem seems rather too ready to convict its tramps (seen as virtually protozoic types) of criminal leisure, and too negligent of the Depression's consequences for such lives as theirs.
15. See Louis Martz's essay in *Wallace Stevens: a Celebration*, eds. Doggett and Buttel (Princeton: Princeton University Press, 1980), pp. 3–29, for a discussion of the earlier Crispin poem.
16. Ibid., p. 10.
17. In 1909 Stevens remembered having in his boyhood watched the organ pump-handle going up and down in Reading's First Presbyterian Church (*L* 125); as a former choirboy in Christ Cathedral, Reading, he would have been alert to the gradations of church music-making.
18. This letter, dated '9 April', is known only because Williams quoted it in his 'Prologue' to *Kora in Hell: Improvisations* (1920), which he also sent to Stevens – who never disputed the letter's authenticity.
19. Pound's comment is a continuation of his remarks about Stevens cited in Chapter 1, and quoted by Filreis in *Modernism from Left to Right*, p. 147; for the alternative titles for '...One of Fictive Music', see *Wallace Stevens: a Celebration*, p. 27.
20. The longer text of '...Pharynx...' is given in Holly Stevens's edition of her father's poetry, *The Palm at the End of the Mind* (see Bibliography). See also her notes on the poem, and on 'Nomad Exquisite', p. 401.
21. In *Wallace Stevens and the Pennsylvania Keystone*, Lombardi notes that there was a casino in Carsonia Park, Reading.
22. 'Floral Decorations for Bananas' has significant continuities of tone and imagery with remarks about Marsden Hartley's paintings made by Paul Rosenfeld in a *Dial* essay (December 1921), as quoted by Martz in *Wallace Stevens: a Celebration* (p. 15).

5. 1923–37: FROM THE EDGE TO THE CENTRE

1. Alfred Kreymborg, *Our Singing Strength* (New York: Coward, McCann, 1929), p. 500.
2. See *L* 246 and Richardson, II, p. 48.
3. My allusion here is to the 1951 essay 'Two or Three Ideas' (*OP2* 259).
4. Unless otherwise referenced, all quotations from reviews are locatable in Doyle's *Wallace Stevens: the Critical Heritage*.
5. Newcomb estimates that the combined circulation of the magazines in which *Harmonium* was reviewed may have been as much as 50 000 (*Wallace Stevens and Literary Canons*, p. 51).
6. See Holly Stevens, 'Holidays in Reality', in *Wallace Stevens: a Celebration* (p. 107).

7.　Chieles, *American Literary Magazines*, p. 142. Filreis and Newcomb also discuss the relations betwen Stevens, Blackmur, and *Hound and Horn*.

8.　In 1919, Stevens had wanted to drop 'Exposition...' from the 'Pecksniffiana' set, in *Poetry* (*L* 214).

9.　Filreis, *Modernism from Right to Left*, p. 49; uncharacteristically, he gives no evidence for this assertion.

10.　*Selected Letters of Conrad Aiken*, ed. Joseph Killorin (New Haven: Yale University Press, 1978), p. 170.

11.　*Stevens' Poetry of Thought* was the title of a 1966 monograph by Frank Doggett.

12.　Filreis gives good reasons to suppose that the two poems were 'written as early as mid-1933'; op. cit., p. 119.

13.　Details about Leippert's life, and the chronology of his interactions with Stevens, derive from Filreis's detailed account of their relationship.

14.　There is some dispute about whether he was referring to 'Anglais Mort à Florence' (*CP* 148) or to 'Waving Adieu, Adieu, Adieu' (*CP* 127): aspects of the 'new regime' seem more visible in the first, but deathbed farewells and floods of colour (the collocation 'ever-jubilant' is repeated) are more obvious in the second.

15.　Stevens did, however, assure 'Latimer' that 'all of the Florida poems have actual backgrounds. The real world seen by an imaginative man may very well seem like an imaginative construction' (*L* 289).

16.　This seems to owe much to Emerson's essay 'Experience' (1844): 'the new statement will comprise the skepticisms, as well as the faiths of society, and out of unbeliefs a creed shall be formed. For, skepticisms are not gratuitous or lawless, but are limitations of the affirmative statement, and the new philosophy must take them in...'.

17.　See Filreis, pp. 83–4.

18.　See George Lensing's account of Stevens's involvement with the Fortune Press in England, in *Wallace Stevens: a Celebration*.

19.　The poem's attitude is not unreminiscent of Carlyle's assertion (quoted by Raymond Williams in *Culture and Society 1780–1950*, p. 80) that 'of all "rights of man," this right of the ignorant man to be guided by the wiser ... is the indisputablest' – although in 'The Sense of the Sleight-of-Hand Man' (1939) Stevens would be more respectful of the capacities of 'the ignorant man' (*CP* 222).

20.　See Filreis on the politics of 'The Men that are Falling' (pp. 31–40).

6. 1937–47: HELPING PEOPLE LIVE THEIR LIVES

1.　Quoted by George Lensing in his essay in *Wallace Stevens: a Celebration* (p. 138).

2.　See Alan Filreis, *Wallace Stevens and the Actual World* (Princeton: Princeton University Press, 1991), pp. 101–2.

3.　See *Wallace Stevens: a Celebration*, pp. 101–3.

4. In 1939 Stevens told Church that poem XII of 'Thirteen Ways...' suggested 'the compulsion frequently back of the things that we do' (*L* 340); in *Wallace Stevens and Modern Art*, MacLeod relates 'Dry Loaf' to Miró's 'Still Life with Old Shoe' (p. 85).

5. Given Stevens's voiced resentments of the world that was too much with him – 'We are close together in every way. We lie in bed and listen to a broadcast from Cairo, and so on. There is no distance. We are intimate with people we have never seen and, unhappily, they are intimate with us' (*NA* 18) – it seems typical that he should choose Wordsworth's vision of the city rendered pastorally amenable by being virtually unpeopled.

6. In 'Wallace Stevens and the Cummington Press: Additions and Reflections', Carolyn Masel offers a useful view of the nature of his relations with Katharine Frazier and the Press; *WSJ* Vol. 20 No. 2 (1996), pp. 199–208.

7. T.S. Eliot, *The Sacred Wood* (2nd edn, London: Methuen, 1928), p. viii.

8. In a cancelled comment from a 1953 lecture he gave, Eliot described the three later Quartets as 'primarily patriotic poems'. For a discussion of their relation to wartime Britain, see the discussion in my *T.S. Eliot: a Literary Life* (Basingstoke: Macmillan, 1991), pp. 151–65.

9. *Swing Time* of the following year, although Jerome Kern's music was hardly less memorable than Irving Berlin's, cast Fred and Ginger as a pair of indigent hoofers struggling to make their way in the gangsterish night-clubs of New York, in what now seems an ill-calculated concession to contemporary realities; perversely, then, *Top Hat* may well have helped people to live their lives better than its more 'relevant' successor.

10. Filreis, op. cit., p. 50.

11. See Filreis, pp. 134–6, for a discussion of the importance of John Crowe Ransom's *Kenyon Review* to the genesis of 'Esthétique du Mal'.

12. Richardson, II, p. 233. In 'Of Holly and Wallace Stevens in a Hartford Light' (see Ch. 4, n. 6), John Crockett briefly describes this marriage.

13. Filreis, pp. 155–60.

14. Simons's 'The Genre of Wallace Stevens' appeared in *Sewanee Review* (1945), and Sypher's 'Connoisseur in Chaos: Wallace Stevens' in *Partisan Review* (1946).

15. In *Poetry and Pragmatism* (London: Faber & Faber, 1992), Richard Poirier has written about 'the virtues of superfluousness, his determination to show that excess is more important than necessity, energy more lasting than any meanings it may toss out to the intellectually sedentary' (p. 37); and although his strict subject is Emerson, this is applicable to Stevens, whom he also considers in the book. Eleanor Cook's *Poetry, Word-Play, and Word-War in Wallace Stevens* (Princeton: Princeton University Press, 1988) is also a valuable study.

7. 1947–55: PRIVATE MAN AS PUBLIC FIGURE

1. With regard to 'Someone Puts a Pineapple Together', 'The Red Fern' (1946; *CP* 365), seems to me a different – and better – version of the same poem, with its implicit repudiation of Emerson's assertion that 'the sun illuminates only the eye of the man, but shines into the eye and heart of the child' (from *Nature*).

2. See the discussion in Newcomb, pp. 170–1.

3. For Stevens's habits of composition, see also letters to Morse (*L* 641), Sweeney (*L* 713), and Van Doren (*L* 844).

4. See the illustration between pp. 284–5, Richardson, II. This inscription recycles one of Steven's 'Adagia'.

5. Filreis gives some insight into attitudes to Stevens's work at Knopf in *Modernism from Right to Left* (p. 357, n. 74).

6. The information here derives from Edelstein and *L* 732n.

7. This (representativeness rather than preservation) potentially defines the difference between selected and collected poems; although Stevens's own later definition was that people read selections but didn't buy them, and bought collections but didn't read them (*L* 829).

8. Sales figures for the British *Selected Poems* are as given by Lensing in *Wallace Stevens: a Celebration* (p. 147).

9. Stevens's comment on the Columbia commission comes from an unpublished letter quoted at greater length by Filreis in *Wallace Stevens and the Actual World* (p. 252). See *L* 834–5 and footnote for his feelings about the poem and the occasion; consenting to its publication in Britain was possibly a sign of how much he despised it!

10. See 'A Letter from Father Hanley on Stevens' Conversion to Catholicism' by Janet McCann in *WSJ* Vol. 18, No. 1 (Spring 1994), pp. 3–5; see also Bates, pp. 296–7 n. Why Elsie might have objected to her husband's joining the church is unclear: Steve Kemper (see Ch. 2, n. 3) quotes the Provost of the Episcopal Church, to which she sold 118 Westerly Terrace at an advantageously low price before her death, as saying that 'the theory was that she took delight in selling it to a church because Wallace was an atheist, and this was one last way to get back at him as part of their dysfunctional relationship'.

11. This comes from a previously unpublished letter quoted by Holly Stevens in 'Flux[2]', *Southern Review* Vol. 12, No. 4 (October 1979), pp. 771–4 (p. 774).

12. See *Modernism from Right to Left*, p. 4. As Terry Eagleton has declared in *Criticism and Ideology*, 'the instalment of the "value-question" at the heart of critical enquiry is a rampantly ideological gesture' (p. 164); in my response to Stevens's poetry I obviously take an evaluative stance that reflects my particular ideological position. Varieties of critical experience have been cogently and combatively set forth by Russell Reising in *The Unusable Past: Theory and the Study of American Literature* (New York & London: Methuen, 1986).

Select Bibliography

PRIMARY

Dates for American publication by Alfred Knopf are given in square brackets, where applicable.

Wallace Stevens, *Collected Poems* (London: Faber & Faber, 1955) [1954]
——, *The Necessary Angel* (London: Faber & Faber, 1960) [1951]
——, *Opus Posthumous* first edition, ed. S.F. Morse (London: Faber & Faber, 1959) [1957]
——, *Opus Posthumous* revised and enlarged edition, ed. M.J. Bates (London: Faber & Faber, 1990) [1989]
——, *The Palm at the End of the Mind* ed. Holly Stevens (New York: Alfred Knopf, 1971)
Holly Stevens, *Letters of Wallace Stevens* (London: Faber & Faber, 1967) [1966]
——, *Souvenirs and Prophecies: The Young Wallace Stevens* (New York: Alfred Knopf, 1977)

BIBLIOGRAPHICAL

J. M. Edelstein, *Wallace Stevens: a Descriptive Bibliography* (Pittsburgh: University of Pittsburgh Press, 1973)
Bates, Milton J., 'Stevens' Books at the Huntington: An Annotated Checklist' *Wallace Stevens Journal* Vol. 2, 3–4 (1978), pp. 45–61; Vol. 3, 1–2 (1979), pp. 15–33; Vol. 3, 3–4 (1979), p. 70
Brazeau, Peter, 'Wallace Stevens at the University of Massachusetts: Check List of an Archive' *WSJ* Vol. 2, 1–2 (1978), pp. 50–4
Moynihan, Robert, 'Checklist: Second Purchase, Wallace Stevens Collection, Huntington Library' *WSJ* Vol. 20, 1 (1996), pp. 76–103

SECONDARY

Bates, Milton J., *Wallace Stevens: a Mythology of Self* (Berkeley and London: University of California Press, 1985)

Bloom, Harold, *Wallace Stevens: the Poems of Our Climate* (Ithaca and London: Cornell University Press, 1977)

Brazeau, Peter, *Parts of a World: Wallace Stevens Remembered* (New York: Random House, 1983)

Brogan, Jacqueline Vaught, *Stevens and Simile* (Princeton: Princeton University Press, 1986)

Buttel, Robert, *Wallace Stevens: a Celebration* co-edited with Frank Doggett (Princeton: Princeton University Press, 1980)

Cook, Eleanor, *Poetry, Word-Play, and Word-War in Wallace Stevens* (New Jersey: Princeton University Press, 1988)

Doyle, Charles, *Wallace Stevens: the Critical Heritage* (London: Routledge and Kegan Paul, 1985)

Filreis, Alan, *Modernism from Right to Left: Wallace Stevens, the Thirties and Literary Radicalism* (Cambridge and New York: Cambridge University Press, 1994)

——, *Wallace Stevens and the Actual World* (New Jersey: Princeton University Press, 1991)

Grey, Thomas C., *The Wallace Stevens Case: Law and the Practice of Poetry* (Cambridge, Mass. and London: Harvard University Press, 1991)

Longenbach, James, *Wallace Stevens: the Plain Sense of Things* (New York: Oxford University Press, 1991)

Lentricchia, Frank, *Ariel and the Police* (Brighton: Harvester Press, 1988)

——, *Modernist Quartet* (Cambridge and New York: Cambridge University Press, 1994)

Macleod, Glenn G., *Wallace Stevens and Company: the* Harmonium *Years 1913–1923* (Ann Arbor: UMI Research Press, 1983)

——, *Wallace Stevens and Modern Art* (New York and London: Yale University Press, 1993)

Newcomb, John T., *Wallace Stevens and Literary Canons* (Jackson and London: University Press of Mississippi, 1992)

Richardson, Joan, *Wallace Stevens: the Early Years 1879–1923* (New York: William Morrow, 1986)

——, *Wallace Stevens: the Later Years 1923–1955* (New York: William Morrow, 1988)

Vendler, Helen, *Wallace Stevens: Words Chosen Out of Desire* (Cambridge, Mass. and London: Harvard University Press, 1986)

Index